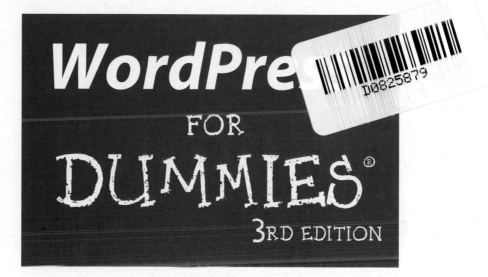

WordPress FOR DUMMIES® 3RD EDITION

by Lisa Sabin-Wilson

Foreword by Matt Mullenweg
Cofounder of WordPress

Wiley Publishing, Inc.

WordPress® For Dummies®, 3rd Edition

Published by
Wiley Publishing, Inc.
111 River Street
Hoboken, NJ 07030-5774

www.wiley.com

Copyright © 2010 by Wiley Publishing, Inc., Indianapolis, Indiana

Published by Wiley Publishing, Inc., Indianapolis, Indiana

Published simultaneously in Canada

For general information on our other products and services, please contact our Customer Care Department within the U.S. at 877-762-2974, outside the U.S. at 317-572-3993, or fax 317-572-4002.

For technical support, please visit www.wiley.com/techsupport.

Wiley also publishes its books in a variety of electronic formats. Some content that appears in print may not be available in electronic books.

Library of Congress Control Number: 2010929417

ISBN: 978-0-470-59274-8

Manufactured in the United States of America

10 9 8 7 6 5 4

WILEY

About the Author

Lisa Sabin-Wilson has worked with the WordPress software since its inception in 2003 and has built her business around providing technical support, hosting, and design solutions for bloggers who use WordPress. She reaches thousands of people worldwide with her WordPress services, skills, and knowledge regarding the product. Lisa is also the author of *BuddyPress For Dummies*.

Lisa operates a few blogs online, all of which are powered by WordPress. Her personal blog (justagirlintheworld.com) has been online since February of 2002; her design business at E.Webscapes (ewebscapes.com) has been online since 1999. She also provides a successful Web hosting service, Blogs About Hosting (blogs-about.com), which caters to blogs and bloggers on a global scale.

When she can be persuaded away from her computer, where she is usually hard at work providing design solutions for her WordPress clients, she sometimes emerges for public speaking appearances on the topics of design, blogging, and WordPress. She has appeared at national conferences such as the annual South By Southwest Interactive Conference, WordCamps around the country, and meet ups local to her Southeastern Wisconsin area like Web414.

Lisa consults with bloggers both large and small. Bloggers come in thousands of different flavors, from business to personal, from creative to technical, and all points in between. Lisa is connected to thousands of them worldwide and appreciates the opportunity to share her knowledge through *WordPress For Dummies*. She hopes you find great value in it, as well!

When she's not designing or consulting with her clients, you can usually find her either at her favorite coffee shop sipping espresso, on a mountaintop somewhere hitting the slopes with her husband and kids, or 100 feet beneath the ocean waters, scuba diving with her husband and swimming with the fishes.

Dedication

To WordPress. . . . and all that entails from the developers, designers, forum helpers, testers, educators, consultants, plugin makers, and theme bakers. Every single person involved in the WordPress community plays a vital role in making this whole thing work, and work well. Kudos to you.

Author's Acknowledgments

Many, many thanks and kudos to Matt Mullenweg, the core development team from Automattic, and every single person involved in making WordPress the best blogging platform available on the Internet today. To the volunteers and testers who destroy all those pesky prerelease bugs for every new version release, the WordPress community thanks you! And to each and every WordPress plugin developer and theme designer who donates his or her time, skills, and knowledge to provide the entire WordPress community of users with invaluable tools that help us create dynamic blogs, thank you a thousand times! Every person mentioned here is an invaluable asset to the overall WordPress experience; I wish I could name you all, individually, except that there are literally thousands of you out there!

Extra special thanks to my friends and colleagues within the WordPress community who inspire and teach me every day.

Huge thanks to Amy Fandrei, and Nicole Haims Trevor from Wiley Publishing for their support, assistance, and guidance during the course of this project. Just the mere fact they had to read every page of this book means that they deserve the Medal of Honor! Also, many thanks to technical editor, Kevin Palmer, and other editors of the project who also worked hard to make sure that I look somewhat literate here.

To my family and close friends whom I have neglected during the process of writing this book, thank you for not abandoning me - your support sustains me!

Finally, I thank my family — my husband, Chris; my children, Ben and Melissa; and my parents, Donald and Penny Sabin — for their unending support for this book, and in life.

Publisher's Acknowledgments

We're proud of this book; please send us your comments through our online registration form located at www.dummies.com/register/.

Some of the people who helped bring this book to market include the following:

Acquisitions and Editorial

Project Editor: Nicole Haims Trevor

(Previous Edition: Rebecca Senninger)

Acquisitions Editor: Amy Fandrei

Technical Editor: Kevin Palmer

Editorial Manager: Jodi Jensen

Editorial Assistant: Leslie Saxman

Sr. Editorial Assistant: Cherie Case

Cartoons: Rich Tennant
(www.the5thwave.com)

Composition Services

Project Coordinator: Katherine Crocker

Layout and Graphics: Ashley Chamberlain, Joyce Haughey

Proofreaders: John Greenough, Toni Settle

Indexer: Potomac Indexing, LLC

Publishing and Editorial for Technology Dummies

Richard Swadley, Vice President and Executive Group Publisher

Andy Cummings, Vice President and Publisher

Mary Bednarek, Executive Acquisitions Director

Mary C. Corder, Editorial Director

Publishing for Consumer Dummies

Diane Graves Steele, Vice President and Publisher

Composition Services

Debbie Stailey, Director of Composition Services

Table of Contents

Foreword..*xiii*

Introduction 1
About This Book 1
Conventions Used in This Book...........................2
What You Are Not to Read 3
Foolish Assumptions 3
How This Book Is Organized 4
    Part I: Introducing WordPress.........................4
    Part II: Using the WordPress
        Hosted Service 4
    Part III: Self-Hosting with WordPress.org........5
    Part IV: Flexing and Extending WordPress 5
    Part V: Customizing WordPress........................5
    Part VI: The Part of Tens 6
Icons Used in This Book 6
Where to Go from Here 6

Part 1: Introducing WordPress 7

Chapter 1: What WordPress Can Do for You.....................9
Discovering the Benefits of WordPress 9
    Getting set up the fast and easy way................10
    Extending WordPress's capabilities 11
    Taking part in the community........................12
Choosing a WordPress Platform...........................13
    Choosing the hosted version from WordPress.com 15
    Self-hosting with WordPress.org......................15

Chapter 2: WordPress Blogging Basics.........................17
This Crazy Little Thing Called Blog 17
Dipping In to Blog Technologies 18
    Archiving your publishing history....................19
    Interacting with your readers through comments 21
    Feeding your readers.................................22
    Tracking back 24
    Dealing with comment and trackback spam 24
Moving On to the Business of Blogging.....................25

Part II: Using the WordPress Hosted Service 27

Chapter 3: Getting Started with WordPress.com 29
Creating a WordPress.com Account 29
Navigating WordPress.com 32
Using the WordPress.com Dashboard 34
    Right Now 35
    Recent Comments 37
    Incoming Links 38
    Your Stuff 38
    What's Hot 38
    QuickPress 38
    Recent Drafts 39
    Stats 39
Setting Important Options Before You Blog 40
    Setting your General options 41
    Adjusting your Date and Time settings 42
    Setting your public profile: Tell us a little about yourself 43
    Setting your personal preferences 49

Chapter 4: Writing and Managing Your Blog 51
Ready? Set? Blog! 51
    Inserting media files into your post 54
    Refining your post options 59
    Publishing your post 61
Organizing Your Blog by Subject 63
    Creating categories and subcategories 63
    Filing posts in categories and subcategories 64
Creating and Categorizing Your Blogroll 65
    Creating link categories 66
    Adding new links to your blogroll 66
Managing and Inviting Users 69
    Managing authors and users 69
    Inviting friends to WordPress.com 70
Managing Comments and Comment Spam 72
    Setting discussion options for your blog 72
    Viewing comments 76
    Managing comment spam with Akismet 78
Creating a Static Page 78
Setting Up Your Front Page 80
Publishing a Public or Private Blog 82
Establishing Trust Relationships with OpenID 83

Chapter 5: Enhancing Your Blog with Themes,
Widgets, and Upgrades 85
Changing Your Blog's Look 85
Widget Wonder: Adding Handy Tools to Your Sidebar 87
    Selecting and activating widgets 87
    Using Text widgets 90
    Using the RSS widget 91

Upgrading Your Hosted Service (For a Fee) 92
Naming Your Domain 94

Part III: Self-Hosting with WordPress.org 95

Chapter 6: Setting Up Blogging Base Camp 97
Establishing Your Domain 97
Understanding domain name extensions 98
Considering the cost of a domain name 98
Registering your domain name 99
Finding a Home for Your Blog 100
Getting help with hosting WordPress 101
Dealing with disk space and bandwidth 102
Transferring Files from Point A to Point B 103
Installing WordPress 104
Setting up the MySQL database 105
Uploading the WordPress files 107
Last step: Running the install script 109

Chapter 7: Understanding the WordPress.org Dashboard 115
Logging In to the Dashboard 115
Navigating the Dashboard 116
Right Now 117
Recent Comments 119
Incoming Links 120
Plugins 121
QuickPress 122
Recent Drafts 123
WordPress Development Blog 123
Other WordPress News 125
Arranging the Dashboard to Your Tastes 125
Setting Options in the Dashboard 128
Configuring the Settings 128
General 129
Writing 132
Reading 134
Discussion 136
Media 142
Privacy 144
Permalinks 144
Creating Your Personal Profile 145
Setting Your Blog's Format 147
Posts 148
Media 148
Links 149
Pages 149
Comments 150
Appearance 150
Plugins 151

Users..152
Tools...152

Chapter 8: Establishing Your Blog Routine **153**
Staying on Topic with Categories......................................153
Changing the name of a category 154
Creating new categories..156
Link Lists: Sharing Your Favorite Sites.............................158
Organizing your links..159
Adding new link loves 160
Editing existing links...165
Examining a Blog Post's Address: Permalinks....................165
Making your post links pretty....................................166
Customizing your permalinks.....................................167
Making sure that your permalinks work with your server...........169
Discovering the Many WordPress RSS Options....................171
Blog It!: Writing Your First Entry 173
Composing your blog post 173
Dressing up your posts with images, video, and audio 176
Refining your post options 176
Publishing your post 178
You are your own editor...180
Look Who's Talking on Your Blog 181
Managing comments and trackbacks...........................181
Moderating comments and trackbacks........................183
Tackling spam with Akismet.......................................183

Part IV: Flexing and Extending WordPress **185**

Chapter 9: Media Management: Images, Audio, and Video **187**
Inserting Images into Your Blog Posts...............................188
Aligning your images 192
Inserting a photo gallery 193
Inserting Video Files into Your Blog Posts.........................197
Inserting Audio Files into Your Blog Posts.........................199
Keeping Media Files Organized...199

Chapter 10: Making the Most of WordPress Plugins **203**
Finding Out What Plugins Are...204
Exploring Manage Plugin page 205
Discovering the one-click plugin upgrade 207
Getting the Most out of the Plugins Included with WordPress 210
Akismet..210
Hello Dolly..213
Using Plugins: Just the Basics..213
Installing Plugins Manually...215
Finding and downloading the files...............................215
Reading the instructions...218

Uploading and Activating Plugins 219
    Uploading the files 219
    Activating the plugin 221
Setting Plugin Options 221
Uninstalling Plugins 222
Understanding the Open Source Environment 224

Chapter 11: Finding and Installing WordPress Themes **227**
Getting Started with Free Themes 227
    Finding free themes 228
    Previewing themes 230
    Downloading themes 231
Activating a New Theme 232
Browsing and Installing Themes from the Dashboard 234
Deciding to Use Premium Themes 236

Part V: Customizing WordPress 239

Chapter 12: Understanding Themes and Templates **241**
Using WordPress Themes: The Basics 242
    Understanding theme structure 242
    Connecting templates 244
Contemplating the Structure of a WordPress Blog 245
Examining the Anatomy of a Template Tag 247
Getting Familiar with the Four Main Templates 248
    The Header template 248
    The Main Index template 254
    The Sidebar template 258
    The Footer template 259
    Other templates 259
Customizing Your Blog Posts with Template Tags 260
Putting a Theme Together 261
Using Tags with Parameters for Sidebars 265
    The Calendar 267
    List pages 267
    Bookmarks (blogroll) 270
    Post archives 272
    Categories 274
    Getting widgetized 276
Checking Out Miscellaneous but Useful Template Tags 278

Chapter 13: Tweaking WordPress Themes **281**
Styling with CSS: The Basics 281
    CSS selectors 282
    Classes and IDs 283
    CSS properties and values 285
Changing the Background Color 286
    Creating a custom background 287
    Changing the background using CSS 289
Using Your Own Header Image 290

Creating Custom Navigation Menus..292
   Adding the Custom Menu feature to your theme.......................293
   Building custom navigation menus 295
Changing Font Styles, Colors, and Sizes......................................296

Chapter 14: Beyond Blogging: WordPress as a Content Management System................................299
Creating the Front Page of Your Web Site....................................300
   Creating the static page 301
   Assigning a static page as the front page 303
Adding a Blog to Your Web Site...304
Defining Specific Templates for Static Pages 306
   Uploading the template...307
   Assigning the template to a static page 308
Creating a Template for Each Post Category 310
Pulling In Content from a Single Category....................................311
   Finding the category ID number 311
   Adding the <query_post> tag 313
Using Sidebar Templates..314
Custom Styles for Sticky, Category, and Tag Posts.......................315
Working with Custom Post Types 317
Optimizing Your WordPress Blog..322
   Planting keywords in your Web site.......................................323
   Optimizing your post titles for search engine success.............324
   Writing content with readers in mind 324
   Creating categories that attract search engines.....................325
   Using the <ALT> tag for images 326

Chapter 15: Hosting Multiple Sites with WordPress..............327
Considering Web Hosting Services 328
Enabling the WordPress Network Feature 329
   Preparing Your Web Server..330
Setting Up the WordPress Network...333
Exploring the Super Admin Dashboard Menu 335
   Configuring network options 336
   Exploring the Network Admin Page...341
   Discovering the Sites Page...342
   Using the Users Page 344
   Enabling network themes 345
   Updating Your Network 347
Using Plugins within Your Network 347

Part VI: The Part of Tens................................. 349

Chapter 16: Ten Great Sites That Use WordPress as a CMS 351
Harvard Gazette...352
Icon Dock 352
Mosaic Consulting, Inc..352
CSS Collection 353

Queensryche 353
Streamy Awards 354
MommyCast 354
Mendocino Beauty..355
John James Jacoby 355
E.Webscapes Design Studio 356

Chapter 17: Ten Popular WordPress Plugins 357
WP Print...357
Subscribe to Comments 358
ShareThis..358
All in One SEO Pack...359
WPtouch iPhone Theme 360
WP-DB-Backup...360
WP Super Cache...360
In Chapter 2, I explain the relationship
  between PHP and MySQL.Twitter Tools.............361
Google XML Sitemaps 362
WordPress.com Stats 362

Chapter 18: Ten Free WordPress Themes 363
Hybrid 363
designPile 364
Elegant Grunge...365
P2...365
Stargaze...366
Carrington Blog...366
iTheme 367
Redoable 368
Corporate..368
Gridline Lite...368

Appendix: Migrating Your Existing Blog to WordPress 369
Movin' On Up 370
Preparing for the Big Move 371
Converting Templates...372
Moving Your Blog..373
    Importing from Blogspot/Blogger...................375
    Importing from LiveJournal..............................376
    Importing from Movable
      Type and TypePad 377
    Importing from WordPress...............................378
    Importing from an RSS feed.............................379
Finding Other Import Resources 380

Index..381

Foreword

· ·

*T*here used to be a program from Microsoft called FrontPage that was the first visual interface for creating Web sites that I saw. It worked like Word or Publisher, so with very little knowledge, I was able to hack together the world's worst Web site in just a few hours without worrying about what was going on under the hood.

Years later when I look back at that Web site, I cringe, but at the time it was incredibly empowering. The software, though crude, helped me publish something anybody in the entire world could see. It opened up a world I had never imagined before.

Now, using software like WordPress, you can have a blog or Web site light-years beyond my first one in both functionality and aesthetics. However, just as my first Web experience whetted my appetite for more, I hope that your experience entices you to explore the thousands of free plugins, themes, and customizations possible with WordPress, many of which are explained in this book.

WordPress is more than just software; it is a community, a rapidly evolving ecosystem, and a set of philosophies and opinions about how to create the best Web experience. When you embrace it, you'll be in good company. WordPress users include old media organizations such as CNN, *The New York Times*, and *The Wall Street Journal*, along with millions of personal bloggers like myself for whom a WordPress blog is a means of expression.

Matt Mullenweg
Cofounder of WordPress

Introduction

● ●

*L*et's see . . . it was 2003 when I discovered the wonders of WordPress. Way back then (and in Internet years, that's actually a lot of time), I was using Movable Type as my blogging platform. My friend Chelle introduced me to the WordPress software. "Try it," she said. "You'll really like it."

As a creature of habit, I felt reluctant to make the change. But I haven't looked back. I've been with WordPress ever since.

Blogs are here to stay. Authors, students, parents, business owners, academics, hobbyists — you name it — use blogs as a matter of course.

WordPress has been a huge part of the blogging boom. Today, it's the most popular blogging platform for personal, business, and corporate bloggers alike.

To a brand-new user, some aspects of WordPress can seem a little bit intimidating. After you take a look under the hood, however, you begin to realize how intuitive, friendly, and extensible the software is.

This book presents an in-depth look at two popular versions of WordPress:

- ✔ The hosted version available at WordPress.com
- ✔ The self-hosted version available at WordPress.org

The book also covers managing and maintaining your WordPress blog through the use of WordPress plugins and themes.

If you're interested in taking a detailed look at the blogging and Web site services provided by WordPress, you happen to have just the right book in your hands.

About This Book

This book covers all the important aspects of WordPress that new users need to know to begin using the software for their own blog (or blogs). I cover the two most popular versions of WordPress, highlighting all the important topics, such as these:

- ✔ Setting up and using a hosted blog at WordPress.com

- ✔ Locating good hosting services for the self-hosted version of the software (available at WordPress.org)

- ✔ Installing and setting up the WordPress.org software

- ✔ Navigating the Dashboards of both the hosted and self-hosted versions of WordPress

- ✔ Adding media files to your blog

- ✔ Finding and installing free themes to use in your WordPress blog

- ✔ Using basic coding to design your own WordPress theme or modify the one you're using

- ✔ Using templates and tags in WordPress

- ✔ Installing, activating, and managing WordPress plugins

- ✔ Choosing to use the multiple-site WordPress Network option to host a network of multiple blogs on your domain

- ✔ Discovering the potential pitfalls associated with each version

- ✔ Understanding the challenges you face when running a WordPress–powered site, such as dodging comment and trackback spam

- ✔ Exploring RSS feed syndication

- ✔ Migrating your existing blog to WordPress (if you are using a different blogging platform, such as Blogspot, Movable Type, or TypePad)

- ✔ Discovering the power of WordPress as a Content Management System (CMS) to create a full Web site, not just a blog

- ✔ Upgrading your WordPress blog and staying up to date and informed about ongoing WordPress software development

- ✔ Finding support, tips, and resources for using the WordPress software

With WordPress, you can truly tailor a blog to your own tastes and needs. All the tools are out there. Some of them are packaged with the WordPress software; others are third-party plugins and add-ons created by members of the WordPress user community. It takes a little research, knowledge, and time on your part to put together a blog that suits your needs and gives your readers an exciting experience that keeps them coming back for more.

Conventions Used in This Book

Throughout the book, I apply the following typography conventions to guide you through some of the information I present:

✔ When I ask you to type something, the text that you're supposed to type is in **bold.**

✔ When I suggest a keyword that you may want to enter in a search engine, that term appears in *italics.*

✔ Text that appears in this `special font` is certain to be a URL (Web address), e-mail address, filename, folder name, or code.

✔ When I use a term that I think you may not be familiar with, I apply *italics* to that term to let you know that I'm defining it.

✔ In some instances, I give you a basic idea of what a Web address or block of code looks like. When the text that you see may be different, depending on your settings and preferences, I apply *italics* to that text.

What You Are Not to Read

Don't read supermarket tabloids. They're certain to rot your brain.

This book covers the details of how to set up, use, and maintain the software for WordPress.com and WordPress.org. I don't intend for you to read this book from cover to cover (unless you're my mother — then I won't forgive you if you don't). Rather, hit the Table of Contents and the Index of this book to find the information you need.

If you never intend to run a hosted WordPress blog on your own Web server, you can skip Chapters 6–8.

If you have no interest in setting up a hosted blog at WordPress.com, skip Chapters 3–5.

If you aren't interested in digging in to the code of a WordPress template, and don't want to find out how to apply CSS or HTML to enhance your design, you can skip Part V of this book (Chapters 12–15).

Long story short: Take what you need, and leave the rest.

Foolish Assumptions

I'll never know what assumptions you've made about me at this point, but I can tell you a few things that I already assume about you:

✔ You know what a computer is. You can turn it on, and you understand that if you spill coffee on your keyboard, you'll have to run out and get a replacement.

✔ You understand how to hook yourself into the Internet and know the basics of using a Web browser to surf Web sites and blogs.

✔ You have a basic understanding of what blogs are, and you're interested in using WordPress to start your own blog. Or you already have a blog, are already using WordPress, and want to understand the program better so that you can do more cool stuff and stop bugging your geeky best friend whenever you have a question about something. Or, even better, you already have a blog on another blogging platform and want to move your blog to WordPress.

✔ You know what e-mail is. You know what an e-mail address is. You actually have an e-mail address, and you send and receive e-mail on a semi-regular basis.

How This Book Is Organized

This book is made up of six parts that introduce you to the WordPress platform, including detailed information on two very popular versions of WordPress: the hosted version of WordPress.com and the self-hosted version of WordPress.org. Also included is detailed information on WordPress themes and templates.

Part 1: Introducing WordPress

The first part gives you an overview of WordPress and the advantages of making it your blogging platform. You may think of WordPress as coming in three "flavors": vanilla (WordPress.com hosted solution), chocolate (WordPress.org self-hosted solution), and Neapolitan (WordPress MU, the multiuser solution). In this part, you also discover some of the fun aspects of blogging, such as RSS feed syndication and reader interaction through comments.

Part II: Using the WordPress Hosted Service

Part II takes you through signing up with the hosted service for a blog. You tour the Administration panel, explore writing and managing your blog, find out how to change the various themes available in this version, and discover how to enhance your blog and widgets.

Part III: Self-Hosting with WordPress.org

Part III explores the single-user version of the WordPress software available at WordPress.org. You install this software on your own hosted Web server, so I give you valuable information about domain registration, Web hosting providers, and a few of the basic tools (such as FTP) that you need to install to set up a WordPress blog. I also familiarize you with the Administration panel, where you personalize your blog and explore many of the settings that you need to manage and maintain your WordPress–powered blog.

Part IV: Flexing and Extending WordPress

This part shows you how to add images to your pages, including how to create a photo gallery on your site.

This part also reveals how to find, install, and use various WordPress plugins to extend the functionality of your blog. It also steps into the world of WordPress themes, showing you where to find free themes, install them, and use them.

Part V: Customizing WordPress

Part V takes an in-depth look at the structure of a WordPress theme by taking you through each of the templates and explaining the template tags each step of the way. You find information on basic CSS and HTML that helps you tweak the free theme that you are using or even create your own theme.

This part also looks at the use of WordPress as a Content Management System (CMS) to power a full-blown Web site as well as a blog. Additionally, this part of the book takes you through how to configure WordPress to allow multiple sites, which gives you the option of running a network of multiple sites with one single installation of the WordPress software.

If the topics covered in this part of the book aren't ones you're interested in getting involved with yourself, the last chapter of this part talks about bringing in the professionals — the consultants who can help you achieve a custom-designed blog, as well as assist you with search engine optimization.

Part VI: The Part of Tens

The Part of Tens is in every *For Dummies* book that you will ever pick up. This part introduces ten Web sites that have really stretched the functionality of WordPress through plugins and themes. This part also shows you ten popular free WordPress themes that you can use to create a nice, clean look for your blog. Further, in this part you discover ten great WordPress plugins that you can use to provide your visitors (and yourself) some great functionality.

Icons Used in This Book

Icons emphasize a point to remember, a danger to be aware of, or information that I think you may find helpful. Those points are illustrated as such:

Tips are little bits of information that you may find useful.

I use this icon to point out dangerous situations.

All geeky stuff goes here. I don't use this icon very often, but when I do, you know you're about to encounter technical mumbo-jumbo.

When you see this icon, read the text next to it two or three times to brand it into your brain so that you remember whatever it was that I think you need to remember.

Where to Go from Here

As I mention in the "What You Are Not to Read" section of this introduction, take what you need, and leave the rest. This book is a veritable smorgasbord of WordPress information, ideas, concepts, tools, resources, and instruction. Some of it will apply directly to what you want to do with your WordPress blog. Other parts deal with topics that you're only mildly curious about, so you may want to skim those pages.

Part I

Introducing WordPress

The 5th Wave   By Rich Tennant

"Hi all. 'Turns out that the rash I posted about last night _is_ contagious..."

In this part . . .

Ready to get started? I know I am! This part of the book provides a brief introduction to WordPress and blogging. WordPress is unique in offering two versions of its software, and I tell you about each version so that you can choose the one that's right for you.

Chapter 1

What WordPress Can Do for You

*I*n a world in which technology advances faster than a speeding locomotive, WordPress is blogging made easy — and free! How else can you get your message out to a potential audience of millions worldwide and spend exactly nothing? There may be no such thing as a free lunch in this world, but you can bet your bottom dollar that there are free blogs to be had. WordPress serves them all up in one nifty package.

The software's free price tag, its ease of use, and the speed at which you can get your blog up and running are great reasons to use WordPress to power your personal or business blog. An even greater reason is the incredibly supportive and passionate WordPress community. In this chapter, I introduce you to the WordPress software so that you can begin to discover how effective it is as a tool for creating your blog or Web site.

Discovering the Benefits of WordPress

I work with first-time bloggers all the time — folks who are new to the idea of publishing on the Internet. One of the questions I'm most frequently asked is "How can I run a blog? I don't even know how to code or create Web sites."

Enter WordPress. You no longer need to worry about knowing the code, because the WordPress blogging software does the code part for you. When you log in to your blog, you have to do only two simple things to publish your thoughts and ideas:

1. Write your post.

2. Click a button to publish your post.

That's it!

WordPress offers the following competitive advantages as the most popular blogging tool on the market:

- **Diverse options:** Two versions of WordPress are available to suit nearly every type of blogger: a hosted turnkey solution and a version to install on the Web server of your choice. I go into detail about each of these versions later in this chapter, in the "Choosing a WordPress Platform" section.

- **Ease of use:** WordPress setup is quick, and the software is easy to use.

- **Extensibility:** WordPress is extremely extensible, meaning that you can easily obtain plugins and tools that let you customize it to suit your purposes.

- **Strong community of users:** WordPress has a large and loyal members-helping-members community via public support forums, mailing lists, and blogs geared to the use of WordPress.

The following sections fill in a few details about these features and point you to places in the book where you can find out more about them.

Getting set up the fast and easy way

WordPress is one of the only blog platforms that can brag about a five-minute installation — and stand behind it! Signing up for the hosted version of WordPress takes approximately the same amount of time.

Mind you, five minutes is an *approximate* installation time. It doesn't include the time required to obtain domain registration and Web hosting services or to set up the options in the Dashboard.

When you complete the installation, however, the world of WordPress awaits you. The Dashboard is well organized and easy on the eyes. Everything is clear and logical, making it easy for even a first-time user to see where to go to manage settings and options.

The WordPress software surely has enough meat on it to keep the most experienced developer busy and happy. At the same time, however, it's friendly enough to make a novice user giddy about how easy getting started is. Each time you use WordPress, you can find out something exciting and new.

Extending WordPress's capabilities

I've found that the most exciting and fun part of running a WordPress blog is exploring the flexibility of the software. Hundreds of plugins and themes are available to let you create a blog that functions the way *you* need it to.

If you think of your blog as a vacuum cleaner, plugins are the attachments. The attachments don't function alone. When you add them to your vacuum cleaner, however, you add to the functionality of your vacuum, possibly improving its performance.

All WordPress blogs are pretty much the same at their core, so by using plugins, you can truly individualize your blog by providing additional features and tools to benefit yourself and your readers. When you come upon a WordPress blog that has some really different and cool functions, 98 percent of the time you can include that function in your own blog by using a WordPress plugin. If you don't know what plugin that blog is using, feel free to drop the blog owner an e-mail or leave a comment. WordPress blog owners usually are eager to share the great tools they discover.

Most plugins are available at no charge. You can find out more about WordPress plugins and where to get them in Chapter 10. Chapter 17 lists my choice of ten popular WordPress plugins available for download.

In addition to using plugins, you can embellish your WordPress blog with templates and themes. WordPress comes with a real nice default theme to get you started. Figure 1-1 shows the default Twenty Ten theme, created by the team from WordPress, which is displayed by default after you install and set up your blog.

The theme's default form is blue and white, with a handy application built in to the preferences that lets you change the background color and insert an image to use as a header image (more about tweaking WordPress themes can be found in Chapter 13).

This theme includes all the basic elements that you need when starting a new WordPress blog. You can extend your WordPress blog in a hundred ways with the use of plugins and themes that have been released by members of the WordPress community, but the Twenty Ten theme is a nice place to start.

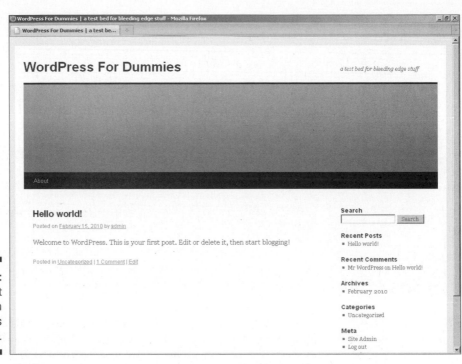

Figure 1-1:
The default
Twenty Ten
WordPress
theme.

Taking part in the community

Allow me to introduce you to the fiercely loyal folks who make up the user base, better known as the vast WordPress community. This band of merry ladies and gentlemen comes from all around the globe, from California to Cairo, Florida to Florence, and all points in between and beyond.

In March 2005, Matt Mullenweg of WordPress proudly proclaimed that the number of WordPress downloads had reached 900,000 — an amazing land-mark in the history of the software. But the real excitement occurred in August 2006, when WordPress logged more than 1 million downloads, and in 2007, when the software had more than 3 million downloads. The number of downloads of WordPress has broken the ceiling since 2007 and continues to grow with each passing day!

Don't let the sheer volume of users fool you: WordPress has bragging rights to the most helpful blogging community on the Web today. You can find users helping other users in the support forums at `http://wordpress.org/ support`. You can also find users contributing to the very helpful **WordPress**

Codex (a collection of how-to documents) at `http://codex.wordpress.org`. Finally, across the blogosphere, you can find multiple blogs about WordPress itself, with users sharing their experiences and war stories in the hope of helping the next person who comes along.

You can subscribe to various mailing lists, too. These lists offer you the opportunity to become involved in various aspects of the WordPress community, as well as in the future development of the software.

Don't worry if you're not a member of the WordPress community. Joining is easy: Simply start your own blog by using one of the two WordPress software options. If you're already blogging on a different platform, such as Blogspot or Movable Type, WordPress makes it simple for you to migrate your current data from that platform to a new WordPress setup. (See the appendix for information about moving your existing blog to WordPress.)

Choosing a WordPress Platform

Among the realities of running a blog today is choosing among the veritable feast of software platforms to find the one that will perform the way you need it to. You want to be sure that the platform you choose has all the options you're looking for. WordPress is unique in that it offers two versions of its software. Each version is designed to meet the various needs of bloggers. The two different versions of WordPress are the following:

- ✔ The hosted version at WordPress.com. (Part II of this book focuses on this version.)
- ✔ The self-installed and self-hosted version available at WordPress.org. (Part III focuses on this version.)

Certain features are available to you in every WordPress blog setup, whether you're using the self-hosted software from WordPress.org or the hosted version at WordPress.com. These features include (but aren't limited to):

- ✔ Quick-and-easy installation and setup
- ✔ Full-featured blogging capability, letting you publish content to the Web through an easy-to-use Web-based interface
- ✔ Topical archiving of your posts, using categories
- ✔ Monthly archiving of your posts, with the ability to provide a listing of those archives for easy navigation through your site.

- ✔ Comment and trackback tools
- ✔ Automatic spam protection through Akismet
- ✔ Built-in gallery integration for photos and images
- ✔ Media Manager for video and audio files
- ✔ Great community support
- ✔ Unlimited number of static pages, letting you step out of the blog box and into the sphere of running a fully functional Web site
- ✔ RSS capability with RSS 2.0, RSS 1.0, and Atom support
- ✔ Tools for importing content from different blogging systems (such as Blogger, Movable Type, and LiveJournal)

Table 1-1 compares the two WordPress versions.

Table 1-1	Exploring the Differences among the Two Versions of WordPress	
Feature	**WordPress.org**	**WordPress.com**
Cost	Free	Free
Software download	Yes	No
Software installation	Yes	No
Web hosting required	Yes	No
Custom CSS control	Yes	$15/year
Template access	Yes	No
Sidebar widgets	Yes	Yes
RSS syndication	Yes	Yes
Access to core code	Yes	No
Ability to install plugins	Yes	No
WP themes installation	Yes	No
Multiauthor support	Yes	Yes
Unlimited number of blog setups with one account	Yes	Yes
Community-based support forums	Yes	Yes

Choosing the hosted version from WordPress.com

WordPress.com is a free service. If downloading, installing, and using software on a Web server sound like Greek to you — and are things you'd rather avoid — the WordPress folks provide a solution for you at WordPress.com.

WordPress.com is a *hosted solution,* which means it has no software requirement, no downloads, and no installation or server configurations. Everything's done for you on the back end, behind the scenes. You don't even have to worry about how the process happens; it happens quickly, and before you know it, you're making your first blog post using a WordPress.com blog solution.

WordPress.com has some limitations. You can't install plugins or custom themes, for example, and you can't customize the base code files. But even with its limitations, WordPress.com is an excellent starting point if you're brand new to blogging and a little intimidated by the configuration requirements of the self-installed WordPress.org software.

The good news is this: If you ever outgrow your WordPress.com hosted blog in the future and want to make a move to the self-hosted WordPress.org software, you can. You can even take all the content from your WordPress.com-hosted blog with you and easily import it into your new setup with the WordPress.org software.

So in the grand scheme of things, your options are really not that limited.

Self-hosting with WordPress.org

The self-installed version from WordPress.org (covered in Part III) requires you to download the software from the WordPress Web site and install it on a Web server. Unless you own your own Web server, you need to lease one — or lease space on one.

Using a Web server is typically referred to as *Web hosting,* and unless you know someone who knows someone, hosting generally isn't free. That being said, Web hosting doesn't cost a whole lot, either. You can usually obtain a good Web hosting service for anywhere from $5 to $10 per month. (Chapter 6 gives you the important details you need to know about obtaining a Web host.) You need to make sure, however, that any Web host you choose to work with has the required software installed on the Web server. Currently, the minimum software requirements for WordPress include

- ✔ PHP version 4.3 or greater
- ✔ MySQL version 4.0 or greater

After you have WordPress installed on your Web server (see the installation instructions in Chapter 6), you can start using it to blog to your heart's content. With the WordPress software, you can install several plugins that extend the functionality of the blogging system, as I describe in Chapter 10. You also have full control of the core files and code that WordPress is built on. So if you have a knack for PHP and knowledge of MySQL, you can work within the code to make changes that you think would be good for you and your blog.

You don't need design ability to make your blog look great. Members of the WordPress community have created more than 1,600 WordPress themes (designs), and you can download them for free and install them on your WordPress blog (see Chapter 11). Additionally, if you're creatively inclined, like to create designs on your own, and know Cascading Style Sheets (CSS), you have full access to the template system within WordPress and can create your own custom themes (see Chapters 12 and 13).

The self-hosted WordPress.org software lets you run an unlimited number of blogs on one installation of its software platform, on one domain. When you configure the Network options within WordPress to enable a multisite interface, you become administrator of a network of blogs. All of the options remain the same, but with the Network options configure you can add additional blogs, domains and allow registered users of your Web site to host their own blog within your network, as well.

What types of sites use the Network options within WordPress?

- ✔ Blog networks, which can have more than 150 blogs. The popular electronics retail store, Best Buy, uses WordPress to power 1,050 local store blogs (example: `http://stores.bestbuy.com/577`).
- ✔ Newspapers and magazines, such as *The New York Times,* and universities such as Harvard Law School that currently use WordPress to manage the blog sections of their Web sites.
- ✔ Niche-specific blog networks, such as Edublogs.org, that use WordPress to manage their full networks of free blogs for teachers, educators, lecturers, librarians, and other education professionals.

Chapter 2

WordPress Blogging Basics

In This Chapter

▶ Considering blog types

▶ Finding out what blog technology can do for you

▶ Outlining your initial blog plan

A lot happens behind the scenes to make your WordPress blog or Web site function. The beauty of it is this: You don't have to worry about what's happening on the back end in order to manage and maintain a WordPress site — unless you really want to. In this chapter, I delve a little bit into the technology behind the WordPress platform, including a brief look at PHP and MySQL, two software components required to run WordPress.

This chapter also covers some of the various blogging technologies that help you on your way to running a successful blog, such as the use of comments and RSS feed technology, as well as information about combating spam.

This Crazy Little Thing Called Blog

Blogging is an evolutionary process, and I have a strong feeling that blogs have evolved beyond personal journals to become tools for real journalism, business, and authorship.

A blog is a fabulous tool for publishing your personal diary of thoughts and ideas; however, blogs also serve as excellent tools for business, editorial journalism, news, and entertainment. Here are some ways that people use blogs:

✔ **Personal:** This type of blogger creates a blog as a personal journal or diary. You're considered to be a personal blogger if you use your blog mainly to discuss topics that are personal to you or your life — your family, your cats, your children, or your interests (for example, technology, politics, sports, art, or photography). My own blog, which you'll find at `http://justa girlintheworld.com`, is an example of a personal blog.

✔ **Business:** This type of blogger uses the power of blogs to promote a company's business services and/or products on the Internet. Blogs are very effective tools for promotion and marketing, and business blogs usually offer helpful information to readers and consumers, such as ad tips and product reviews. Business blogs also let readers provide feedback and ideas, which can help a company improve its services. ServerBeach is a good example of a business that keeps a blog on the hosted WordPress. com service at `http://serverbeach.wordpress.com`.

✔ **Media/journalism:** More and more popular news outlets such as Fox News, MSNBC, and CNN are adding blogs to their Web sites to provide information on current events, politics, and news on a regional, national, and international level. These news organizations often have editorial bloggers as well. Editorial cartoonist Daryl Cagle, for example, maintains a blog on MSNBC's Web site at `http://cagle.msnbc.com/news/blog`, where he discusses his cartoons and the feedback he receives from readers.

✔ **Citizen journalism:** The emergence of citizen journalism coincided with the swing from old media to new media. In old media, the journalists and news organizations direct the conversation about news topics.

With the popularity of blogs and the millions of bloggers who exploded onto the Internet, old media felt a change in the wind. Average citizens, using the power of their voices on blogs, changed the direction of the conversation. Citizen journalists often fact-check traditional media news stories and expose inconsistencies, with the intention of keeping the media or local politicians in check. An example of citizen journalism is the Power Line Blog at `http://powerlineblog.com`.

✔ **Professional:** This category of blogger is growing every day. Professional bloggers are paid to blog for individual companies or Web sites. Blog networks, such as WeblogsInc.com, hire bloggers to write on certain topics of interest. Also, several services match advertisers with bloggers, so that the advertisers pay bloggers to make blog posts about their products. Is it possible to make money as a blogger? Yes, and making money is becoming common these days. If you're interested in this type of blogging, check out Darren Rowse's ProBlogger blog at `http://problogger.net`. Darren is considered to be the grandfather of all professional bloggers.

Dipping In to Blog Technologies

The WordPress software is a personal publishing system that uses a PHP-and-MySQL platform, which provides you everything you need to create your own blog and publish your own content dynamically, without having to know how to program those pages yourself. In short, all your content is stored in a MySQL database in your hosting account.

PHP (which stands for *PHP Hypertext Preprocessor*) is a server-side scripting language for creating dynamic Web pages. When a visitor opens a page built in PHP, the server processes the PHP commands and then sends the results to the visitor's browser. MySQL is an open source relational database management system (RDBMS) that uses Structured Query Language (SQL), the most popular language for adding, accessing, and processing data in a database. If that all sounds like Greek to you, just think of MySQL as a big filing cabinet where all the content on your blog is stored.

Every time a visitor goes to your blog to read your content, he makes a request that's sent to a host server. The PHP programming language receives that request, obtains the requested information from the MySQL database, and then presents the requested information to your visitor through his Web browser.

In using the term *content* as it applies to the data that's stored in the MySQL database, I'm referring to your blog posts, comments, and options that you set up in the WordPress Dashboard. The theme (design) you choose to use for your blog — whether it's the default theme, one you create for yourself, or one that you have custom-designed for you — isn't part of the content in this case. Those files are part of the file system and aren't stored in the database. So it's a good idea to create and keep a backup of any theme files that you're currently using. See Part IV for further information on WordPress theme management.

When you look for a hosting service, keep an eye out for the hosts that provide daily backups of your site, so that your content/data won't be lost in case something happens. Web hosting providers that offer daily backups as part of their services can save the day by restoring your site to its original form.

Archiving your publishing history

Packaged within the WordPress software is the capability to maintain chronological and categorized archives of your publishing history, automatically. WordPress uses PHP and MySQL technology to sort and organize everything you publish in an order that you, and your readers, can access by date and category. This archiving process is done automatically with every post you publish to your blog.

When you create a post on your WordPress blog, you can file that post under a category that you specify. This feature makes for a very nifty archiving system in which you and your readers can find articles/posts that you've

placed within a specific category. The archives page on my personal blog
(see it at http://justagirlintheworld.com/archives) contains a
Topical Archive Pages section, where you find a list of categories I've created
for my blog posts. Clicking the Blog Design link below the Topical archive
pages heading takes you to a listing of posts that I wrote on that topic (see
Figure 2-1 and Figure 2-2).

Figure 2-1:
A list of cat-
egories in a
WordPress
blog site.

Figure 2-2: A
page with a
list of posts
made in my
Blog Design
category.

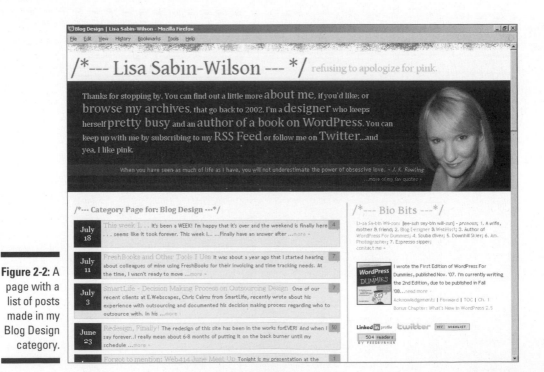

WordPress lets you create as many categories as you want for filing your blog posts by topic. I've seen blogs that have just one category and blogs that have up to 1,800 categories — WordPress is all about personal preference and how you want to organize your content. On the other hand, using WordPress categories is your choice. You don't have to use the category feature if you'd rather not.

Interacting with your readers through comments

One of the most exciting and fun aspects of blogging with WordPress is getting feedback from your readers the moment you make a post to your blog. Feedback, referred to as *blog comments,* is akin to having a guestbook on your blog. People can leave notes for you that are published to your site, and you can respond and engage your readers in conversation about the topic at hand (see Figure 2-3 and Figure 2-4). Having this function in your blog creates the opportunity to expand the thoughts and ideas that you presented in your blog post by giving your readers the opportunity to add their two cents' worth.

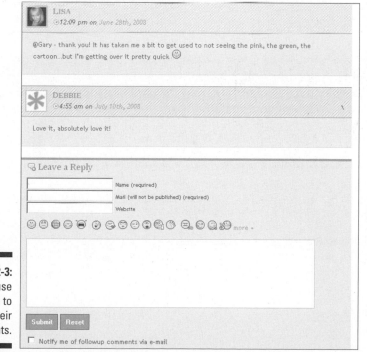

Figure 2-3:
Readers use the form to leave their comments.

/*--- 50 Responses to "Redesign, Finally!" ---*/

LINDSEY
⏱9:32 pm on June 23rd, 2008

This looks so much like you! I love that it all looks like code, yet it's still feminine. And the use of your rockin' headshot is great - that is a fantastic picture 😊 ! Glad you were finally able to spend a little time on YOU!! Wonderful design - worth the wait 😊

MICHAEL
⏱9:40 pm on June 23rd, 2008

The design is absolutely beautiful (even though it is pink. 😊) It took me a while to remember why the formatting of the type looked so familiar and then it hit me when I opened my current design project. Its eye pleasing and geeky at the same time.

LISA
⏱9:43 pm on June 23rd, 2008

Lindsey - thank you! It's been a while in the making..every time I thought I had a day or two to work on it... that day (or two) vaporized somewhere else. It's nice to finally have it done and dusted!

Glad you like the headshot - - I always struggle with actually LIKING pictures of myself... so moving away from the cartoon to my actual face is a little therapy lol

LISA
⏱9:44 pm on June 23rd, 2008

Michael - thanks for stopping by and leaving your comments. I tried to make the design a little reminiscent of CSS code that I bury myself eyebrow deep in on a daily basis. Glad to hear the pink isn't too offensive 😊

Figure 2-4:
My blog fans comment on my blog about this book.

In the WordPress Dashboard, you have full administrative control over who can and can't leave comments. In addition, if someone leaves a comment with questionable content, you can edit the comment or delete it. You're also free to choose not to allow any comments on your blog.

Some blog users say that a blog without comments isn't a blog at all. This belief is common in the blogging community, because experiencing visitor feedback through the use of comments is part of what has made blogging so popular. It's a personal choice. Allowing comments on your blog invites your audience members to actively involve themselves in your blog by creating a discussion and dialogue about your content. By and large, readers find commenting to be a satisfying experience when they visit blogs, because comments make them part of the discussion.

Feeding your readers

RSS stands for *Really Simple Syndication*. An *RSS feed* is a standard feature that blog readers have come to expect. So what is it, really?

The Introduction to RSS page on the resource site WebReference.com (`www.webreference.com/authoring/languages/xml/rss/intro/`) defines RSS as "a lightweight XML format designed for sharing headlines and other Web content. Think of it as a distributable 'What's New' for your site."

Readers can use tools called *feed readers* to download your feed — that is, their feed readers are set up to automatically discover new content (such as posts and comments) from your blog and download that content for their consumption. Table 2-1 lists some of the most popular feed readers on the market today.

Table 2-1	Popular RSS Feed Readers	
Reader	*Source*	*Description*
Bloglines	`http://bloglines.com`	Bloglines is a free online service for searching, subscribing to, and sharing RSS feeds. You have no software to download or install; Bloglines is all Web based. You need to sign up for an account to use this service.
Google Reader	`http://google.com/reader`	This free online service is provided by Internet search giant Google. With Google Reader, you can keep up with your favorite blogs and Web sites that have syndicated (RSS) content. You have no software to download or install to use this service, but you need to sign up for an account with Google.
FeedDemon	`http://feeddemon.com`	This is a free service that requires you to download the RSS reader application to your own computer.

For your blog readers to stay updated with the latest and greatest content you post to your site, they need to subscribe to your RSS feed. Most blogging platforms allow the RSS feeds to be *autodiscovered* by the various feed readers — meaning that the reader needs only to enter your site's URL, and the program will automatically find your RSS feed.

 Most browser systems today alert visitors to the RSS feed on your site by displaying the universally recognized orange RSS feed icon, shown in the margin.

WordPress has built-in RSS feeds in several formats. Because the feeds are built in to the software platform, you don't need to do anything to provide your readers an RSS feed of your content. Check out Chapter 8 to find out more about using RSS feeds within the WordPress program.

Tracking back

The best way to understand trackbacks is to think of them as comments, except for one thing: Trackbacks are comments that are left on your blog by other blogs, not by actual people. Sounds perfectly reasonable, doesn't it?Actually, it does.

A trackback happens when you make a post on your blog, and within that post, you provide a link to a post made by another blogger in a different blog. When you publish that post, your blog sends a sort of electronic memo to the blog you've linked to. That blog receives the memo and posts an acknowledgment of receipt in a comment to the post that you linked to.

That memo is sent via a *network ping* (a tool used to test, or verify, whether a link is reachable across the Internet) from your site to the site you link to. This process works as long as both blogs support trackback protocol.

Sending a trackback to a blog is a nice way of telling the blogger that you like the information she presented in her blog post. Every blogger appreciates the receipt of trackbacks to their posts from other bloggers.

Dealing with comment and trackback spam

Ugh. The absolute bane of every blogger's existence is comment and track-back spam. When blogs became the "It" things on the Internet, spammers saw an opportunity. If you've ever received spam e-mail, the concept is similar and just as frustrating.

Before blogs came onto the scene, you often saw spammers filling Internet guestbooks with their links but not leaving any relevant comments. The reason is simple: Web sites receive higher rankings in the major search engines if they have multiple links coming in from other sites. Enter blog software, with comment and trackback technologies — prime breeding ground for millions of spammers.

Because comments and trackbacks are published to your site publicly — and usually with a link to the commenters' Web sites — spammers got their site links posted on millions of blogs by creating programs that automatically seek Web sites with commenting systems and then hammer those systems with tons of comments that contain links back to their own sites.

No blogger likes spam. As a matter of fact, blogging services such as WordPress have spent untold hours in the name of stopping these spammers in their tracks, and for the most part, they've been successful. Every once in a while, however, spammers sneak through. Many spammers are offensive, and all of them are frustrating because they don't contribute to the ongoing conversations that occur in blogs.

All WordPress systems have one very major, very excellent thing in common: Akismet, which kills spam dead. Chapter 10 tells you more about Akismet, which is brought to you by Automattic, the maker of WordPress.com.

Moving On to the Business of Blogging

Before getting started with blogging, you need to take a long look at your big plans for your Web site. A word of advice: Organize your plan of attack before you start. Have a good idea of what types of information you want to publish, how you want to present and organize that information, and what types of services and interaction you want to provide your audience.

Ask this question out loud: "What am I going to blog about?" Go ahead — ask it. Do you have an answer? Maybe you do, and maybe not — either way, it's all right. There's no clear set of ground rules you must follow. Having an idea of what you're planning to write about in your blog makes planning your attack a little easier. You may want to write about your personal life. Maybe you plan to share only some of your photography and provide very little commentary to go along with it. Or maybe you're a business owner, and you want to blog about your services and current news within your industry.

Having an idea of your subject matter will help you determine how you want to deliver that information. My design blog, for example, is where I write about Web design projects, client case studies, and news related to design and blogging. You won't find pictures of my cats there, but you will find those pictures on my personal blog. I keep the two blogs separate, much in the same way that most of us like to keep a distinct line of separation between our personal and professional lives, no matter what industry we work in.

When you have your topic and plan of delivery in mind, you can move forward and adjust your blog settings to work with your plan.

Part II
Using the WordPress Hosted Service

The 5th Wave   By Rich Tennant

"He saw your laptop and wants to know if he can post a new blog."

In this part . . .

If installing software on a Web server and hosting your
own blog sound like things you'd like to avoid,
WordPress.com may be your answer. In this section, you
find out how to get — and use — a free hosted blog from
WordPress.com.

Chapter 3

Getting Started with WordPress.com

In This Chapter

▶ Signing up for a blog

▶ Familiarizing yourself with the Dashboard

▶ Important options to set before you begin

▶ Finding the help you need

*1*f you're just starting out and don't want to spend money purchasing a domain name and hosting your site with a third-party Web host, then WordPress.com has a great alternative for you.

This part takes a complete look at the hosted service offered at WordPress. com, and in this chapter, you discover how to create a free blog through this service. You also find out how to get your hosted blog up and running.

Don't confuse WordPress.com with the blogging software available for download at WordPress.org! The two were created and developed by the same folks, and they do have the same name; however, they are different varieties of WordPress. (See Part III for information on installing and using the self-hosted version of WordPress.org.)

Creating a WordPress.com Account

To create your WordPress.com user account, follow these steps:

1. **In your browser, enter the URL** `http://wordpress.com`.

2. **On the page that appears, click the big Sign Up Now! button (shown in Figure 3-1).**

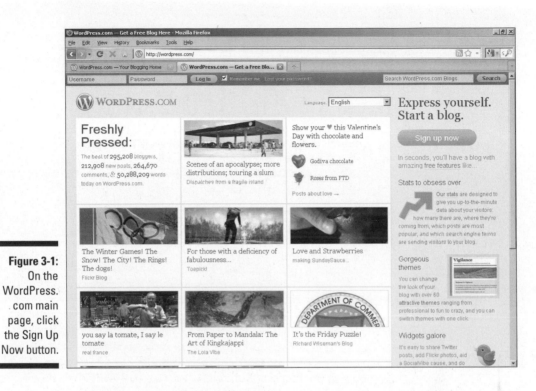

Figure 3-1:
On the
WordPress.
com main
page, click
the Sign Up
Now button.

You're taken to the WordPress.com signup page at `http://wordpress.com/signup`.

3. **In the Username text box, enter the name you want to use to log in to your blog from now until forever.**

   This username must be at least four characters in length with letters and numbers only. This username cannot be changed for the blog you are creating right now. In the future, you can sign up for a new WordPress.com account with a new username; you also start over with a new blog.

4. **Enter a password of your choice first in the Password box and then in the Confirm box.**

   You use this password to log in to your new WordPress.com account. Choose, and then type, a password that you will remember, but not one that would be easy for any outside users to guess. Your password must be at least four characters in length.

5. **Enter your e-mail address in the Email Address box.**

   This address isn't made public on your blog; rather, it's used for communication between you and WordPress.com. You can change this address later, in the Options section in your WordPress.com Dashboard.

6. **Select the check box in the Legal Flotsam section.**

   Selecting the Legal Flotsam box lets the WordPress.com folks know that you've read its terms of service.

7. **Select either Gimme a Blog! or Just a Username, Please.**

   The Gimme a Blog! option signs you up with a WordPress.com account and sets you up with a new WordPress.com blog. The Just a Username, Please option just signs you up with a new WordPress.com account, without the blog-setup part. You may want only to reserve a username in WordPress.com for now, which is why you might choose the second option.

8. **Click the Next button.**

9. **In the Blog Domain text box, enter what you choose as your blog domain name.**

   Whatever you enter here becomes the URL address of your blog. It must be at least four characters (letters and numbers only), and you can't change it later, so choose carefully! (The domain name of your blog does not have to be the same as your username, although WordPress.com already fills in this text box for you, with your username. You can choose any domain name you want; WordPress.com lets you know whether that domain name is available within its network.) Keep in mind that search engines catalog your content based on your chosen URL, so it's a good idea to use a domain name that relates well to your site's content (see Chapter 14 for more information about search engine optimization).

10. **In the Blog Title text box, enter the name you've chosen for your blog.**

    Your blog title doesn't have to be the same as your username, and you can change it later in the Options section in your Dashboard.

11. **Choose your language preference from the Language drop-down menu.**

    Choose the primary language that you will be blogging in.

12. **Select the Privacy check box if you want your blog to be public. Deselect this box if you want your blog to be private and not show up in search engines. (By default, this box is checked for you.)**

    Some bloggers actually do not want their blogs to be indexed by search engines, amazingly enough. Like them, you may want to run a private blog for which you decide who can, and cannot, view the contents of your blog.

13. **Click the Sign-Up button, and you're done!**

    A new page opens with a message telling you that WordPress.com has sent you an e-mail containing a link to activate your account. As you wait for that e-mail to arrive, take a moment to fill out the form on this page that invites you to update your profile. Enter your first name, last name, and a few sentences about yourself. Then click the Save Profile button.

14. Check your e-mail and click the link contained within it to activate your new WordPress.com blog.

A page loads with a message that your blog is now active. That page also displays your username and password. You receive another e-mail from WordPress.com that contains your username and password, as well as some useful links for navigating around WordPress.com — for example, the sign-in page, the Write Post page, and so on.

Your new blog is yours to use for the life of your blogging career at WordPress.com. You can log in to your blog any time by going to http://wordpress.com and filling in the login form shown in the top-left corner of the WordPress.com Web site (refer to Figure 3-1).

Have you ever signed up for a service on the Web, only to forget your user-name and/or password for that service mere weeks after the fact? Yep, me, too. It's a *very* good idea to file that e-mail from WordPress.com in a safe place for future reference. Just make sure that you remember where you put it. Or you can tell WordPress.com to remember you each time you enter the site. To do so, select the Remember Me check box. WordPress.com places a cookie in your browser files that tells it to remember your login credentials the next time you visit the site. (You need to have cookies enabled in your browser configurations for this feature to work.)

If you delete your cookies in your browser and then visit WordPress.com again, you won't see the WordPress.com menu bar and have to log in again. Likewise, after you delete the cookies in your browser, when you visit your new blog, it appears to you as though you are a visitor (that is, you see no menu bar with quick links for logging in to your Dashboard). In this case, you have to revisit the WordPress.com main site to log in again.

You can get help and support for your WordPress.com account in the Support Forums here: http://wordpress.com/forums. Find answers to frequently asked questions here: http://faq.wordpress.com.

Navigating WordPress.com

When you've successfully logged in to your new account, WordPress returns you to the main WordPress.com Web site — only this time, you see some-thing slightly different at the top. The page now displays the WordPress.com menu bar, shown in Figure 3-2. The WordPress.com menu bar contains some shortcut links to some important areas of your Dashboard.

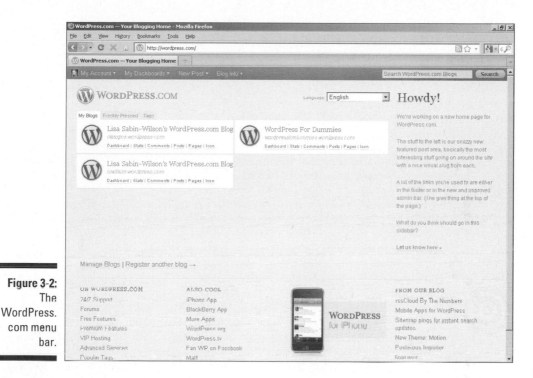

Figure 3-2:
The
WordPress.
com menu
bar.

The WordPress.com menu bar also appears at the top of any WordPress.com blog you surf to, as long as you are logged in to your WordPress.com account. The WordPress.com menu bar consists of several helpful quick links for you to access your account, your Dashboard, and various options. From left to right, these quick links include

✔ **My Account:** Hover your mouse pointer over this link, and you see a drop-down menu that consists of the following:

- *Global Dashboard:* Takes you to the Dashboard panel.

- *Stats:* Takes you to your statistics page in your WordPress.com Dashboard that displays information about your blog such as how many visitors you have on a daily basis, referrers, and keywords.

- *Blog Surfer:* Takes you to the Blog Surfer page, where you can search for and add new blogs to track and stay updated on.

- *Tag Surfer:* Takes you to the Tag Surfer, where you can find out what people are talking about based on keywords.

- *My Comments:* Takes you to the My Comments section in the WordPress Dashboard, where you can view all comments you've left anywhere within the WordPress.com network of blogs.

- *Edit Profile:* Takes you to the Your Profile section in your Dashboard, where you can edit your own user profile.

- *Support:* Takes you to an area where you can get assistance from the folks who run WordPress.com (`http://support.wordpress.com`).

- *WordPress.com:* Takes you to the main WordPress.com Web site.

- *Logout:* Lets you log out.

✔ **My Dashboard:** Click this link to go to the Dashboard page. I discuss the Dashboard page in detail in the next section.

✔ **New Post:** Click this link to go to the Write Post page, where you can write and publish a new post to your blog. If you want to get started right away with a new post, see Chapter 4.

✔ **Blog Info:** Hover your mouse pointer over this link to see a drop-down menu with the following elements:

- *Random Post:* Loads, in the same window, a random post from the blog you are visiting.

- *Follow this Blog:* Loads the Blog Surfer page within your Dashboard, allowing you to subscribe to the blog you're visiting.

- *Add to Blogroll:* Automatically adds the blog you are visiting to your blogroll.

- *Get Shortlink:* Pops open a dialog box on your computer with a short-ened version of the Web address of the page you're currently visiting.

- *Report as spam:* Reports the blog to WordPress.com administration as a spam blog.

- *Report as mature:* Reports the blog to WordPress.com administra-tion as a blog containing mature content.

Using the WordPress.com Dashboard

When you click the My Dashboard link in the WordPress.com menu bar (covered in the preceding section), you go directly to your WordPress.com Dashboard, starting at the Dashboard page (see Figure 3-3). Several modules within your Dashboard provide you with information about your blog, as well as actions you can take to navigate to other areas of the Dashboard, such as writing a new post, and adding a new link or blogroll.

The Dashboard modules are configurable; you can move them around on your Dashboard page and change the way the modules display. Hover your mouse pointer over the title bar of the module you want to move. Click and drag the module to the spot you'd like to move it and release the mouse button. This drag 'n' drop capability is available not only on the Dashboard

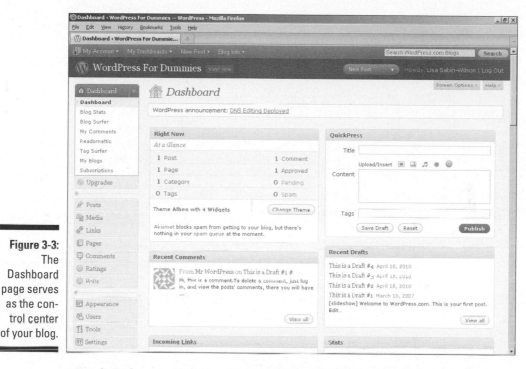

Figure 3-3:
The
Dashboard
page serves
as the con-
trol center
of your blog.

page, but also on all the inner pages of the WordPress Dashboard so you can really configure the panel to suit your needs. You can also expand (open) and collapse (close) the individual modules by clicking your mouse anywhere within the grey title bar of the module. This feature is really nice because it allows you to use the Dashboard to see just those modules that you use regularly. The concept is easy: Keep the modules you use all the time open and close the ones that you only use occasionally — you can open those modules only when you really need them.

The navigation menu in the WordPress Dashboard appears on the left side of your browser window. When you need to get back to the WordPress Dashboard, click the Dashboard link that appears at the top of the navigation menu of any of the pages within your WordPress Dashboard. Each navigation item that appears in the menu has an arrow to the right of the header — clicking that arrow expands (open) the menu for that item. Likewise, clicking the arrow again collapses (close) the submenu.

Right Now

The Right Now module of the Dashboard gives you some stats on what's happening in your blog this very second. Figure 3-3 shows what was happening in my WordPress.com blog when I took a picture of it.

The Dashboard displays the following information under the At a Glance header:

- ✔ **The number of posts:** The number here always reflects the total number of posts you currently have in your WordPress blog. Figure 3-3 shows I currently have one post on my blog. The number is blue; click the number, and you go to the Edit Posts page, where you can edit the posts on your blog. I cover editing posts in Chapter 4.

- ✔ **The number of pages:** This is the current number of pages on your blog, which will change as you add or delete pages. (*Pages,* in this context, refer to the static pages you have created in your blog.) Figure 3-3 shows that my blog has 1 page.

  Clicking this link takes you to the Edit Pages page, where you can view, edit, and delete your current pages. (Find the difference between WordPress posts and pages in Chapter 4.)

- ✔ **The number of categories:** This is the current number of categories you have on your blog, which will change as you add and delete categories. Figure 3-3 shows that I currently have 1 category for my blog.

  Clicking this link takes you to the Categories Page, where you can view, edit, and delete your current categories or add brand new ones. (For details about the management and creation of categories, see Chapter 4.)

- ✔ **The number of tags:** This is the current number of tags you have in your blog, which will change as you add and delete categories in the future. Figure 3-3 shows that I have no tags.

  Clicking this link takes you to the Tags page, where you can add new tags and view, edit, and delete your current tags. (You can find more information about Tags in Chapter 4.)

- ✔ **The number of comments:** This is the total number of the comments that are currently on your blog. Figure 3-3 shows that I have 1 Comment, 1 Approved, 0 Pending (waiting to be approved), and 0 Spam. Clicking any of these four links takes you to the Edit Comments page, where you can manage the comments on your blog. I cover the management of comments in Chapter 4.

The last section of the Dashboard's Right Now module in the Dashboard shows the following information:

- ✔ **Which WordPress theme you're using:** Figure 3-3 shows that I'm using the Albeo theme. The theme name is a link that, when clicked, takes you to the Manage Themes page where you can view and activate themes on your blog.

- ✔ **How many widgets you've added to your blog:** This is the number of WordPress widgets you're using in your blog. Figure 3-3 shows that I have 4 widgets. The number is a link that, when clicked, takes you to the Widgets page, where you can change your widget options by editing them, moving them, or removing them. (I cover widgets in detail in Chapter 5.)

✔ **Change Theme:** Clicking this button takes you to the Manage Themes page, which lists your currently active and all available themes for your WordPress blog.

✔ **Akismet Spam stats:** This is the last statement in the Right Now section, and it gives you a quick look into how many spam comments and trackbacks the Akismet application has successfully blocked from your site. Figure 3-3 shows that Akismet has not blocked any spam comments on my site yet, because it's brand new.

Recent Comments

The next module is Recent Comments. Within this module, you find

✔ **Most recent comments published to your blog:** WordPress displays a maximum of five comments in this area.

✔ **The author of each comment:** The name of the person who left the comment appears below it. This section also displays the author's picture (or avatar), if they have one.

✔ **A link to the post the comment was left on:** The post title appears to the right of the commenter's name. Click the link, and you go to that post in the Dashboard.

✔ **An excerpt of the comment:** This is a short snippet of the comment left on your blog.

✔ **Comment management links:** Hover your mouse over the comment, and five links appear that give you the opportunity to manage those comments right from your Dashboard (I discuss Comment management later in Chapter 4):

  • *Unapprove:* This link only appears if you have comment moderation turned on.

  • *Edit:* This link opens the Edit Comment page where you can edit the comment.

  • *Reply:* This link displays a text box where you can quickly reply to the comment right from your Dashboard.

  • *Spam:* Clicking this link marks that comment as spam.

  • *Trash:* Clicking this link deletes the comment from your blog.

✔ **View All button:** This button invites you to see all the comments that have been left on your blog. Clicking the View All button takes you to the Edit Comments page, where you can view and edit, moderate, or delete any comments that have been left for your blog.

You'll find even more information on managing your comments in Chapter 4.

Incoming Links

Directly to the right of the Recent Comments section in the Dashboard is the Incoming Links section, which lists all the blog-savvy people who wrote blog posts that link to your blog. Figure 3-3, earlier in this chapter, shows that I don't have any incoming links to my blog. How sad is that? Because my blog is brand new, people haven't discovered it yet, but I'm sure as soon as they do, my Incoming Links list will start filling up in no time.

In the meantime, a message in the Incoming Links section says, "This dashboard widget queries Google Blog Search so that when another blog links to your site it will show up here. It has found no incoming links . . . yet. It's okay — there's no rush." The phrase Google Blog Search is underlined because it's a link; when you click it, you go to the Google Blog Search page, which is a search engine for blogs only.

Your Stuff

In the Your Stuff section of the Dashboard, you see the following sections:

- **Today:** Click the links here to go to a page with options that let you manage today's posts. This page contains new or updated posts you've made during the current day.
- **A While Ago:** Click the links here to go to a page with options that let you manage posts and updates you made in past days.

What's Hot

Last but not least, the What's Hot section provides information about happenings in and around WordPress.com, including WordPress.com news, top blogs, top posts, fastest-growing blogs, and the latest posts made to blogs on WordPress.com. This section helps you stay in touch with the WordPress.com community as a whole.

QuickPress

The QuickPress module is a handy form that allows you to write, save, and publish a blog post right from your WordPress Dashboard. The options are very similar to the ones I cover in the section on writing posts in Chapter 4.

Recent Drafts

If you're using a brand new WordPress.com blog, the Recent Drafts module displays the message: *There are no drafts at the moment.* That's because you have not written any drafts. As time goes on, however, and you have written a few posts in your blog, you may save some of those posts as drafts to be edited and published at a later date. These drafts will be shown in the Recent Drafts module. Figure 3-3 shows that I have four recent drafts showing in this box.

WordPress displays up to five drafts in this module and displays the title of the post, the date it was last saved, and a short excerpt. Click the View All button to go to the Manage Posts page where you can view, edit, and manage your blog posts. Check out Chapter 4 for more information on that.

Stats

The last module of the Dashboard page is Stats (see Figure 3-4). It includes a visual graph of your blog stats for the past several days. These stats represent how many visitors your blog received each day. The right side of the Stats module shows some specific information:

- ✔ **Top Posts:** This display lists the most popular posts in your blog, determined by the number of visits each post received. It also shows you exactly how many times each post has been viewed. Figure 3-4 shows that my post titled About Lisa Sabin-Wilson has been viewed 70 times. You can click the title of a post, and WordPress loads that post in your browser window.

- ✔ **Top Searches:** This area tells you the top keywords and search phrases people used to find your blog in search engines. Figure 3-4 shows that people used these search phrases to find my blog: *WordPress MU For Dummies* and *WordPress For Dummies.* It's nice to know how people are finding your site in the search engines!

- ✔ **Most Active:** This area tells you which posts in your blog are the most active, as determined by the number of comments left on each post. You can click the title of a post, and WordPress loads that post in your browser window.

If you find that you don't use a few modules on your Dashboard page, you can completely get rid of them altogether by following these few steps:

Figure 3-4:
The Stats
section
of the
WordPress.
com
Dashboard.

1. **Click the Screen Options button shown at the top of the Dashboard.**

   This button is located at the top of the Dashboard page, on the right side. Clicking this button drops down the Screen Options menu, displaying the title of each module with check boxes to the left of each title.

2. **Deselect the module you want to hide on your Dashboard.**

   The check mark is removed from the box, and the module you deselected disappears from your Dashboard. If you have hidden one module and find later that you really miss having it on your Dashboard, you can simply enable that module again by selecting it from the Screen Options menu.

Setting Important Options Before You Blog

The options in this section help you get started and well on your way to managing your own WordPress.com blog. In this section, you discover how to set the primary options that personalize your blog, including creating your user profile, setting the date and time stamp (based on your own time-zone settings), and uploading a picture of yourself.

Setting your General options

To begin personalizing your WordPress.com blog by setting the General options, follow these steps:

1. **Click the Settings menu in the navigation menu.**

2. **Click the General link on the Settings menu.**

   The General Settings page opens (see Figure 3-5).

3. **Enter the name of your blog in the Blog Title text box.**

   You can revisit this page any time and change the blog name as often as you like.

4. **In the Tagline text box, enter a slogan or a motto that describes you or your blog.**

   The tagline should be a short (one line) phrase that sums up the tone and premise of your blog. Figure 3-5 shows I used a quote from a song by a group called Timbuk 3: "The future's so bright, I gotta wear shades." Although my tagline doesn't give you a description of my blog, it does give you an idea of my optimistic nature.

Figure 3-5: The General Settings page in the WordPress Dashboard.

5. **From the drop-down Language menu, choose the language in which you want to publish your blog.**

Below the drop-down menu is a link that says *modify the interface language* — referring to the language in the WordPress Dashboard. So you can have your blog published in English but have the Dashboard displayed in Spanish, for example.

6. **Type your e-mail address in the E-Mail Address box.**

Enter the e-mail address that you used to sign up with WordPress.com. You can change this address, but be warned: If you change the e-mail address here, it won't become active until you confirm that you are in fact the owner of said e-mail address. This confirmation is accomplished through a simple process: WordPress.com sends an e-mail to that address, providing a link you can click to confirm that you are the owner. This e-mail address is used for administrative purposes only, which consists mainly of communication between you and WordPress.com.

Adjusting your Date and Time settings

After you configure the General options that I discuss in the preceding section, you can use the last section of the General Settings page to set your local time, so that your blog posts are published with a time stamp in your own time zone no matter where in the world you are. Use the following options to establish your settings in this area, as shown in Figure 3-6.

Figure 3-6: Date and time settings for your WordPress.com blog.

✔ **Timezone section:** Choose your UTC time from the drop-down menu. This setting refers to the number of hours that your local time differs from Coordinated Universal Time (UTC). This setting ensures that all your blog posts and comments left on your blog are time-stamped with the correct time. If you're lucky enough, like me, to live on the frozen tundra of Wisconsin, which is in the Central time zone (CST), you would choose –6 from the drop-down menu because that time zone is 6 hours off UTC.

If you're unsure what your UTC time is, you can find it at the Greenwich Mean Time (http://wwp.greenwichmeantime.com) Web site. GMT is essentially the same thing as UTC.

The Timezone option doesn't update automatically for daylight saving time (DST). If you live in an area of the world that practices DST, you have to update the Timezone option manually when it occurs.

✔ **Date Format:** Select how you want to display the date. The default format is F j, Y (F = the full month name; j = the two-digit day; Y = the four-digit year), which gives you the output of January 1, 2008. Select a different format by clicking the circle to the left of the option.

✔ **Time Format:** Select how you want to display the time. The default format is g:i a (g = the two-digit hour; i = the two-digit minute; a = lower-case ante meridiem and post meridiem, or a.m. or p.m.), which gives you the output of 12:00 a.m. Select a different format by clicking the circle to the left of the option. You can also customize the date display by selecting the Custom option and entering your preferred format in the text box provided; find out how at http://codex.wordpress.org/Formatting_Date_and_Time.

✔ **Week Starts On:** From the drop-down menu, choose the day the week starts in your calendar. The display of the calendar in the sidebar of your blog is optional. If you choose to display the calendar, you can select the day of the week you want your calendar to start with.

Click the Save Changes button at the bottom of any page where you set new options. If you don't click Save Changes, your settings aren't saved, and WordPress reverts to the previous options.

Setting your public profile: Tell us a little about yourself

The next set of options you need to update is your profile. This area lets you configure your personal settings to individualize your WordPress.com blog and tell the world a little more about yourself. This blog is, after all, about you, and this is your opportunity to brag and promote!

To get started telling the world about yourself, follow these steps:

1. **Click the Users menu in the navigation menu.**

2. **Click the My Profile link on the Users menu.**

   The My Public Profile page opens, as shown in Figure 3-7.

You can adjust all sorts of personal settings to let your visitors get to know you better. You can be liberal with the information you want to share or as stingy as you want. It's *your* blog, after all.

Choose carefully the information you share on your blog, especially if you have a public blog on WordPress.com — public blogs can (and are!) viewed by a worldwide audience! If you don't want people to know your real name, use a nickname. If you don't want to share a picture of yourself for fear of shattering computer monitors worldwide, you can choose not to upload any picture at all or to upload a picture of something that reflects the essence of you. (You can post a picture of a book if you're an avid reader, a picture of a camera if you're a photographer, and so on.)

Make your blog your own. Stake your claim and mark your territory in this section!

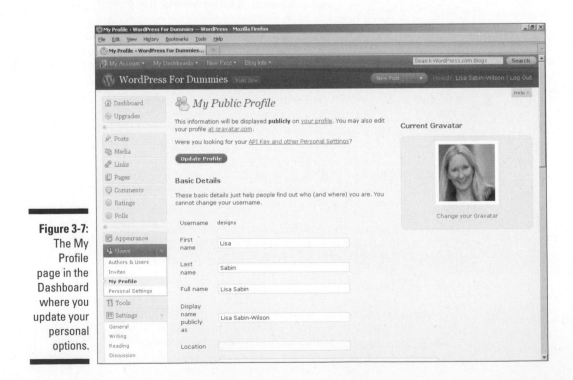

Figure 3-7:
The My
Profile
page in the
Dashboard
where you
update your
personal
options.

Basic details

In the first section of the My Public Profile page, you can see seven settings for your blog, only six of which you can change:

✔ **Username:** This displays your current username, which you can't change.

✔ **First Name:** Type your first name in the text box provided.

✔ **Last Name:** Type your last name in the text box provided.

✔ **Full Name:** Type your full name in the text box provided.

✔ **Display name publicly as:** Type in the name you would like displayed publicly.

✔ **Location:** Type your location in the text box provided.

✔ **About you:** In this section, you can provide a little biography, as well as change the password for your blog. Figure 3-8 shows this section in detail.

Contacts

In the section of the My Public Profile page, you can add different types of contact information and make them public on your profile. Followers of the blog will use this information to keep in touch with you and ask you questions. Here's what's included (you don't need to fill in all this information):

✔ **Home Phone, Work Phone, Mobile Phone:** Type these phone numbers if you so desire.

✔ **Public Email:** Type your e-mail address in the text box.

✔ **AIM, Live Messenger, Yahoo!, ICQ, Jabber:** If you want to share this information, enter your identities in the appropriate text boxes.

✔ **GTalk and Skype:** Type your Google Talk and Skype names in the text boxes if you'd like to share them.

Photos

To include several different photographs on your WordPress.com profile, click the Add photo through Gravatar button to upload photos from your computer. Any photos you add in this section will be displayed on your Profile page on WordPress.com.

Links

Add any links to Web sites that you'd like to have listed on your Profile page. For example, if you have several different Web sites other than the one you're creating on WordPress.com, you can add the links to those Web sites here so that they appear on your public profile for other people.

To add links, simply type the link URL in the URL text box, and the name of the page in the Title text box. Then click the Add Link button. You can edit and delete links in this area of the My Public Profile page anytime you want.

Verified External Services

Verified external services are other online services, such as social networking and social bookmarking sites, that you use in addition to your WordPress blog. WordPress.com wants you to include your online identities with these services because, in the words of WordPress, "they help people to confirm that you are in fact who you say you are." Your verified external services will be listed on your public profile. The different types of external services available in this section include

- Blogger
- Digg
- Facebook
- Friendfeed
- LinkedIn
- MySpace
- Posterous
- Tumblr
- Twitter
- Vimeo
- WordPress
- Yahoo!
- YouTube

Current Gravatar

Want to show the world your pretty picture? In the Current Gravatar section of the My Public Profile page, you can upload a picture of yourself or an image that represents you. This image is called a *gravatar*. This section is located on the right side of the My Public Profile page (refer to Figure 3-7, earlier in this chapter).

The picture/avatar that you insert into your WordPress.com is used in several ways:

- **The WordPress.com Blog of the Day page (`http://botd.wordpress.com/top-posts`):** This page lists the top posts from the top blogs of the day. If your blog is included in this list, a smaller version of the picture you've uploaded to your profile appears next to the listing.

- **The WordPress.com Hawt Post:** Also called a "hot" post, this appears on the main page at `http://wordpress.com`. If the WordPress spotlight shines in your direction, your picture will be displayed here for your own 15 minutes of WordPress.com fame.

- **The WordPress.com directory (by topic) of its community blogs:** This directory is called the Tags page (`http://wordpress.com/tags`). Bloggers on WordPress.com can tag their posts with keywords that help define the topics of their posts; WordPress.com collects all those tagged posts and sorts them by name on the Tags page.

- **On Tag pages:** This blogging page (`http://wordpress.com/tag/blogging`) allows you to find the most recent posts that WordPress.com bloggers have made on the topic of blogging. If your blog appears in this directory, a thumbnail of your picture appears, as well.

Follow these steps to insert a picture or avatar into your profile:

1. **Choose the image you want to attach to your profile, and save it to your computer.**

   Upload an image that is at least 128 pixels wide and 128 pixels tall. Later in these steps, you see how you can crop a larger image to the perfect size.

2. **In the Current Gravatar section of the My Public Profile page, click the Change Your Gravatar link.**

   The Gravatar.com window appears. Click the Upload a New Image from Your Computer link. The Select File from Your Computer window opens.

3. **Click the Browse button and select an image from your computer.**

4. **Click the Next button.**

   No matter what size image you chose, the Gravatar.com page allows you to crop your image to the correct size and lets you decide which part of your image to use for your picture display. When you click the Next button, the Crop Image page appears, and you can crop your chosen picture to the right size (see Figure 3-8).

5. **Use the crop tool to highlight the area of the picture that you want to remain after cropping.**

   In Figure 3-8, the box with a dotted line outlines the image I've chosen to use. This dotted outline indicates the size the picture will be when I'm done cropping it. You can move that dotted box around to choose the area of the image you want to use as your avatar. The Gravatar.com crop tool gives you two previews of your cropped image on the right side of the window: Small Preview and Large Preview.

6. **Click the Crop and Finish! button.**

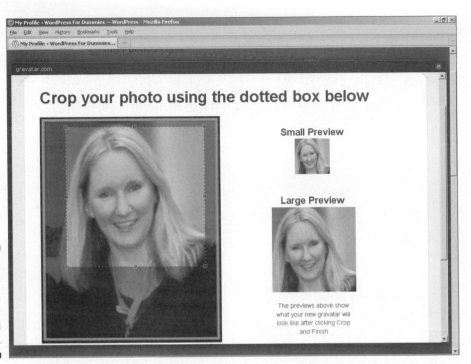

Figure 3-8:
Using the
WordPress.
com image-
cropping
interface.

The Choose a Rating page opens, where you can choose a rating for your new Gravatar.

7. Choose a rating.

The rating system works very much like the movie rating system we're all familiar with: G, PG, R, and X. A G rating means that your Gravatar is suitable for all ages, whereas an X rating means that your Gravatar contains some unmentionables that you would not want any kids to see.

8. Choose an e-mail address.

You can assign your Gravatar to a particular e-mail address so that your Gravatar images appear on any blog you comment on, provided you use your assigned e-mail address to do so.

When you're done, you get a message from Gravtar.com that says "Your new Gravatar is now being applied."

9. Click the X in the upper-right corner of the window to return to the Profile page in your WordPress.Com Dashboard

The My Public Profile page now displays your newly uploaded Gravatar. Visit this page again, anytime, to change your Gravatar.

Setting your personal preferences

WordPress.com gives you the ability to set a few different preferences based on your individual tastes for publishing, proofreading, and passwords. In the WordPress.com Dashboard, click the Personal Settings link in the User menu to load the Personal Settings page. Here, you have several different options available to you.

Personal Options

- ✔ **Fun:** Place a checkmark in this box to tell WordPress.com to set up all of the options for you. This is what they call *Fun Mode*, because WordPress.com will set random configurations for the Personal Settings, so you may be surprised with what you get.

- ✔ **Visual Editor:** Place a check in this box to indicate that you want to use the Visual Editor when writing your posts. Leave this box blank if you prefer not to use the Visual Editor. For information about the Visual Editor, including reasons why you would or would not want to use it, see Chapter 4.

- ✔ **Admin Color Scheme:** This option changes the colors in your WordPress Dashboard, which uses the Gray color scheme by default. The other option is Blue — the choice is yours!

- ✔ **Keyboard Shortcuts:** These shortcuts are designed to save you time navigating through the different areas of the Dashboard and Dashboard. Click the More Information link to read about how you can use keyboard shortcuts in your WordPress.com Dashboard.

- ✔ **Twitter API:** Enable this option to connect to WordPress.com using the Twitter program of your choice. This option also allows you to follow other blogs via Twitter as well as to post status updates to the WordPress.com blog of your choice from Twitter. More information, including recommendations for Twitter programs for your desktop and mobile phone, can be found on the WordPress.com Web site here: `http://support.wordpress.com/twitter-api`.

- ✔ **Browser Connection:** You can select whether use the HTTPS connection when visiting your WordPress.com Dashboard. HTTPS refers to a secure browser connection called SSL-encrypt, which protects your Internet connection and keeps out potential hackers.

- ✔ **Interface Language:** The Interface Language option refers to the language that you want to set for the Dashboard only. Don't confuse this setting with the Language option on the General Settings page, which determines the language you publish your blog in. If you want to view the settings in your WordPress Dashboard in Italian but want your published blog to appear in English, you set the Interface Language option (shown in Figure 3-7) to Italian and the Language option (shown in Figure 3-5) to English. Capiche?

✔ **Primary Blog:** This option is the URL of your primary WordPress.com blog. Figure 3-7 shows that the URL of my primary WordPress.com blog is `lswilson.wordpress.com`. Because WordPress.com allows you to have several blogs under one account, if you have more than one blog, a drop-down menu appears here, and you can use it to choose the blog you want to set as your primary blog.

✔ **Proofreading:** WordPress.com allows you to proofread your blog posts and page content. This section gives you several different options to choose from:

- Clichés
- Duplicate words
- Double negatives
- Jargon
- Redundant phrases

Click the link that says *Learn more* about these options to read about how the proofreader can help you publish better content on your blog.

The two areas of this section are

✔ **Account Details:** Type your e-mail address in the E-mail text box and the address to your Web site in the Website URL text box (this is the URL that your name will be linked to when you leave a comment on your blog. It also appears when you comment on another WordPress.com blog.

✔ **New Password:** When you want to change the password for your blog, type your new password in the first text box (refer to Figure 3-8). To confirm your new password choice, type it again in the second text field.

Directly below the two New Password text boxes is a little password helper. WordPress.com assists you in creating a secure password by giving you a tip about the password you have chosen. WordPress.com alerts you if the password is too short or not secure enough (by telling you that it's Bad).

When you create a new password, use a combination of letters, numbers, and symbols to make it hard for anyone to guess what it is (for example, aty89!#4j). When you have created a password that WordPress thinks is a good one, it says the password is Strong.

Change your password frequently. I can't recommend this practice strongly enough. Some people on the Internet make it their business to attempt to hijack blogs for their own malicious purposes. If you change your password monthly, you lower your risk by keeping the hackers guessing.

When you finish setting all the options on the Personal Settings page, don't forget to click the Save Changes button to save your changes.

Chapter 4

Writing and Managing Your Blog

In This Chapter

▶ Writing your first post and making it look nice

▶ Organizing and categorizing your blog

▶ Inviting friends and establishing their permissions

▶ Moderating discussions — even when you aren't logged in

▶ Combating comment spam

▶ Deciding what shows up on your front page

▶ Protecting your blog's privacy

▶ Initiating trusting relationships with OpenID

*T*he first chapter in this part covers the signup process and a few important settings and options that you configure when you first log in to your new WordPress.com blog. Now it's time to make a blogger out of you. In this chapter, I show you the tools you need to write your first post. When you understand that process, the blogging world is right at your fingertips.

This chapter also shows you the basics of categorizing your posts and links, uploading images to your blog posts, setting discussion and reading options for your blog, using static pages, and managing your users and authors. I don't have the space in this chapter to cover every option available, but I hit the high points of what you need to know.

Ready? Set? Blog!

In the Dashboard, click the Add New link on the Posts menu to display the Add New Post page, where you write, organize, and publish your first post. Start by thinking up a name for your post and entering it in the Title text box, shown in Figure 4-1.

You can make the name snappy and fun if you want, but don't be cryptic. Use titles that give your readers a basic idea of what they're about to read in the posts. No set of hard-and-fast rules exists when it comes to creating titles for your blog posts, of course. Have fun with your title, and let it reflect your personality and style of writing. After giving your post a title, you can write the content of your post in the Post text box.

Title text box   HTML tab

Post text box   Visual tab

Figure 4-1:
The area in
which you
write your
post.

The area in which you write your post is in Visual Editing mode, as indicated by the Visual tab that appears above the text. Visual Editing mode is how WordPress provides WYSIWYG (What You See Is What You Get) options for formatting. Rather than have to embed HTML code within your post, you can simply type your post, highlight the text you'd like to format, and click the buttons (shown in Figure 4-1) that appear above the box in which you type your post.

If you've ever used a word processing program such as Microsoft Word, you'll recognize many of these buttons:

- **Bold:** Embeds the `<strong> </strong>` tag to emphasize the text in bold (example: **bold text**).

- **Italics:** Embeds the `<em> </em>` tag to emphasize the text in italics (example: *italic text*).

✔ **Strikethrough:** Embeds the `<strike> </strike>` tag to put a line through your text (example: `strikethrough text`).

✔ **Unordered List:** Embeds the `<ul><li> </li></ul>` tag to create an unordered, or bulleted, list.

✔ **Ordered List:** Embeds the `<ol><li> </li></ul>` tag that creates an ordered, or numbered, list.

✔ **Blockquote:** Inserts the `<blockquote> </blockquote>` tag to indent the selected paragraph or section of text.

✔ **Align Left:** Inserts the `<p align="left"> </p>` tag to align the selected paragraph or section of text against the left margin.

✔ **Align Center:** Inserts the `<p align="center"> </p>` tag to position the selected paragraph or section of text in the center of the page.

✔ **Align Right:** Inserts the `<p align="right"> </p>` tag to align the selected paragraph or section of text against the right margin.

✔ **Insert/Edit Link:** Applies the `<a href=" "> </a>` tag to the selected text to create a hyperlink.

✔ **Unlink:** Removes a hyperlink from selected text.

✔ **Insert More Tag:** Inserts the `<!--more-->` tag to split the display on your blog page. It publishes the text written above this tag with a Read More link, which takes the user to a page with the full post. This feature is good for really long posts.

✔ **Toggle Spellchecker:** This is a perfect tool for you, if you make spelling errors while you type. Use it to check your spelling before you post.

✔ **Toggle Full Screen Mode:** Expands the Post text box to occupy the full height and width of your browser screen. Use this tool to focus on writing without being distracted by all the other options on the page. To bring that Post text box back to its normal state, click the Toggle Full Screen Mode button again, and voilà — it's back to normal.

✔ **Show/Hide Kitchen Sink:** Displays a new formatting menu, providing options for underlining, font color, custom characters, undo and redo, and so on — a veritable kitchen sink full of options! I saw this option and thought, "Wow! WordPress does my dishes, too!" Unfortunately, the option's name is a metaphor to describe the advanced formatting options available with the Visual Editor.

If you'd rather embed your own HTML and skip the Visual Editor, click the HTML tab that appears to the right of the Visual tab above the Post text box. If you type HTML in your post — using a table or embedding video files, for example — you have to click the HTML tab before you insert that code. If you don't, the Visual Editor formats your code, and it most likely looks nothing like you intended it to.

At this point, you can skip to the "Publishing your post" section, later in this chapter, for information on publishing your post to your blog, or continue with the following sections to discover how to include images in your blog post and refine the options for your post.

WordPress.com has a nifty autosave feature that saves your work while you're typing and editing a new post. If your browser crashes, or you accidentally close your browser window before you've saved your post, the post is there for you when you get back. Those WordPress.com folks are so thoughtful!

Inserting media files into your post

Pictures, images, video, and audio files can greatly enhance the content of a post by adding visual and/or auditory effects to the words that you've written. Look right above the formatting buttons on the Write Post page (refer to Figure 4-1), and you see an Add Media toolbar. Have a look again; it's pretty small, but it's there! The Add Media toolbar has four small buttons:

- Add an Image
- Add Video
- Add Audio
- Add Media
- Add Poll

As of this writing, if you don't have any blog space upgrades purchased for your account, you can only upload images (jpg, jpeg, png, gif), documents (pdf, doc) and presentations (ppt) files. If you've purchased a space upgrade, you can upload other files — audio (mp3, mp4a, wav) and video (avi, mp4, mpg, mov, wmv) files. Chapter 5 has information on the upgrades that are available for your WordPress.com blog.

Adding an image

Adding an image or photo to your post is easy. Start by clicking the Add an Image button, which is the first button on the Add Media toolbar. The Add an Image window opens, letting you choose images from your hard drive or from the Web (see Figure 4-2).

Figure 4-2:
The
WordPress.
com media
uploader.

To add an image from the Web after you click the Add an Image button, follow these steps:

1. **Click the From URL tab.**

2. **Type the URL (Internet address) of the image in the Image URL text box.**

   Type the full URL, including the `http` and www portion of the address. You can find the URL of any image on the Web by right-clicking it and selecting Properties.

3. **Type a title for the image in the Image Title box.**

   This gives the image a title so you can easily identify the image later when using the Media Library. A title also assists in search engine optimization because WordPress inserts a `<title>` tag in the HTML markup that looks like this: `title="your image title here"`, which helps search engines identify the type of content on your page.

4. **(Optional) Type a description of the image in the Image Caption box.**

   The description of the image provides image ALT tags, which help search engines find and list your site in their directories — so it's a good idea to provide a description if you can. Some WordPress themes also display the caption directly underneath your image on your blog.

5. **Choose your alignment option by selecting the None, Left, Center, or Right radio button.**

6. **Type a link or choose not to link the image:**

- *None:* You don't want to link the image to anything.

- *Link to Image:* You want to link the image to its individual URL or you can type any URL you like to link an image to another Web site or page.

7. **Click the Insert into Post button.**

To add an image from your hard drive after you click the Add an Image button, follow these steps:

1. **Click the From Computer tab.**

2. **Click the Select Files button.**

   A dialog box opens, letting you choose an image from your hard drive.

3. **Choose an image or multiple images to upload.**

4. **Click Open.**

   The image is uploaded from your computer to your Web server. WordPress displays a progress bar on the upload and displays an image options box when the upload is finished.

5. **Edit the details for the image(s) by filling in the fields provided for you in the Add an Image box:**

- *Title:* Type a title for the image.

- *Alternate text:* Provides image ALT tags, which help search engines find and list your site in their directories. It's a good idea to provide a description if you can.

- *Caption:* Type a caption for the image (such as **This is a flower from my garden**).

- *Description:* Type a description of the image.

- *Link URL:* Type the URL you want the image linked to. Whatever option you choose from the following three options determines where your readers go when they click the image you've uploaded:

  None: You don't want the image to be clickable.

  File URL: Readers can click through to the direct image itself.

  Post URL: Readers can click through to the post that the image appears in. You can type your own URL in the Link URL text box.

- *Alignment:* Choose None, Left, Center, or Right. (See Table 4-1, in the following section, for styling information regarding image alignment.)

- *Size:* Choose Thumbnail, Medium, Large, or Full Size.

6. **Click the Edit Image button (as shown in Figure 4-3) to edit the appearance of the image.**

   Figure 4-4 shows the following image editor options:

   - **Crop:** Click this button to cut the image down to a smaller size.

   - **Rotate counter-clockwise:** Click this button to rotate the image to the left.

   - **Rotate clockwise:** Click this button to rotate the image to the right.

   - **Flip vertically:** Click this button to flip the image upside down, and back again.

   - **Flip horizontally:** Click this button to flip the image from right to left, and back again.

   - **Undo:** Click this button to undo any changes you've made.

   - **Redo:** Click this button to redo images edits that you've made.

   - **Scale Image:** Click this link to see a drop-down menu that you can use to set a specific width and height for the image.

7. **Click the Insert into Post button.**

   The HTML code needed to display the image within your published post is inserted automatically. The media uploader window closes and returns you to the Write Post page. (Alternatively, you can click the Save All Changes button to save the options you've set for the image(s) and then return at a later date to insert the image(s) in your post, without having to reset those options again.)

Along with inserting just one image into your post, you can use the media uploader to insert a full gallery of images. Go through the steps I outline in this section to upload images, but don't click the Insert into Post button. Instead, click the Gallery link at the top of the media uploader window (refer to Figure 4-2).

You can configure the options for each image by clicking the Show link to the right of the image (as explained in Step 3 of the preceding steps). When you're done, click the Insert Gallery into Post button. A short piece of code is inserted that looks like this: `[gallery]`. That piece of code tells WordPress to display your gallery of images inside the post you are about to publish.

The interface that WordPress.com uses for file upload is Flash-based. Adobe Flash contains a specific set of multimedia technologies programmed to handle media files on the Web. Some browsers and operating systems aren't configured to handle Flash-based applications. If you experience difficulties with the media uploader, WordPress.com gives you a handy alternative method. In the media uploader (refer to Figure 4-2), click the Browser Uploader link to upload files in an interface that is not Flash-based.

Figure 4-3:
Setting
options for
the image
after you
upload it.

Figure 4-4:
Image editor
options.

Using audio, video, and other media files

The Add Media toolbar contains four other buttons:

- ✔ **Add Video:** Click this button, and the media uploader box opens. In the URL box, type the URL for the video file you want to use in the URL field. WordPress.com also provides you instructions (and the correct code) for inserting a video from YouTube, Google Video, DailyMotion, and VodPod. Click the Insert into Post button to use that video in your blog post.

- ✔ **Add Audio:** Click the button, and the media uploader box opens. In the URL box, type the URL for the audio file you want to use; then type the title of that file in the Title box. Click the Insert into Post button to insert a link to that audio file into your blog post.

- ✔ **Add Media:** Click the button, and the media uploader box opens. In the URL box, type the URL for the media file you want to use; then type the title of that file in the Title box. Click the Insert into Post button to insert a link to that media file into your blog post.

- ✔ **Add Poll:** You can automatically set up an account with WordPress. com's sister company, Poll Daddy, to create and insert polls on your WordPress.com blog.

How do media files differ from image, video, and audio files? Media files include Microsoft PowerPoint presentation files (.ppt), Microsoft Word documents (.doc), and Adobe Portable Document Format (.pdf) files. While these types of files can also contain images, video, and audio files, you can use the media uploader to upload these files to your WordPress.com account so that you can display and link to them on your blog.

WordPress.com gives you 3GB of disk space for your free blog, and though it would take a lot of files to use up that amount of space, if you upload large image files, that space can go a lot quicker than you think. Keep the actual file size of the images you upload in mind when you use this feature; you can eat that disk space up before you know it.

Refining your post options

After you write the post, you can choose a few extra options before you publish it for the entire world to see. These settings are applied only to the post you're working on; they don't apply automatically to any future or past posts you make. You can find these options (see Figure 4-5) underneath and to the right of the Post text box.

Figure 4-5:
Several
options for
your blog
post.

Here are the options:

- **Excerpt:** Excerpts are short summaries of your posts. Many bloggers use snippets to show teasers of their blog posts, thereby encouraging the reader to click the Read More link to read posts in their entirety. Type your short summary in the Excerpt box. Excerpts have no word limit, but the idea is to keep them short and sweet.

- **Send Trackbacks:** I discuss trackbacks in Chapter 2, if you want to refresh your memory banks on what they are. If you want to send a trackback to another blog, enter that blog's Trackback URL in the Sent Trackbox To box. You can send trackbacks to more than one blog; just be sure to separate trackback URLs with spaces.

- **Discussion:** Decide whether to allow readers to submit feedback through the comment system and whether to allow pings and trackbacks (read more about pings and trackbacks in Chapter 2) by selecting the boxes here or leaving them blank.

- **Publish:** These are the publishing options for your blog post. I cover these options in detail in the "Publishing your post" section.

- **Tags:** Tags are a nice feature of WordPress.com; they let you add searchable and archived keywords for your posts in small subtopics. Type your chosen tags (or keywords) in the Tags box. Tags can be single words or several words; just make sure to separate tags with commas (for example: **books, movies, pop culture, and entertainment**).

✔ **Categories:** You can file your posts in different categories to organize them by subject. (See more about organizing your posts in the "Organizing Your Blog by Subject" section, later in this chapter.) Select the box to the left of the category name you want to use. Don't see the category you need listed here? Click the Add New Category link at the bottom of the Categories box, and you can add a new category.

When you finish setting the options for your post, don't navigate away from this page, because your options have not yet been fully saved. You need to scroll all the way back up to the top and click the Save Draft button on the top right side of the page. Before you do that, however, you probably want to check out the next section, which discusses publishing options for your new blog post.

Publishing your post

You have given your new post a title and written the content of your new blog post. Maybe you've even added an image or other type of media file to your blog post and have configured the tags, categories, and other options for your post. Now the question is: Publish? Or not to publish (yet)?

WordPress.com gives you three options for saving or publishing your post when you are done writing it. Figure 4-6 shows the Publish Status section, which is located on the right side of the Write Post page.

Figure 4-6:
WordPress.
com post
publishing
status
section.

> **Publish**
>
> [**Save Draft**]   (Preview)
>
> Status: **Draft** <u>Edit</u>
>
> Visibility: **Public** <u>Edit</u>
>
> 📅 Publish **immediately** <u>Edit</u>
>
> (**Publish**)

The Publish Status drop-down menu offers three options:

✔ **Status:** Click the Edit link next to the Status option, and a new menu appears with the following options:

  • *Pending Review:* Select this option to set the post status as Pending; the post shows up in your list of drafts next to a Pending Review header. This option lets the administrator of the blog know that contributors have entered posts that are waiting for administrator review and approval (helpful for blogs with multiple authors).

- *Draft:* Select this option to save the post, but not publish it to your blog. Your post is saved in draft form, allowing you to return at a later time.

Click OK when you're done to save your settings.

✔ **Visibility:** Click the Edit link next to the Visibility option and a new menu appears with the following options:

- *Public:* Choosing this option publishes your post to your blog for the entire world to see. Choose Stick This Post to Your Front Page if you want to publish this post to the very top of your blog, and keep it there until you come back and edit the status at a later date.

- *Password Protect This Post:* You can password-protect a post by entering a password in this box. When you do, you can share the password with only the readers you want to let read that post. This feature is perfect for those times when you'd love to make a blog post about all the stupid things your boss did today but don't want your boss to see it. This feature also hides the post from search engines so that it doesn't show up in search results. If you don't want to password-protect the post, leave this box blank.

- *Password Protected:* This option allows you to password protect a post, which publishes it to your blog; however; for a reader to view the post, they have to know the password. When you select this option, a text box appears where you type the password for this post.

Click OK when you're done to save your settings.

✔ *Publish Immediately:* Click the Edit link next to the Publish Immediately option, and a new menu appears where you can set the date (or time-stamp) of the post and publish the post right away. The date settings here allow you to set a date in the future for the post to publish, or you can back-date a post to publish on a date in the past.

Click OK when you are done to save your settings.

When you have chosen a publishing status, click the Publish button. WordPress saves your publishing-status option. Successfully published blog posts show up on the front page of your blog.

If you want to publish your blog post right away, skip the drop-down menu options, and click the Publish button, which sends your new blog post to your blog in all its glory.

If you click Publish and for some reason don't see the post you just published to the front page of your blog, you probably left the Publish Status drop-down menu set to Unpublished. Look for your new post among the draft posts.

Organizing Your Blog by Subject

Categorizing your posts in WordPress provides an organizational structure for your blog. Each blog post that is assigned to a category is grouped with other posts in the same category. When your blog is a few months old, this structure creates a nice topical directory of posts for you and your readers.

Category lists generally appear in two places on your blog, letting your readers find all your posts by subject very easily. Almost all WordPress themes list categories within the blog post itself. Most themes also provide a list of your categories in the sidebar of your blog so that your readers can click a topic of interest.

Each category in a WordPress.com blog has its own RSS feed, making it easy for your readers to subscribe to a feed and keep updated on what you have to say in your blog about a certain topic.

Creating categories and subcategories

A brand-new WordPress.com blog has only one category to begin with: Uncategorized, as shown in Figure 4-7.

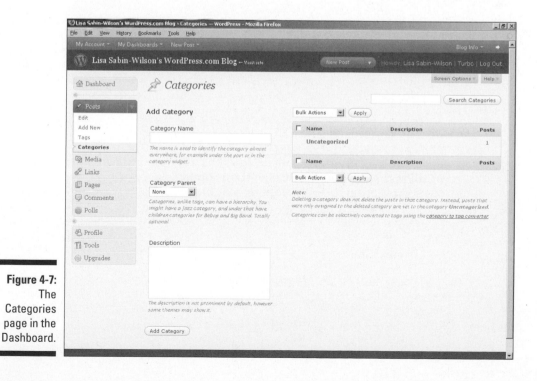

Figure 4-7:
The Categories page in the Dashboard.

You can create new categories (and categories within those categories) by following these steps:

1. **Click the Categories link on the Posts menu.**

   The Categories page opens (refer to Figure 4-7).

2. **Under the Add Category heading, type the name of your category in the Category Name text box.**

3. **Leave the Category Parent drop-down menu set to the default option (None).**

   The Category Parent drop-down menu lets you create subcategories. If you have a main category called Books, for example, Books appears in the Category Parent drop-down menu. To create a subcategory of the Books category, follow Steps 1 and 2 and then choose Books from the Category Parent drop-down menu.

4. **(Optional) Enter a description of the category in the Description text box.**

   Do this step now so that later, you'll know what you were thinking of when you created this category. A short summary will do. (Also, some WordPress themes are coded to display the category description in the sidebar of your blog.)

5. **Click the Add Category button.**

Categories you create now aren't set in stone. You can edit or delete them by revisiting the Categories page and clicking the name of the category you want to edit. The Edit Category page opens, and you can edit the category name, category parent, and description.

Filing posts in categories and subcategories

The preceding section tells you how to create categories and subcategories. When you've created those categories and subcategories, you don't ever have to re-create them — they are always there for you to assign your blog posts to.

To assign existing posts to a category, follow these steps:

1. **Click the Edit link in the Posts menu.**

   The Edit Posts page appears, displaying a list of posts you've made.

2. **Click the name of the post you want to categorize.**

   The Edit Post page opens, displaying your post content and saved options.

3. **In the Categories section to the right of the Post text box, select the check box next to the category or subcategory (you can select more than one category and subcategory) that you want to assign to the post.**

   You can also use the Categories section before you publish a new post to assign it to the categories you'd like.

4. **Scroll up to the top of the Edit Post page, and click the Update Post button.**

   WordPress.com refreshes the Edit Post page, displaying the post you just edited; it reflects the changes you just made.

Creating and Categorizing Your Blogroll

A *blogroll* is a list of links that you display on your blog. In this section, I show you how to add and manage the links in your blogroll.

To view your default blogroll, click the Links menu. The Edit Links page opens, and you see the default links that are already included in your WordPress.com blog. See Figure 4-8.

Figure 4-8: Manage your WordPress.com blogroll here.

If you want to remove a link from your blogroll, select the box to the left of the link name; select Delete from the Bulk Actions drop-down menu at the top of the page, then click the Apply button (refer to Figure 4-8).

Creating link categories

WordPress.com lets you have an unlimited number of link categories on your blog. Link categories, much like the post categories discussed earlier in this chapter, provide you a way of separating your blogrolls (or list of links) into topical categories.

By default, WordPress.com sets up a link category for you called — by no coincidence — Blogroll. To add a new category, click the Link Categories link on the Links menu.

You add a new link category the same way you add new post categories (see the "Creating categories and subcategories" section, earlier in this chapter).

Adding new links to your blogroll

To add a new link to your blogroll, click the Links subtab and then click the Add New link. The Add New Link page opens, as shown in Figure 4-9.

Follow these steps to add your new link:

1. **In the Name text box, type the name of the Web site you're adding.**

2. **In the Web Address text box, type the URL, making sure to include the** http:// **part.**

3. **(Optional) In the Description text box, type a short description of the Web site.**

4. **In the Categories box, select the box to the left of the category you want this link to appear in.**

5. **(Optional) Select the target for your link in the Target box.**

    The target tells your browser how you want this link to load in your visitor's browser window after the visitor clicks it. You have three choices:

    • *_blank:* Loads the link in a new browser window.

    • *_top:* Loads the link in the top frame (if your site is designed with frames).

    • *None:* Loads the link in the same browser window (the default setting, should you choose to overlook the Target option).

Figure 4-9:
Add a link to
your blogroll
by using this
tool from
WordPress.
com.

The third option — None — is my personal preference and recommendation. I like to let my visitors decide whether they want a bunch of new browser windows to open every time they click a link on my site.

6. (Optional) Select the Link Relationship (XFN) option, and define why you're providing this link.

XFN stands for XHTML Friends Network and allows you to indicate the relationship you have with the people you are linking to by defining how you know, or are associated with, them. Table 4-1 lists the different relationships you can assign to your links.

7. (Optional) Select advanced options for your link in the Advanced box:

- *Image Address:* This option associates an image with the link, and some WordPress themes display the image on your site along with the link. Type the URL for the image in the Image Address box. For this purpose, you need to know the direct URL to the image (for example, `http://yourdomain.com/images/image.jpg`).

- *RSS Address:* Type the RSS feed URL for the blog you are linking to. WordPress displays the link to the site's RSS feed alongside the link that appears on your site. Not all WordPress themes accommodate this feature.

- *Notes:* Type your notes in the Notes box. These notes aren't displayed on your site, so feel free to leave whatever notes you need to further define the details of this link. A month from now, you may not remember who this person is or why you linked to her, so you can add notes to remind yourself.

- *Rating:* Use the Rating drop-down menu to rate this link from 0 to 10, 0 being the worst and 10 being the best. Some WordPress themes display your blogroll in the order in which you've rated your links, from best to worst.

8. Scroll to the top of the page, and click the Save button.

Your new link is saved, and a blank Add New Link page opens, ready for you to add another new link to your blogroll(s). Additionally, in the Save section at the top right, you can choose to keep this link private — this option, if checked, will not display the link publicly on your blog. It would be kept protected and for your eyes only.

Table 4-1	Link Relationships (XFN) Defined
Link Relationship	*Description*
Identity	Select this check box if the link is to a Web site you own.
Friendship	Select the option (Contact, Acquaintance, Friend, or None) that most closely identifies the relationship.
Physical	Select this check box if you've met the person you're linking to face to face. Sharing pictures over the Internet doesn't count. This selection identifies a person you've physically met.
Professional	Select one of these check boxes if the person you're linking to is a co-worker or colleague.
Geographical	Select Co-Resident if the person you're linking to lives with you. Or select Neighbor or None, depending on which option applies to your relationship with the person you're linking to.
Family	If the blogger you're linking to is a family member, select the option that tells how the person is related to you.
Romantic	Select the option that applies to the type of romantic relationship you have with the person you're linking to. Do you have a crush on him? Is she your creative muse? Is he someone you consider to be a sweetheart? Select the option that most closely identifies the romantic relationship, if any.

You can find more information on XFN at `http://gmpg.org/xfn`.

Revisit the Manage Links page any time you want to add a new link, edit an old link, or delete an existing link. You can create an unlimited amount of blogroll categories to sort your blogrolls by topics. I know one blogger who has 50 categories for his links, so the options are limitless.

Managing and Inviting Users

What's a blog without blog users? Of course, your WordPress.com blog always has at least one user: you. To see your list of users, click the Users link that is in the navigation menu. The Users page opens and the Users menu expands to show three different links:

- ✔ Authors & Users
- ✔ Your Profile (See Chapter 3 for information on the Profile page.)
- ✔ Invites

Managing authors and users

The Users page tells you about all the users on your blog. It lists each user's username, name, e-mail address, role on your blog, and number of posts made to your blog. This page also has the Add User from Community section, where you can add a new user to your blog. (By *user,* WordPress means simply a person who is a member of your blog as a contributor, an author, an editor, or an administrator. You can have an unlimited amount of users on one WordPress.com blog.)

To manage user roles, you need to understand the distinct differences among the roles. The following list explains the type of access each role provides:

- ✔ **Contributor:** A Contributor can upload files and write/edit/manage her own posts. When a Contributor writes a post, however, that post is saved as a draft to await administrator approval; Contributors can't publish their posts. This feature is a nice way to moderate content written by new authors.

- ✔ **Author:** In addition to having the access and permissions of a Contributor, an Author can publish his own posts without administrator approval. Authors can also delete their own posts.

- ✔ **Editor:** In addition to having the access and permissions of an Author, an Editor can moderate comments, manage categories, manage links, edit pages, and edit other Authors' posts. Editors can also read and edit private posts.

✔ **Administrator:** An Administrator has the authority to change any of the Administration options and settings in the WordPress blog. You, as the account owner, are listed as an Administrator already. You can also assign other users as Administrators.

WordPress.com lets you have an unlimited amount of users and authors on one blog, which is a nice feature if running a multiauthor blog is something you'd like to do.

At the bottom of the Authors & Users page, in the Add User from Community section, you can add new users to your blog. Enter the person's e-mail address, assign a user role, and click the Add User button. The user you add must be a registered user in the WordPress.com system. If you enter someone who isn't registered, WordPress.com gives you the option to send that person an invitation to become a member. (The WordPress people have thought of everything, haven't they?)

To change a user's role, follow these steps:

1. **Find that person's username on the Users page.**
2. **Select the box next to the username.**
3. **From the Change Role To drop-down menu at the top the page, choose the role you want to assign; then click the Change button.**

   The Users page refreshes with the new role assignment applied.

To view all the posts made by an author, click the number that appears below the Posts column for that user.

Inviting friends to WordPress.com

Now that you've experienced the fun, ease, and excitement of having your very own WordPress.com blog, why not tell your friends, so that they can tell their friends, and their friends can tell their friends, and so on?

Click the Invites link on the Users menu, and you can do just that. Figure 4-10 shows the form that lets you invite people you know to sign up for WordPress.com accounts. You can also tell WordPress to add a user to your blogroll after she joins. Additionally, you can tell WordPress to add the new member to your own blog as a Contributor, if you want. (This option is especially helpful if you're setting up new users or authors for your own WordPress.com blog.)

Figure 4-10:
WordPress.
com Invites
page.

Follow these instructions to invite as many people as you want to join WordPress.com:

1. **Click the Invites link on the Users menu.**

   The Invites page opens.

2. **In the appropriate text boxes, type the user's first name, last name, and e-mail address.**

3. **Type a personal message to the prospective member in the Personal Message text box, or use the default message WordPress.com provides.**

4. **(Optional) Select the Add to My Blogroll after Signup check box if you also want to add this person to your own WordPress.com blogroll.**

5. **(Optional) Select the Add User to My Blog as a Contributor check box if you want to add this user to your blog as a Contributor after he signs up.**

6. **Click the Send Invite button to send the invitation to the prospective member via e-mail.**

When you complete these steps, WordPress sends you confirmation that the invitation was sent.

Managing Comments and Comment Spam

As I describe in Chapter 2, comments provide a great way for readers to interact with you, and vice versa. Readers of your blog can post comments by using the comment form that appears on the same page as each of the published posts on your blog. You need to be able to exercise control over the comments that appear, however.

Setting discussion options for your blog

Click the Discussion link on the Settings menu. On the Discussion Settings page, you can set the options, such as notification settings, for your posts; determine how comments and comment spam are handled on your WordPress.com blog; and specify whether you want to use avatars on your blog. The Discussion Settings page has six settings you can configure for your blog, each of which I discuss in the following sections.

When you're done setting up your options, click the Save Changes button at the bottom of the page to make the changes take effect. You can revisit this page as often as you need to so you can keep your settings current and to your liking.

Default Article Settings

The Default Article Settings section is where you tell WordPress.com how to handle post notifications. Three options are available to you:

- **Attempt to Notify Any Blogs Linked to from the Article (Slows Down Posting):** Enabled by default, this option makes your blog send a notification, via a ping, to any site you've linked to in your blog post. This feature is very similar to a trackback (which I discuss in Chapter 2) and can slow the process of posting just a bit, because of the time it takes for your blog to talk to another blog to let it know that you're talking about it.

- **Allow Link Notifications from Other Blogs (Pingbacks and Trackbacks):** Enabled by default, this option tells WordPress that you want your blog to be notified via pings and trackbacks that other people have linked to you. WordPress lists any ping and trackback notifications on your site as comments in the Comments section. If you deselect this option, your ears may tingle, but you won't know when other people are talking about, or linking to, you on other blogs.

- **Allow People to Post Comments on the Article:** Enabled by default, this option lets people leave comments on your blog.

Other Comment Settings

The Other Comment Settings tell WordPress how to handle comments:

- ✔ **Comment Author Must Fill Out Their Name and E-Mail:** Enabled by default, this option requires everyone who comments on your blog to fill in the Name and E-Mail field when leaving a comment. This option is very helpful in combating comment spam. (See Chapters 2 and 10 for information on comment spam.) Clear this check box to disable this option.

- ✔ **Users Must Be Registered and Logged in to Comment:** Not enabled by default, this option allows you to accept comments on your blog from only those people who have registered and are currently logged in as a user on your blog. If a user is not logged in, he or she sees a message that says: *You must be logged in in order to leave a comment.*

- ✔ **Automatically Close Comments on Articles Older Than *X* Days:** Check the box next to this option to tell WordPress you would like comments on older articles to be automatically closed. Fill in the text box provided with the number of days you would like to wait before WordPress closes comments on older articles.

  This is a very effective anti-spam technique that many bloggers use to limit the comment and trackback spam on their blogs.

- ✔ **Enable Threaded (Nested) Comments *X* Levels Deep:** This drop-down menu allows you to choose the level of threaded comments you'd like to have on your blog. The default is 1; you can choose up to 10 levels. Instead of all comments being displayed on your blog in chronological order (as it is by default), nesting them allows you and your readers to reply to comments within the comment itself.

- ✔ **Break Comments into Pages with *X* Comments Per Page:** Fill in the text box with a number of comments you want to display on one page. Setting a limit is very helpful for blogs that receive a large number of comments. It lets you break the long string of comments into several pages, which makes it easier to read and helps speed up the load time of your site, because the page isn't loading such a large number of comments at once.

- ✔ **Comments Should Be Displayed with the Older/Newer comments at the Top of Each Page:** Use the drop-down menu to select Older or Newer. Selecting Older displays the comments on your blog in the order of oldest to newest. Selecting Newer displays comments from newest to oldest.

E-Mail Me Whenever

The two options in the E-Mail Me Whenever section, Anyone Posts a Comment and A Comment Is Held for Moderation, are selected by default. This feature tells WordPress that you want to receive an e-mail any time

anyone leaves a comment on your blog and/or any time a comment is awaiting your approval in the moderation queue. This feature can be very helpful,
particularly if you don't visit your blog daily. Everyone likes to get comments
on his blog posts, and it's good to be notified when it happens so that you
can revisit that post, respond to your readers, and keep the conversation
active. You can disable this feature, however, by deselecting these options.

Before a Comment Appears

The three options in the Before a Comment Appears section tell WordPress how
you want WordPress to handle comments before they appear in your blog:

- **An Administrator Must Always Approve the Comment:** Selecting this
  option holds every new comment on your blog in the moderation queue
  until you log in and approve it. This feature is particularly helpful if you
  want to review the content of comments before they're published to
  your blog.

- **Comment Author Must Have a Previously Approved Comment:** When
  this box is selected, the only comments that are approved and published on your blog are those that have been left by commenters who
  have already been approved by you. Their e-mail addresses are stored
  in the database, and WordPress runs a check on their e-mails. If the
  e-mail address matches a previously approved comment, the new comment is published automatically. If no match occurs, WordPress places
  the comment in the moderation queue, awaiting your approval. This
  measure is yet another feature that helps prevent comment spam.

Comment Moderation

In the Comment Moderation section, you can set options to specify what
types of comments are held in the moderation queue to await your approval.
Frequently, comment spammers try to spam your blog with a *ton* of links in
the hope of promoting their own sites through your comment form. You can
set the number of links that are allowed in a comment before it is tossed into
the moderation queue to await approval. The default is 2. Give that a try, and
if you find that you're getting lots of spam comments with multiple links, you
may want to revisit this page and increase that number.

The text box below the link setting is where you can set keywords, URLs,
e-mail addresses, or IP addresses to be flagged for moderation. One popular topic that comment spammers like to spam with is Viagra; they fill their
comments with links to sites where you can purchase Viagra. Really, if you
wanted to know about those sites, wouldn't you seek them out? Well, that's
beside the point. If you're getting a lot of Viagra spam, you can enter **Viagra**
in the Comment Moderation list rather than in the Comment Blacklist list,
because you may actually receive a legitimate comment with the word *Viagra*

in it that you would like to approve. A visitor to my blog left a comment —
"Espresso is Viagra for my brain!" — in response to a post I made about my
love for espresso. That comment is legitimate but probably got thrown into
my moderation queue because I have that term in my Comment Moderation
list.

By default, WordPress.com automatically discards spam on older posts on
your blog. You can switch this option off by checking the Don't Discard Spam
on Old Posts box at the top of this section.

Comment Blacklist

In contrast to the Comment Moderation list, the Comment Blacklist is a list
of words, URLs, e-mail addresses, and IP addresses that you want to flat-out
ban from ever making it to your blog. Items placed here don't even make it
into your Comment Moderation queue; they're filtered as spam by the system
and completely disregarded. The words I have placed in my Blacklist are not
family friendly and have no place in a nice book like this.

Are you getting the feeling that comment spam is a real issue for bloggers?
It's huge — probably bigger than you imagine it to be. Much of the comment-
spam prevention is done behind the scenes, so you don't even see half of
what's going on. All the options on the Discussion Settings page are geared
toward decreasing or eliminating comment or trackback spam from your blog.
If, during the course of your blogging experience on WordPress.com, you find
that you're having an issue with spam, you may want to revisit these options
and make adjustments.

Comment Reply via E-mail

Check the box that is labeled Enable sending comment replies via e-mail, and
WordPress.com will not only publish your comment replies to your readers
on your blog, but it will also send your reply via e-mail to the reader you're
replying to. That e-mail will contain the body of your reply and link back to
your blog.

Subscribe to Comments

Check the box labeled Show a Subscribe to Comments option in the comment
form if you want to allow the readers of your blog to subscribe to individual
comment threads on your blog. When you enable this option, your readers
can opt to receive e-mails every time there is a new comment posted to a
specific post on your blog. This option also puts a comment subscription
management page on your blog that allows readers to view and manage their
comment subscriptions. This is a really great tool to keep readers coming
back to your blog over and over again, and a great way to keep lively discussions going!

Subscribe to Blog

Check the box labeled Show a Subscribe to Blog option in the comment form if you want to give your readers an easy way to subscribe to your blog via e-mail. With this option enabled, readers who select this option will receive an update in their e-mail box every time you publish a new post to your blog. This is a fantastic way to keep your readers informed and coming back to your blog time and time again for more of your great published content.

Avatars

Avatars are photos or images that represent your commenters (and you) on your blog. Figure 4-12, later in this chapter, shows a small avatar to the left of the comment. You can choose to display avatars on your blog by selecting the Show Avatars option. You can also set the maximum rating for the avatars, much like the movie rating system we're all used to. If your site is family friendly, you probably don't want to display R- or X-rated avatars on your blog. You can select G, PG, R, or X ratings for the avatars that display on your blog. You can also select an image to use as the default avatar for those users who do not yet have avatars assigned to their e-mail.

For WordPress.com users, the avatars displayed are the images they uploaded to their profiles (see Chapter 3). Users who are not registered with WordPress. com still have the option of having an avatar displayed when they comment on your blog by signing up for one at `http://gravatar.com`.

Viewing comments

You open the Edit Comments page by clicking the Comments menu. The Edit Comments page shows all the comments on your blog, from the very first day you started. Here, you can view the comments, edit them, mark them as spam, or flat-out delete them.

If you've set your Comments options so that comments aren't published until you approve them, you can approve comments in this section as well. To accomplish this task, of course, you have to have comments on your blog, and if your blog is new, you may not have any yet. Figure 4-11 shows what a comment looks like in this area.

To manage a comment, find one that you want to edit, delete, unapprove (or remove it from your blog page), or mark as spam. If you need to, you can find a specific comment by using the search feature. Just type a keyword in the search box located in the top-right corner of the page and click the Search Comments button.

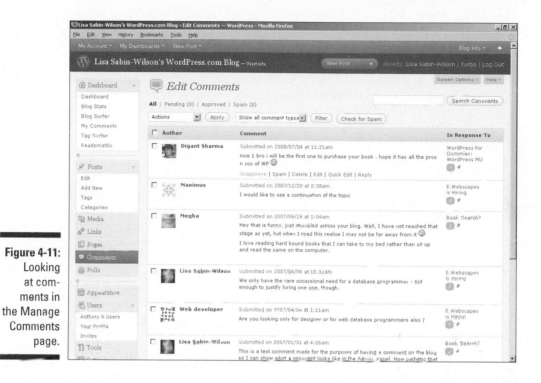

Figure 4-11:
Looking
at com-
ments in
the Manage
Comments
page.

When you've found the comment you want to manage, hover your mouse over the comment, and six different links appear beneath the comment text, and include:

- **Approve or Unapprove:** If the comment has not yet been approved, the Approve link appears here. Click Approve to publish the comment to your blog. If the comment was approved, click the Unapprove link to . . . well, unapprove it. This link puts the comment back into the moderation queue.

- **Reply:** This link drops down a text box on the same page to allow you to reply to the comment right from the Edit Comments page.

- **Quick Edit:** This link accomplishes the same as the Edit link except instead of taking you to a new Edit Comment page, it drops down a quick edit text box that allows you to do a fast edit right on the same page.

- **Edit:** Clicking this link takes you to the Edit Comment page where you can edit the text of the comment, if you need to (correcting typos, anyone?).

- **Spam:** This link tells WordPress that this comment is spam and removes it from your blog.

- **Trash:** This link deletes the comment from your blog.

Managing comment spam with Akismet

Comment spam, as I discuss in Chapter 2, is a sneaky method that spammers are fond of using to post links to their sites on yours. Akismet is the answer to combating comment and trackback spam; it kills spam dead. Created by the Automattic team, headed by Matt Mullenweg, Akismet is a "collaborative effort to make comment and trackback spam a non-issue and restore innocence to blogging, so you never have to worry about spam again," according to Akismet.com.

Click the Spam link on the Edit Comments page to view the comments and trackbacks that were caught by Akismet's spam filters. Akismet keeps the past two weeks' worth of comments and trackbacks that were stopped by its filters because the rare legitimate comment can get caught up in the spam filters. If that happens, you can visit this section and de-spam the comment by clicking the Not Spam button.

I usually don't have to visit the Akismet Spam page. My readers usually are pretty quick to let me know if they've left a comment that didn't get published. In such a case, I check the Akismet Spam page to see whether it was caught in the spam filters. Then I de-spam it and move on.

Creating a Static Page

You can create pages on your blog that are treated differently from posts. These pages, called *static pages,* appear as separate pages on your blog rather than posts within your blog. You use nearly the same process of writing a static page as you do to write a post. You can easily create an unlimited number of static pages, which can serve as nice complements to your overall site content.

You can use this feature to write, for example, an About Me page, on which you give all the wild and wooly details about yourself. (See Figure 4-12 for an example of an About page.) If you use the Page Sidebar widget, the pages you create are listed in your sidebar. (See Chapter 5 for more about widgets.)

You can create these pages by logging in to your WordPress.com Dashboard and following these steps:

1. **Click the Add New link in the Pages menu.**

    The Add New Page page appears where you can compose your static page.

2. **Type the title of your page in the Title text box.**

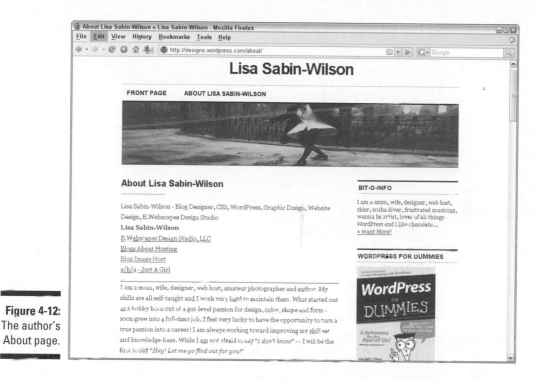

Figure 4-12:
The author's
About page.

3. **Type the body of your page in the Page text box.**

   You can use the Virtual Text Editor and insert media files into your page by using the same techniques discussed in the "Ready? Set? Blog!" section, earlier in this chapter.

4. **Set the options for your page by using the option boxes below the Page text box.**

   To display these boxes, click the white arrow to the left of each option title. The following options appear:

   • *Discussion:* By default, the Allow Comments and Allow Pings boxes are selected. Deselect them if you don't want to allow comments or pings.

   • *Parent:* Choose the page parent from the drop-down menu if you want to make the static page a subpage of another page you've created.

   • *Template:* If the WordPress.com theme you're using has page templates available, choose from this drop-down menu the template you want to use for the page.

- *Order:* Enter a number in the text box that reflects the order in which you want this page to display on your site. If you want this page to be the third page listed, for example, enter **3**.

- *Page Author:* Choose the author of this blog from the drop-down menu. This step isn't necessary if you're the only author of this blog; if you have multiple authors, however, you may find this option helpful.

5. **Scroll back to the top of the page, and choose options from the Publish Status drop-down menu.**

   These options are the same as the Publish Status options that are available when you're writing a new blog page. I covered the available options in the "Ready? Set? Blog!" section earlier in this chapter.

6. **Click the Save or Publish button when you're done to save your work.**

Your static pages aren't included in your Recent Posts list, in categories, or in your monthly archive.

Setting Up Your Front Page

On the Reading Settings page (click the Reading link in the Settings menu), you can set how many blog posts show up on the front page of your blog and/or change your front page to display a static page rather than displaying your most recent blog posts. (See the "Creating a Static Page" section, earlier in this chapter, for more information on creating static pages.) You can also determine how many blog posts your readers can see in your RSS feed. Figure 4-13 shows the options that are available.

The Reading Settings page gives you control of the settings that let you make these decisions for your blog:

- **Front Page Displays:** This setting determines what appears on the front page of your site.

  - *Your Latest Posts:* Select this option if you want your blog posts to display on the front page of your blog.

  - *A Static Page:* Select this option if you want a static page to display on the front page of your blog.

  - *Front Page:* If you choose to display a static page, choose from this drop-down menu which page to display.

  - *Posts Page:* If you choose to display a static page, use this drop-down menu to tell WordPress which page to display your posts on.

Figure 4-13:
The Reading
Settings
page.

✔ **Blog Pages Show at Most *X* Posts:** If you choose to display your blog posts on your front page, this step is where you set the number of blog posts to display per page. Figure 4-13, in the following section, shows that I've decided to display ten posts on my front page.

✔ **Syndication Feeds Show the Most Recent *X* Posts:** This setting determines how many posts show in your RSS feed at one time. See the next section for details.

✔ **For Each Article in a Feed, Show:** Indicate here which portion of each article you want to show in your feed:

   • *Full Text:* Select this radio button if you want the entire text of each post to be displayed in your RSS feed.

   • *Summary:* Select this radio button if you want only excerpts of your posts to be displayed in your RSS feed.

✔ **For Each Article in an Enhanced Feed, Show:** Here, you have the option of showing several more details about your blog, as well as giving the reader the opportunity to add your article to several social bookmark sites:

   • Categories

   • Tags

- Comment Count

- Add to Stumbleupon

- Add to Del.icio.us

- Add to Digg.com

- Add to Reddit

✔ **Encoding for Pages and Feeds:** UTF-8 is the default, and recommended, character encoding for your blog. *Character encoding* is code that handles the storage and transmission of the text from your blog through the Internet connection. Your safest bet is to leave the default in place, because it is the most commonly accepted character encoding and supports a wide range of languages.

✔ **E-mail Settings:** When people subscribe to your blog for the first time, an e-mail is sent to them welcoming them to your blog. The text box in the E-mail Settings area provides default text for that e-mail. You can change this text to suit your needs.

When you change any settings in the Reading Settings page, make sure that you click the Save Changes button in the bottom-left corner to save your preferences.

Publishing a Public or Private Blog

This section contains one very simple option for you to set; this option lets you determine how you want to deal with publicity on your blog. Figure 4-14 shows your choices. To access the privacy options for your blog, click the Privacy link on the Settings menu. You can choose one of these three options in the Privacy Settings page:

✔ **I Would Like My Blog to Be Visible to Everyone, Including Search Engines (Like Google, Sphere, Technorati) and Archivers:** Select this option if you want to freely allow search engines to visit your blog and include its content in their search directories.

✔ **I Would Like to Block Search Engines, but Allow Normal Visitors:** Select this option if you don't want search engines to visit and include your site in their directories. This option is helpful if you want normal (read: human) visitors but don't want the publicity that search engines provide.

✔ **I Would Like My Blog to Be Visible Only to Users I Choose:** Select this option if you want to make your blog available only to the people you choose. This option keeps your blog completely private and away from prying eyes — except for those users you allow.

When you select and save this option, WordPress.com provides a form where you can enter the WordPress.com usernames for the people you want to invite to view your private blog. (WordPress.com lets you add up to 35 users at no cost; you can pay an annual fee to add more.)

When you finish making your decision, be sure to click the Save Changes button to make the changes take effect.

Establishing Trust Relationships with OpenID

OpenID is a third-party, Internet-community identification system that lets an Internet user create an online identity that she can use anywhere on the Web where OpenID is supported. With WordPress.com, you already have an OpenID identity.

In the WordPress Dashboard, click the OpenID link on the Settings menu to see the OpenID Trusted Sites page, which tells you what your OpenID is. (It's usually your main WordPress.com domain: `http://username.wordpress.com`.) You can also add the URLs of what you consider to be trusted sites. After you enter the URL of a trusted site and click the Add to List button, you aren't asked whether you trust the site when you attempt to log in to it. In a nutshell, this setting means that you can use your WordPress.com OpenID to log in to any Web site that supports OpenID.

Chapter 5

Enhancing Your Blog with Themes, Widgets, and Upgrades

In This Chapter

▶ Giving your blog a new look

▶ Adding widgets to your sidebar

▶ Upgrading your free WordPress.com blog

*Y*ou don't want your blog to look identical to everyone else's, do you? Although WordPress.com doesn't give you the vast array of design options that you'd have by hosting your own blog, you do have some flexibility.

The great thing about the WordPress hosted service is how easily you can change your theme to one of the alternative designs available. What's not so hot is that you can't create your own custom theme. As noted later in this chapter, you can pay a fee to customize the CSS of the template you've chosen to use, but you need to be familiar with CSS to use this upgrade — and there again, you're limited to customizing only the templates that WordPress provides.

In this chapter, you discover the WordPress.com themes that let you choose a design and format for your blog. You have some fabulous themes to choose among, all created by WordPress users. At this writing, 86 themes are available. You also explore the fun of using sidebar widgets to rearrange how your blogroll, category and monthly archive lists, and page lists are displayed.

This chapter also discusses enhancing your blog with custom CSS (Cascading Style Sheets), choosing a domain name, and increasing the amount of hard drive space on your WordPress.com account through its upgrade feature (for a fee).

Changing Your Blog's Look

It's time to choose a theme for your WordPress.com blog. In this case, the word *theme* is synonymous with the words *design* and *template*. All three words describe the very same things: the visual layout and appearance of your blog.

Follow these steps to find your theme:

1. **In the Dashboard, click the Themes link on the Appearance menu.**

   A page full of themes appears (as shown in Figure 5-1), along with a thumbnail image of the theme so that you can get a basic idea of what it looks like.

2. **Scroll through the themes, and when you find a theme you like, click its name or the thumbnail image associated with it.**

   You can page through the list of available themes by using the handy buttons at the top-right and bottom-right corners of the Available Themes section. Or you can use the drop-down menu in the top-left corner of the Available Themes section to filter your theme choices by color, columns, width, and option refer to Figure 5-1.

   What happens next is pretty nifty! A box pops up, showing you a pre-view of what your own blog would look like with that particular theme.

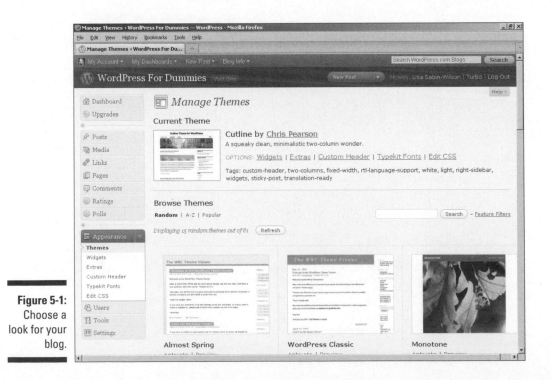

Figure 5-1:
Choose a
look for your
blog.

3. **Click the Activate link in the top-right corner to activate the theme on your own blog, or click the X in the top-left corner if you decide you'd rather not use that theme.**

No, really — it's just that easy. If you get tired of that theme, go to the Design tab and click a different theme name, and you're done.

It really is that easy!

Widget Wonder: Adding Handy Tools to Your Sidebar

WordPress widgets are very helpful tools built in to the WordPress.com application. They allow you to easily arrange the display of content in your blog sidebar, such as your blogroll(s), recent posts, and monthly and category archive lists. With widgets, arrange and display the content in the sidebar of your blog without having to know a single bit of PHP or HTML.

Selecting and activating widgets

Click the Widgets link on the Appearance menu in the Dashboard. The Widgets page displays the available widgets, as shown in Figure 5-2. This feature is a big draw because it lets you control what features you use and where you place them — all without having to know a lick of code.

On the left side of the Widgets page is a listing of all widgets available for your WordPress.com blog.

On the right side of the Widgets page are the widgets you're using in your sidebar. Figure 5-2 shows that I am using the following widgets in my sidebar:

- Recent Posts
- Categories
- Archives

The Widgets page also includes a drop-down menu in the Current Widgets section (refer to Figure 5-2). If you're using a theme that has only one sidebar, the Widgets page has only one sidebar for you to configure. If you are using a theme with two sidebars (usually called a three-column layout), use the drop-down menu to toggle between Sidebar 1 and Sidebar 2. When you want to configure widgets for Sidebar 1, be sure that Sidebar 1 is selected in the

Figure 5-2:
WordPress.
com
Widgets
page.

drop-down menu; when you want to configure widgets for the second sidebar, choose Sidebar 2. Click the Show button to load the widgets for that sidebar on your screen.

To add a new widget to your sidebar, follow these steps:

1. **Choose the widget you want to use.**

   You find all the widgets are listed in the Available Widgets section. For the purpose of these steps, choose the Archives widget.

2. **Click the Widget menu bar.**

   Use your cursor to drag and drop the widget over to the Sidebar section on the right side of the page. The widget is now located in your sidebar, and the content of the widget now appears on your site in the sidebar.

3. **Click the arrow you see to the right of the widget title.**

   Click the arrow to see drop-down menu with options for the widget. Each widget has different options that you can configure. The Archives widget, for example, lets you configure the title, the display of the post counts, and the display of the archives (see Figure 5-3).

4. **Select your options and click the Save button.**

   The options you've set are now saved. Click the Close link to close the widget options menu.

5. **Arrange your widgets in the order in which you want them to appear on your site by clicking a widget and dragging it above or below another widget.**

   Repeat this step until your widgets are arranged the way you want them.

To remove a widget from your sidebar, click the arrow to the right of the widget title to open the options menu, and then click the Delete link. WordPress removes the widget from the Current Widgets list on the right side of this page and places it back in the Available Widgets list.

After you've selected and configured all your widgets, click the Visit Site button at the top of your WordPress Dashboard (you'll see it to the right of your site name), and your blog's sidebar matches the content (and order of the content) you've arranged in the sidebar on the Widgets page. How cool is that? You can go back to the Widgets page and rearrange the items, as well as add and remove items, to your heart's content.

Figure 5-3:
Configuring
widget
options.

Using Text widgets

The Text widget in WordPress.com is a little different from the rest of the widgets you encounter on the Widgets page. Add the Text widget just as you would any other, using the steps I outline in the preceding section. After you have it settled in the sidebar, click the arrow to the right of the Widget title. A text box drops down to let you type text or HTML code to insert a hyperlink or include an image file (see Figure 5-4). You can't, however, include any executable code, such as PHP or JavaScript, in a Text widget.

You have no real options to configure, but you can use this simple text box for several things. Here are a couple of examples of what you can use a Text widget for:

✔ Type a short paragraph of text, such as a bio.

✔ Insert the HTML code to display an image in your sidebar. (See Chapter 13 for some information on basic HTML codes you can use.)

Figure 5-4: Text widget text box.

Using the RSS widget

The RSS widget lets you display content from another blog in your sidebar. If I wanted to display a list of recent posts from another blog that I have somewhere else, for example, I would use the RSS widget to accomplish this task. Follow these steps to add the RSS widget to your blog:

1. **Add the RSS widget to your sidebar on the Widgets page.**

   Follow the steps in the "Selecting and activating widgets" section, earlier in this chapter, to add the widget.

2. **Click drop-down arrow to the right of the RSS widget's name.**

   A box drops down, displaying the different options you can configure for the RSS widget.

3. **In the Enter the RSS URL Here text box, type the RSS URL of the blog you want to add.**

   You can usually find the RSS Feed URL of a blog listed in the sidebar.

4. **Type the title of the RSS widget.**

   This title is what will appear in your blog above the links from this blog. If I wanted to add the RSS feed from my personal blog, for example, I would type **Lisa Sabin-Wilson's blog**.

5. **Select the number of items to display**

   The drop-down menu here gives you a choice of 1-20 — select the number of items from the RSS feed that you would like displayed on your site.

6. **(Optional) Select the Display the Item Content box.**

   Checking this box tells WordPress that you also want to display the content of the feed (usually, the content of the blog post from the feed URL). If you want to display only the title, leave the box unchecked.

7. **(Optional) Select the Display Item Author, If Available box.**

   Select this option if you want to display the author's name along with the item's title.

8. **(Optional) Select the Display Item Date box.**

   Select this option if you want to display the date the item was published, along with the item title.

9. **Click the Save Changes button.**

   WordPress saves all the options you've just set and reloads the Widgets page with your RSS widget intact.

Figure 5-5 shows my WordPress.com blog displaying the content from my personal blog in thc sidebar. I used the RSS widget to make this happen!

Figure 5-5:
Content
from
another blog
shown in
my sidebar
via the RSS
widget.

Upgrading Your Hosted Service (For a Fee)

Although WordPress.com is a free service, it offers enhancements for a fee. WordPress.com calls these items *upgrades,* and you can purchase credits for them at the cost of $1 (USD) per credit. (The prices I give here are current as of this book's printing, but they are, of course, subject to change.) Click the Upgrades link in the Upgrades menu to display the Upgrades page, shown in Figure 5-6.

Following is a list of the current upgrades you can purchase to enhance your WordPress.com account, with the prices reflecting the annual cost:

- **Add A Domain:** This upgrade allows you to add your own domain name to your WordPress.com account; see the section "Naming Your Domain," later in this chapter. This service costs $5.00 for the domain registration and $9.97 for the domain mapping.

- **VideoPress:** This upgrade equips you with the ability to upload, store, and share your videos from your WordPress.com account. This service covers the storage space that your video files take up on the WordPress.com servers. It costs $59.97 per year.

- **Custom CSS:** This upgrade lets you customize the Cascading Style Sheets (CSS) for the theme you're currently using in the WordPress.com system. Recommended for users who understand the use of CSS, this upgrade currently costs $14.97 per year.

✔ **Space Upgrades:** With the free WordPress.com blog, you have 3GB of hard drive space for use in your upload directory. The various space upgrades add more, letting you upload more files (images, videos, audio files, and so on). Currently, you can add 5GB for $19.97 per year, 15GB for $49.97 per year, or 25GB for $89.97 per year.

✔ **No Ads:** For the cost of $29.97 per year, you can ensure that your WordPress.com blog is ad-free. Occasionally, WordPress.com does serve ads on your blog pages to try and defray the costs of running a popular service. If you'd rather not have those ads appearing on your blog, pay for the No Ads upgrade and you'll be ad-free!

✔ **Unlimited Private Users:** With a free account, you're limited to 35 private users — if you choose to publish your WordPress.com blog as a private blog — giving access to only those users whom you authorize. This upgrade removes that limit, letting you have unlimited private users for your blog (provided that those users are already WordPress.com account holders). The cost is $29.97 per year.

Figure 5-6:
The
WordPress.
com
Upgrades
page.

Naming Your Domain

The URL for your WordPress.com blog is `http://username.wordpress.com`, with *username* being your username. My username is `designs`; therefore, my WordPress.com domain is `http://designs.wordpress.com`.

WordPress.com lets you use your own domain name for your WordPress.com blog. Using the Domains feature in WordPress.com is not free, however. At this writing, this feature costs $5.00 for the domain registration and $9.97 for the domain mapping.

When you have your domain registered, go to your WordPress.com Dashboard, click the Domains link in the Upgrades menu, click the Domains tab, and type your domain name in the Add a Domain text box (see Figure 5-7). Then follow the prompts to fully set up your domain name.

When you've configured your domain name correctly, your old WordPress.com URL redirects to your new domain name. If my domain name is `LisaSabin-Wilson.com`, my WordPress.com blog at `http://designs.wordpress.com` redirects to `http://lisasabin-wilson.com`.

Figure 5-7:
Use your own domain in WordPress.com by upgrading on the Domains page.

Part III
Self-Hosting with WordPress.org

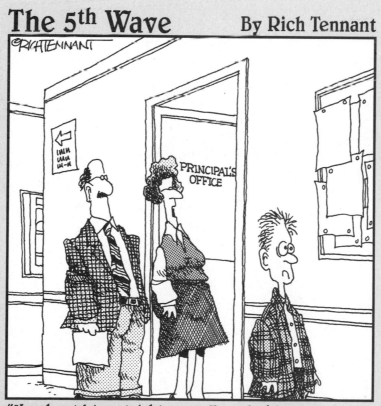

The 5th Wave   By Rich Tennant

"He should be alright now. I made him spend two and a half hours reading prisoner blogs on the state penitentiary Web site."

In this part . . .

In this part, you really dig into the guts of WordPress.org. I tell you how to get your own domain name and Web host and take you through the installation procedure and features of the Administration panel that you'll want to know about when getting started.

Chapter 6

Setting Up Blogging Base Camp

· ·

In This Chapter

▶ Finding and buying a domain name

▶ Finding Web hosting

▶ Brushing up on FTP

▶ Installing WordPress

· ·

*B*efore you can start blogging with WordPress.org, you have to set up your base camp. Doing so involves more than simply downloading and installing the WordPress software. You also need to establish your *domain* (your blog address) and your *Web hosting service* (the place that houses your blog). Although you initially download your WordPress software onto your hard drive, your Web host is where you install it.

Obtaining a Web server and installing software on it are much more involved projects than simply obtaining an account with the hosted version of WordPress that's available at WordPress.com (covered in Part II). You have to consider many factors in this undertaking, as well as cope with a learning curve, because setting up your blog through a hosting service involves using some technologies that you may not feel comfortable with at first. This chapter takes you through the basics of those technologies, and by the last page of this chapter, you'll have WordPress successfully installed on a Web server with your own domain name.

Establishing Your Domain

You've read all the hype. You've heard all the rumors. You've seen the flashy blogs on the Web powered by WordPress. But where do you start?

The first steps toward installing and setting up a WordPress blog are making a decision about a domain name and then purchasing the registration of that name through a domain registrar. A *domain name* is the *unique* Web address that you type in a Web browser's address bar to visit a Web site. Some examples of domain names are WordPress.org and Google.com.

Domain names: Do you own or rent?

In reality, when you "buy" a domain name, you don't really own it. Rather, you're purchasing the right to use that domain name for the period of time specified in your order. You can register a domain name for one year or up to ten years. Be aware, however, if you don't renew the domain name when your registration period ends, you lose it — and most often, you lose it right away to someone who preys on abandoned or expired domain names. Some people keep a close watch on expiring domain names, and as soon as the buying window opens, they snap the names up and start using them for their own Web sites, in the hope of taking full advantage of the popularity that the previous owners worked so hard to attain for those domains.

I emphasize the word *unique* because no two domain names can be the same. If someone else has registered the domain name you want, you can't have it. With that in mind, it sometimes takes a bit of time to find a domain that isn't already in use and is available for you to use.

Understanding domain name extensions

When registering a domain name, be aware of the *extension* that you want. The `.com`, `.net`, `.org`, `.info`, or `.biz` extension that you see tagged on to the end of any domain name is the *top-level domain extension.* When you register your domain name, you're asked to choose the extension you want for your domain (as long as it's available, that is).

A word to the wise here: Just because you have registered your domain as a `.com` doesn't mean that someone else doesn't, or can't, own the very same domain name with a `.net`. So if you register MyDogHasFleas.com, and it becomes a hugely popular site among readers with dogs that have fleas, someone else can come along and register MyDogHasFleas.net, and run a similar site to yours in the hope of riding the coattails of your Web site's popularity and readership.

You can register your domain name with all available extensions if you want to avert this problem. My business Web site, for example, has the domain name EWebscapes.com; however, I also own EWebscapes.net, EWebscapes.biz, and EWebscapes.info.

Considering the cost of a domain name

Registering a domain costs you anywhere from $3 to $30 per year, depending on what service you use for a registrar and what options (such as privacy options and search-engine submission services) you apply to your domain name during the registration process.

When you pay the domain registration fee today, you need to pay another registration fee when the renewal date comes up again in a year, or two, or five — however many years you chose to register your domain name for. (See the "Domain names: Do you own or rent?" sidebar.) Most registrars give you the option of signing up for a service called Auto Renew to automatically renew your domain name and bill the charges to the credit card you have set up on that account. The registrar sends you a reminder a few months in advance, telling you it's time to renew. If you do not have Auto Renew set up, you need to log in to your registrar account before it expires and manually renew your domain name.

Registering your domain name

Domain registrars are certified and approved by the Internet Corporation for Assigned Names and Numbers (ICANN). Although hundreds of domain registrars exist today, the ones in the following list are popular because of their longevity in the industry, competitive pricing, and variety of services they offer in addition to domain name registration (such as Web hosting and Web site traffic builders):

- **GoDaddy:** http://GoDaddy.com
- **Register.com:** http://register.com
- **Network Solutions:** http://networksolutions.com
- **NamesDirect:** http://namesdirect.com

No matter where you choose to register your domain name, here are the steps you can take to accomplish this task:

1. **Decide on a domain name.**

   Doing a little planning and forethought here is necessary. Many people think of a domain name as a *brand* — a way of identifying their Web sites or blogs. Think of potential names for your site; then you can proceed with your plan.

2. **Verify the domain name's availability.**

   In your Web browser, enter the URL of the domain registrar of your choice. Look for the section on the registrar's Web site that lets you enter the domain name (typically, a short text field) to see whether it's available. If the domain name isn't available as a .com, try .net or .info.

3. **Purchase the domain name.**

Follow the domain registrar's steps to purchase the name using your credit card. After you complete the checkout process, you receive an e-mail confirming your purchase, so be sure to use a valid e-mail address during the registration process.

The next step is obtaining a hosting account, which I cover in the next section.

Some of the domain registrars have hosting services that you can sign up for, but you don't have to use those services. Often, you can find hosting services for a lower cost than most domain registrars offer. It just takes a little research.

Finding a Home for Your Blog

When you have your domain registered, you need to find a place for it to live — a Web host. Web hosting is the second piece of the puzzle that you need to complete before you begin working with WordPress.org.

A *Web host* is a business, group, or individual that provides Web server space and bandwidth for file transfer to Web site owners who don't have it. Usually, Web hosting services charge a monthly or annual fee — unless you're fortunate enough to know someone who's willing to give you server space and bandwidth for free. The cost varies from host to host, but you can obtain quality Web hosting services for $3 to $10 per month to start.

Web hosts consider WordPress to be a *third-party application.* What this means to you is that the host typically won't provide technical support on the use of WordPress (or any other software application), because support isn't included in your hosting package. To find out whether your chosen host supports WordPress, always ask first. As a WordPress user, you can find WordPress support in the official forums at `http://wordpress.org/support`.

Several Web hosting providers also have WordPress-related services available for additional fees. These services can include technical support, plugin installation and configuration, and theme design services.

Hosting services generally provide (at least) these services with your account:

- ✔ Hard drive space
- ✔ Bandwidth (transfer)
- ✔ Domain e-mail with Web mail access
- ✔ File Transfer Protocol (FTP) access
- ✔ Comprehensive Web site statistics

> ✔ MySQL database(s)
> ✔ PHP

Because you intend to run WordPress on your Web server, you need to look for a host that provides the minimum requirements needed to run the software on your hosting account, which are

> ✔ PHP version 4.3 (or greater)
> ✔ MySQL version 4.0 (or greater)

The easiest way to find out whether a host meets the minimum requirement is to check the FAQ (Frequently Asked Questions) section of the host's Web site, if it has one. If not, find the contact information for the hosting company, and fire off an e-mail requesting information on exactly what it supports. Any Web host worth dealing with will answer your e-mail within a reasonable amount of time (12–24 hours is a good barometer).

Getting help with hosting WordPress

The popularity of WordPress has given birth to services on the Web that emphasize the use of the software. These services include WordPress designers, WordPress consultants, and — yes — Web hosts that specialize in using WordPress.

Many of these hosts offer a full array of WordPress features, such as an automatic WordPress installation included with your account, a library of WordPress themes, and a staff of support technicians who're very experienced in using WordPress.

Here is a list of some of those providers:

> ✔ **Blogs About Hosting:** `http://blogs-about.com`
> ✔ **Laughing Squid:** `http://laughingsquid.net`
> ✔ **BlueHost:** `http://bluehost.com`
> ✔ **DreamHost:** `http://dreamhost.com`

A few Web hosting providers offer free domain name registration when you sign up for hosting services. Research this topic and read their terms of service, because that free domain name may come with conditions. Many of my clients have gone this route, only to find out a few months later that the Web hosting provider has full control of the domain name, and they aren't allowed to move that domain off the host's servers, either for a set period (usually, a year or two) or for infinity. It's always best to have the control in *your* hands, not someone else's, so try and stick with an independent domain registrar, such as Network Solutions.

Dealing with disk space and bandwidth

Web hosting services provide two very important things with your account:

- ✔ Disk space
- ✔ Bandwidth transfer

Think of your Web host as a garage that you pay to park your car in. The garage gives you the place to store your car (disk space). It even gives you the driveway so that you, and others, can get to and from your car (bandwidth). It won't, however, fix your rockin' stereo system (WordPress or any other third-party software application) that you've installed — unless you're willing to pay a few extra bucks for that service.

Managing disk space

Disk space is nothing more complicated than the hard drive on your own computer. Each hard drive has the capacity, or space, for a certain amount of files. An 80GB (gigabyte) hard drive can hold 80GB of data — no more. Your hosting account provides you a limited amount of disk space, and the same concept applies. If your Web host provides you 10GB of disk space, that's the limit on the file size that you're allowed to have. If you want more disk space, you need to upgrade your space limitations. Most Web hosts have a mechanism in place for you to upgrade your allotment.

Starting out with a self-hosted WordPress blog doesn't take much disk space at all. A good starting point for disk space is between 3–5GB of storage space. If you find that you need additional space in the future, contact your hosting provider for an upgrade in space.

Choosing the size of your bandwidth pipe

Bandwidth refers to the amount of data that is carried from point A to point B within a specific period (usually, only a second or two). I live out in the country — pretty much the middle of nowhere. The water that comes to my house is provided by a private well that lies buried in the backyard somewhere. Between my house and the well are pipes that bring the water to my house. The pipes provide a free flow of water to our home so that everyone can enjoy their long, hot showers while I labor over dishes and laundry, all at the same time. Lucky me!

The very same concept applies to the bandwidth available with your hosting account. Every Web hosting provider offers a variety of bandwidth limits on the accounts it offers. When I want to view your Web site in my browser window, the bandwidth is essentially the pipe that lets your data flow from your "well" to my computer and appear on my monitor. The bandwidth limit is kind of like the pipe connected to my well: It can hold only a certain amount of water before it reaches maximum capacity and won't bring the water from the well any longer. Your bandwidth pipe size is determined by how much bandwidth your Web host allows for your account — the larger the number, the bigger the pipe. A 50MB bandwidth limit makes for a smaller pipe than does a 100MB limit.

Web hosts are pretty generous with the amount of bandwidth they provide in their packages. Like disk space, bandwidth is measured in gigabytes (GB). Bandwidth provision of 10–50GB is generally a respectable amount to run a Web site with a blog.

Web sites that run large files — such as video, audio, or photo files — generally benefit from higher disk space compared with sites that don't involve large files. Keep this point in mind when you're signing up for your hosting account. Planning now will save you a few headaches down the road.

Transferring Files from Point A to Point B

This section introduces you to the basic elements of File Transfer Protocol (FTP). The ability to use FTP with your hosting account is a given for almost every Web host on the market today. FTP is the method you use to move files from one place to another — for example, from your computer to your Web hosting account. This method is referred to as *uploading*.

Using FTP to transfer files requires an FTP client. Many FTP clients are available for download. Following are some good (and free) ones:

- **WS_FTP:** www.ipswitch.com/_download/wsftphome.asp
- **SmartFTP:** www.smartftp.com/download
- **FileZilla:** http://sourceforge.net/projects/filezilla
- **Cyberduck (for Mac users):** http://cyberduck.ch
- **FTP Explorer:** www.ftpx.com

Earlier in this chapter, in "Finding a Home for Your Blog," you find out how to obtain a Web hosting account. Your Web host gives you a username and password for your account, including an FTP IP address. (Usually, the FTP address is the same as your domain name, but check with your Web host, as addresses may vary.) It is this information — the username, password, and FTP IP address — that you insert into the FTP program to connect it to your hosting account.

Figure 6-1 shows my FTP client connected to my hosting account. The directory on the left is the listing of files on my computer; the directory on the right shows the listing of files on my hosting account.

Figure 6-1:
Using an
FTP client
makes file
transfers
easy.

FTP clients make it easy to transfer files from your computer to your hosting account by using a drag-and-drop method. You simply click the file on your computer that you want to transfer, drag it over to the side that lists the directory on your hosting account, and drop it. Depending on the FTP client you've chosen to work with, you can refer to its user manuals or support documentation for detailed information on how to use the program.

Installing WordPress

By the time you're finally ready to install WordPress.org, you should have done the following things:

- ✔ Purchased the domain name registration for your account
- ✔ Obtained a hosting service on a Web server for your blog
- ✔ Established your hosting account username, password, and FTP address
- ✔ Acquired an FTP client for transferring files to your hosting account

If you've missed any of the items listed, you can go back to the beginning of this chapter to reread the portions you need.

Some Web hosts now offer a one-click installation process for WordPress. If this is the case for you, you can simply follow the instructions provided by your Web host. The instructions in this section are for those of you who are doing a manual install of WordPress on your Web server.

If you have to install WordPress manually, here's where the rubber meets the road — that is, you're putting WordPress's famous five-minute installation to the test. Set your watch, and see whether you can meet that five-minute mark.

The famous five-minute installation includes the time it takes to install the software only. It does not include the time to register a domain name; the time to obtain and set up your Web hosting service; or the time to download, install, configure, and learn how to use the FTP software.

Without further ado, go get the latest version of the WordPress software here: `http://wordpress.org/download`.

WordPress gives you two compression formats for the software: `zip` and `tar.gz`. I recommend getting the zip file, as it's the most common format for compressed files.

Download the WordPress software to your computer and decompress (or unpack, or unzip) it to a folder on your computer's hard drive. These steps are the first in the installation process for WordPress. Having the program on your own computer isn't enough, however; you also need to *upload* (transfer) it to your Web server account (the one you obtained in "Finding a Home for Your Blog," earlier in this chapter). Before installing WordPress on your Web server, you need to make sure that you have a MySQL database all set up and ready to accept the WordPress installation. The next section tells you what you need to know about MySQL.

Setting up the MySQL database

The WordPress software is a personal publishing system that uses a PHP-and-MySQL platform, which provides everything you need to create your own blog and publish your own content dynamically without having to know how to program those pages yourself. In short, all your content (options, posts, comments, and other pertinent data) is stored in a MySQL database in your hosting account.

Every time visitors go to your blog to read your content, they make a request that's sent to your server. The PHP programming language receives that request, obtains the requested information from the MySQL database, and then presents the requested information to your visitors through their Web browsers.

Every Web host is different in how it gives you access to set up and manage your MySQL database(s) for your account. In this section, I use a popular hosting interface called cPanel. If your host provides a different interface, the same basic steps apply; just the setup in the interface that your Web host provides may be different.

To set up the MySQL database for your WordPress blog with cPanel, follow these steps:

1. **Log in to the administration interface with the username and password assigned to you by your Web host.**

   I'm using the cPanel administration interface, but your host may provide NetAdmin or Plesk, for example.

2. **Locate the MySQL Database Administration section.**

   In cPanel, click the MySQL Databases icon.

3. **Choose a name for your database, and enter it in the Name text box.**

   Be sure to make note of the database name, because you will need it during the installation of WordPress later.

   For security reasons, make sure that your password isn't something that sneaky hackers can easily guess. Usually, I give my database a name that I will easily recognize later. This practice is especially helpful if you're running more than one MySQL database in your account. If I name this database something like *WordPress* or *wpblog,* I can be reasonably certain — a year from now, when I want to access my database to make some configuration changes — that I know exactly which one I need to deal with.

4. **Click the Create Database button.**

   You get a message confirming that the database has been created.

5. **Click the Go Back link or the Back button on your browser toolbar.**

6. **Choose a username and password for your database, enter them in the Add New User text boxes, and then click the Create User button.**
   You get a confirmation message that the username was created with the password you specified.

   Make absolutely sure that you note the database name, username, and password that you set up during this process. You *will* need them in the next section before officially installing WordPress on your Web server. Jot them down on a piece of paper, or copy and paste them into a text-editor window; either way, just make sure that you have them immediately handy.

7. **Click the Go Back link or the Back button on your browser toolbar.**

8. **In the Add Users to Database section, choose the user you just set up from the User drop-down menu; then choose the new database from the Database drop-down menu.**

The MySQL Account Maintenance, Manage User Privileges page appears in cPanel.

9. **Assign user privileges by selecting the All Privileges check box.**

   Because you're the administrator (owner) of this database, you need to make sure that you assign all privileges to the new user you just created.

10. **Click the Make Changes button.**

    A page opens with a confirmation message that you've added your selected user to the selected database.

11. **Click the Go Back link.**

    You go back to the MySQL Databases page.

Uploading the WordPress files

To upload the WordPress files to your host, return to the folder on your computer where you unpacked the WordPress software that you downloaded earlier. You'll find all the files you need (shown in Figure 6-2) in a folder called /wordpress.

Figure 6-2: WordPress software files to be uploaded to your Web server.

Using your FTP client, connect to your Web server, and upload all these files to your hosting account, into the root directory.

If you don't know what your root directory is, contact your hosting provider and ask, "What is my root directory for my account?" Every hosting provider's setup is different. On my Web server, my root directory is the public_html folder; some of my clients have a root directory in a folder called httpdocs. The answer really depends on what type of setup your hosting provider has. When in doubt, ask!

Here are a few things to keep in mind when you're uploading your files:

- ✔ **Upload the *contents* of the /wordpress folder to your Web server — not the folder itself.** Most FTP client software lets you select all the files and drag 'n' drop them to your Web server. Other programs have you highlight the files and click a Transfer button.

- ✔ **Choose the correct transfer mode.** File transfers via FTP have two different forms: ASCII and binary. Most FTP clients are configured to auto-detect the transfer mode. Understanding the difference as it pertains to this WordPress installation is important, so that you can troubleshoot any problems you have later:

    - *Binary transfer mode* is how images (such as .jpg, .gif, .bmp, and .png files) are transferred via FTP.

    - *ASCII transfer mode* is for everything else (text files, PHP files, JavaScript, and so on).

  For the most part, it's a safe bet to make sure that the transfer mode of your FTP client is set to autodetect. But if you experience issues with how those files load on your site, retransfer the files using the appropriate transfer mode.

- ✔ **You can choose a different folder from the root.** You aren't required to transfer the files to the root directory of your Web server. You can make the choice to run WordPress on a subdomain, or in a different folder, on your account. If you want your blog address to be http://yourdomain.com/blog, you would transfer the WordPress files into a folder named /blog.

- ✔ **Choose the right file permissions.** *File permissions* tell the Web server how these files can be handled on your server — whether they're files that can be written to. As a general rule, PHP files need to have a permission (chmod) of 666, whereas file folders need a permission of 755. Almost all FTP clients let you check and change the permissions on the files, if you need to. Typically, you can find the option to change file permissions within the menu options of your FTP client.

Some hosting providers run their PHP software in a more secure format called *safe mode*. If this is the case with your host, you need to set the PHP files to 644. If you're unsure, ask your hosting provider what permissions you need to set for PHP files.

Last step: Running the install script

The final step in the installation procedure for WordPress is connecting the WordPress software you uploaded to the MySQL database. Follow these steps:

1. **Type this URL in the address window of your browser, replacing** *yourdomain.com* **with your own domain name:**

   ```
   http://yourdomain.com/wp-admin/install.php
   ```

   If you chose to install WordPress in a different folder from the root directory of your account, make sure you indicate this fact in the URL for the install script. If you transferred the WordPress software files to a folder called /blog, for example, you would point your browser to the following URL to run the installation: `http://yourdomain.com/blog/wp-admin/install.php`.

   Assuming that you did everything correctly (see Table 6-1 for help with common installation problems), you see the message shown in Figure 6-3.

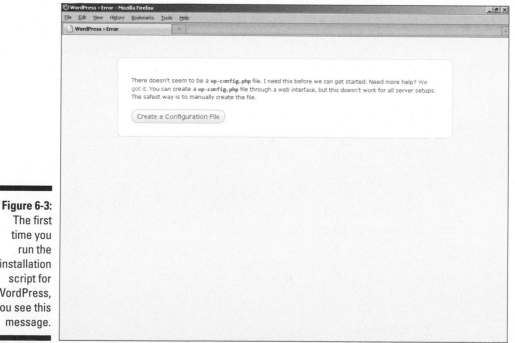

Figure 6-3: The first time you run the installation script for WordPress, you see this message.

2. **Click the Create a Configuration File button.**

   The next page that opens is a Welcome to WordPress message, which gives you the information you need to proceed with the installation.

3. **Click the Let's Go button at the bottom of that page.**

4. **Dig out the database name, username, and password that you saved earlier, and use that information to fill in the following fields (shown in Figure 6-4):**

   • *Database Name:* Type the database name you used when you created the MySQL database before this installation. Because hosts differ in configurations, you need to enter either the database name or the database name with your hosting account username appended.

   If you named your database *wordpress,* for example, you would enter that in this text box. Or if your host requires you to append the database name with your hosting account username, you would enter **username_wordpress**, substituting your hosting username for *username.* My username is *lisasabin,* so I entered **lisasabin_wordpress**.

   • *User Name:* Type the username you used when you created the MySQL database before this installation. Depending on what your host requires, you may need to append this username to your hosting account username.

   • *Password:* Type the password you used when you set up the MySQL database. You don't need to append the password to your hosting account username here.

   • *Database Host:* Ninety-nine percent of the time, you'll leave this field set to *localhost.* Some hosts, depending on their configurations, have different hosts set for the MySQL database server. If *localhost* doesn't work, you need to contact your hosting provider to find out the MySQL database host.

   • *Table Prefix:* Leave this field set to *wp_.*

5. **When you have all that information filled in, click the Submit button.**

   You see a message that says, "*All right, sparky! You've made it through this part of the installation. WordPress can now communicate with your database. If you're ready, time now to run the install!*"

6. **Click the Run the Install button.**

   You see another welcome page with a message welcoming you to the famous five-minute WordPress installation process.

Figure 6-4:
At this step of the WordPress installation phase, you need to enter the database name, username, and password.

[WordPress Setup Configuration screenshot showing fields: Database Name "wordpress", User Name "username", Password "password", Database Host "localhost", Table Prefix "wp_", with a Submit button]

7. **Enter or possibly change this information (shown in Figure 6-5):**

   • *Blog Title:* Enter the title you want to give your blog. The title you enter isn't written in stone; you can change it at a later date, if you like.

   • *User Name:* This is the name you will use to log in to WordPress. By default, the username is **admin**, and you can leave it that way. However, for security reasons, it's recommended practice to change your username to something unique to you.

   • *Password:* Type your desired password in the first text box. Then type it again in the second text box to confirm that you've typed it correctly. If the two versions of your password don't match, WordPress alerts you with an error message. If you don't enter a password, one will automatically be generated for you.

   For security reasons (and so other people can't make a lucky guess), passwords should be at least seven characters long and use as many different characters in as many combinations as possible. Use a mixture of uppercase and lowercase letters, numbers, and symbols (like ! " ? $ % ^ &).

   • *Your E-Mail:* Enter the e-mail address you want to use to be notified of administrative information about your blog. You can change this address at a later date, too.

Figure 6-5:
Information
needed to
finish the
WordPress
installation.

- *Allow My Blog to Appear in Search Engines Like Google and Technorati:* By default, this check box is selected, which lets the search engines index the content of your blog and include your blog in search results. To keep your blog out of the search engines, deselect this check box.

8. Click the Install WordPress button.

The WordPress installation machine works its magic and creates all the tables within the database that contain the default data for your blog. WordPress displays the login information you need to access the WordPress Dashboard. Make note of this username and password before you leave this page. Scribble it down on a piece of paper or copy it into a text editor such as Notepad.

After you click the Install WordPress button, you're sent an e-mail with the login information and login URL. This information is handy if you're called away during this part of the installation process. So go ahead and let the dog out, answer the phone, brew a cup of coffee, or take a 15-minute power nap. If you somehow get distracted away from this page, the e-mail sent to you contains the information you need to successfully log in to your WordPress blog.

9. **Click the Log In button to log in to WordPress.**

If you happen to lose this page before clicking the Log In button, you can always find your way to the login page by entering your domain followed by the call to the login file (for example, `http://yourdomain.com/wp-login.php`).

You know that you're finished with the installation process when you see the login page, as shown in Figure 6-6. Check out Table 6-1 if you experience any problems during this installation process; it covers some of the common problems users run into.

So do tell — how much time does your watch show for the installation? Was it five minutes? Stop by my blog sometime (`http://lisasabin-wilson.com`), and let me know whether WordPress stood up to its famous five-minute-installation reputation. I'm a curious sort.

The good news is — you're done! Were you expecting a marching band? WordPress isn't that fancy . . . yet. Give them time, though; if anyone can produce it, the folks at WordPress can.

Figure 6-6:
You know
you've run a
successful
WordPress
installation
when you
see the
login page.

Table 6-1	Common WordPress Installation Problems	
Error Message	*Common Cause*	*Solution*
Error Connecting to the Database	The database name, username, password, or host was entered incorrectly.	Revisit your MySQL database to obtain the database name, username, and password, and reenter that information.
Headers Already Sent Error Messages	A syntax error occurred in the `wp-config.php` file.	Open the `wp-config.php` file in a text editor. The first line should contain only this line: `<?php`. The last line should contain only this line: `?>`. Make sure that those lines contain nothing else — not even white space. Save the file changes.
500: Internal Server Error	Permissions on PHP files are set incorrectly.	Try setting the permissions (`chmod`) on the PHP files to 666. If that change doesn't work, set them to 644. Each Web server has different settings for how it lets PHP execute on its servers.
404: Page Not Found	The URL for the login page is incorrect.	Double-check that the URL you're using to get to the login page is the same as the location of your WordPress installation (such as `http://yourdomain.com/wp-login.php`).
403: Forbidden Access	An `index.html` or `index.htm` file exists in the WordPress installation directory.	WordPress is a PHP application, so the default home page is `index.php`. Look in the WordPress installation folder on your Web server. If there is an `index.html` or `index.htm` file in there, delete it.

Let me be the first to congratulate you on your newly installed WordPress blog! When you're ready, log in and familiarize yourself with the Dashboard, which I describe in Chapter 7.

Chapter 7

Understanding the WordPress.org Dashboard

In This Chapter

▶ Signing in to the Dashboard

▶ Finding your way around the Dashboard

▶ Customizing the Dashboard

▶ Applying your own settings

▶ Personalizing your profile

▶ Deciding how your blog will look

*W*ith WordPress.org successfully installed, you can explore your new blogging software. This chapter guides you through the preliminary setup of your new WordPress blog using the Dashboard. When you blog with WordPress, you spend a lot of time in the Dashboard, which is where you make all the exciting, behind-the-scenes stuff happen. In this panel, you find all the settings and options that enable you to set up your blog just the way you want it. (If you still need to install and configure WordPress, check out Chapter 6.)

Feeling comfortable with the Dashboard sets you up for successful entrance into the WordPress blogging world. You will tweak your WordPress settings several times throughout the life of your blog. In this chapter, as I go through the various sections, settings, options, and configurations available to you, understand that nothing is set in stone. You can set options today and change them at any time.

Logging In to the Dashboard

I find that the direct approach (also known as jumping in) works best when I want to get familiar with a new software tool. To that end, just follow these steps to log in to WordPress and take a look at the guts of the Dashboard:

1. **Open your Web browser, and type the WordPress login-page address (or URL) in the address box.**

   The login-page address looks something like this (exchange that `.com` for a `.org` or a `.net` as needed:

   ```
   http://www.yourdomain.com/wp-login.php
   ```

   If you installed WordPress in its own folder, include that folder name in the login URL. If you installed WordPress in a folder ingeniously named `wordpress`, the login URL becomes `http://www.yourdomain.com/wordpress/wp-login.php`.

2. **Type your username in the Username text box and your password in the Password text box (see Figure 6-6 in the previous chapter).**

   In case you forget your password, WordPress has you covered. Click the Lost Your Password? link (located near the bottom of the page), enter your username and e-mail address, and then click the Submit button. WordPress resets your password and e-mails the new password to you.

   After you request a password, you receive two e-mails from your WordPress blog. The first e-mail contains a link that you click to verify that you requested the password. After you verify your intentions, you receive an e-mail containing your new password.

3. **Select the Remember Me check box if you want WordPress to place a cookie in your browser.**

   The cookie tells WordPress to remember your login credentials the next time you show up. The cookie set by WordPress is harmless and stores your WordPress login on your computer. Because of the cookie, WordPress remembers you the next time you visit. Also, because this option tells the browser to remember your login, I don't advise checking this option on public computers. Avoid selecting Remember Me when you're using your work computer, or a computer at an Internet café.

   Note: Before you set this option, make sure that your browser is configured to allow cookies. (If you aren't sure how to do this, check the help documentation of the Internet browser you're using.)

4. **Click the Log In button.**

After you've logged in to WordPress, you see the Dashboard page.

Navigating the Dashboard

You can consider the Dashboard to be a Control Panel of sorts, because it offers several quick links and areas that provide information about your blog, starting with the actual Dashboard page, shown in Figure 7-1.

(W)WORDPRESS

Username
UserName

Password
●●●●●●●●

☐ Remember Me   Log In

Lost your password?

Figure 7-1:
Log in to the
WordPress
Dashboard.

You can change how the WordPress Dashboard looks, at least in terms of the order the modules appear on it. You can expand (open) and collapse (close) the individual modules by clicking your mouse anywhere within the grey title bar of the module. This feature is really nice because you can utilize the Dashboard for just those modules that you use regularly. The concept is easy: Keep the modules you use all the time open and close the ones that you only use occasionally — you can open those modules only when you really need them. You save space and you can customize your Dashboard to suit your own needs.

When you view your Dashboard for the very first time, all of the modules in the Dashboard appear in the expanded (open) position by default (refer to Figure 7-1).

The navigation menu in the WordPress Dashboard appears on the left side of your browser window. When you need to get back to the WordPress Dashboard, click the Dashboard link that appears at the top of the navigation menu of any of the pages within your WordPress Dashboard.

In the following sections, I cover the Dashboard page as it appears when you log in to your WordPress Dashboard for the very first time; later in this chapter, I show you how to configure the appearance of your Dashboard so that it best suits how you use the available modules.

Right Now

The Right Now module in the Dashboard shows what is going on in your blog right now, right this very second! Figure 7-2 shows the expanded Right Now module in my brand-spanking-new WordPress blog.

Figure 7-2:
The Right
Now mod-
ule in the
Dashboard
expanded
to see the
available
features.

Right Now		
At a Glance		
1 Post		1 Comment
1 Page		1 Approved
1 Category		0 Pending
0 Tags		0 Spam
Theme **Twenty Ten** with **0 Widgets**		Change Theme
You are using **WordPress 3.0-alpha**.		

The Right Now module shows the following default information under the At a Glance header:

- **The number of posts you have:** This number reflects the total number of posts you currently have in your WordPress blog; I have 1 post on my blog. The number is blue, which means it's a link that you can click. When you do, you go to the Edit Posts page, where you can edit the posts on your blog. I cover editing posts in Chapter 8.

- **The number of pages:** This is the current number of pages on your blog, which changes as you add or delete pages. (*Pages,* in this context, refer to the static pages you have created in your blog.) Figure 7-2 shows that my blog has 1 page.

  Clicking this link takes you to the Edit Pages page, where you can view, edit, and delete your current pages. (Find the difference between WordPress posts and pages in Chapter 8.)

- **The number of categories:** This is the current number of categories you have on your blog, which changes as you add and delete categories. Figure 7-2 shows that I have 1 category for my blog.

  Clicking this link takes you to the Categories Page, where you can view, edit, and delete your current categories; or add brand new ones. (For details about the management and creation of categories, see Chapter 8.)

- **The number of tags:** This is the current number of tags you have in your blog, which changes as you add and delete categories in the future. Figure 7-2 shows that I have 0 tags.

  Clicking this link takes you to the Tags page, where you can add new tags and view, edit, and delete your current tags. (You can find more information about tags in Chapter 8.)

- **The number of comments:** This is the total number of the comments that are currently on your blog. Figure 7-2 shows that I have 1 Comment, 1 Approved, 0 Pending, and 0 marked as spam.

Clicking any of these four links takes you to the Edit Comments page, where you can manage the comments on your blog. I cover the management of comments in the "Comments" section, later in this chapter.

The last section of the Dashboard's Right Now module in the Dashboard shows the following information:

- **Which WordPress theme you are using:** Figure 7-2 shows that I'm using the theme Twenty Ten. The theme name is a link that, when clicked, takes you to the Manage Themes page where you can view and activate themes on your blog.

- **How many widgets you've added to your blog:** This is the number of WordPress widgets you're using in your blog. Figure 7-2 shows that I have 0 widgets. The number 0 is a link that, when clicked, takes you to the Widgets page, where you can change your widget options by editing them, moving them, or removing them. (I cover widgets in detail in Chapter 5 if you want to check that out — although that chapter is in the WordPress.com part of this book, the method of using sidebar widgets is the same for self-hosted WordPress.org blogs.)

- **Change Theme:** Clicking this button takes you to the Manage Themes page, which lists your currently active and all available themes for your WordPress blog. Your active theme (the theme that's visible on your active blog) is shown at the top below the Current Theme header. All other available themes are listed below Available Themes. Click any theme on this page to use it on your blog.

- **The version of WordPress you're using:** This is the last statement in the Right Now section. Figure 7-2 shows that I'm using WordPress version 3.0. In the future, this version announcement will change if you are using an older version of WordPress. When WordPress software is upgraded, this statement will tell you that you are using an outdated version of WordPress and encourage you to upgrade to the latest version.

Recent Comments

The next module is called Recent Comments — within this module, you find:

- **Most recent comments published to your blog:** WordPress displays a maximum of five comments in this area.

- **The author of each comment:** The name of the person who left the comment appears below it. This section also displays the author's picture (or avatar), if she has one.

✔ **A link to the post the comment was left on:** The post title appears to the right of the commenter's name. Click the link, and you go to that post in the Dashboard.

✔ **An excerpt of the comment:** This is a short snippet of the comment this person left on your blog.

✔ **Comment management links:** When you hover over the comment with your mouse cursor, five links appear underneath the comment. These links give you the opportunity to manage those comments right from your Dashboard: The first link is Unapprove, which appears only if you have comment moderation turned on. (Find out more about moderating comments in the "Comments" section, later in this chapter.) The other four links are Edit, Reply, Spam, and Trash.

✔ **View All button:** This button invites you to see all the comments that have been left on your blog. Clicking the View All button takes you to the Edit Comments page, where you can view and edit, moderate, or delete any comments that have been left for your blog.

You'll find even more information on managing your comments in the "Comments" section, later in this chapter.

Incoming Links

The next module visible in the Dashboard is Incoming Links. It lists all the blog-savvy people who wrote a blog post that links to your blog. When your blog is brand new, you won't see any incoming links listed in this section. Don't despair, however; as time goes on, you will see this listing of links fill up as more and more people discover you and your inspired writings!

In the meantime, the Incoming Links module shows *"This dashboard widget queries Google Blog Search so that when another blog links to your site it will show up here. It has found no incoming links ... yet. It's okay — there is no rush."* The phrase *Google Blog Search* is a link; when you click it, you go the Google Blog Search directory, which is a search engine for blogs only.

The following steps show you what how you can edit the Incoming Links module:

1. **Hover your mouse over the title of the Incoming Links module, and a new link appears directly to the right of the title labeled Configure. Click that link.**

   Now you can change the settings of the Incoming Links module (see Figure 7-3).

Figure 7-3:
Changing
the set-
tings of the
Incoming
Links
module by
clicking the
Configure
link.

Incoming Links   Cancel

Enter the RSS feed URL here:

http://blogsearch.google.com/blogsearch_feeds?scoring

How many items would you like to display? 10 ▼

☐ Display item date?

(Submit)

2. **Add a URL in the Enter the RSS Feed URL Here box.**

   You can enter the URL of any RSS feed you want to display incoming
   links to your site. Examples of feeds you can use include Technorati
   (http://technorati.com), Yahoo! Search (http://search.
   yahoo.com) or Social Mention (www.socialmention.com). You're
   not restricted to using the Google Blog Search engine (http://blog
   search.google.com) to provide your Incoming Links information.

3. **Specify how many items you want to display.**

   The default number is 5, but making a different choice from the drop-
   down menu lets you display up to 20 items (incoming links).

4. **Specify whether to display the item date.**

   Check the Display Item Date? box if you want each incoming link to display the date the link was created. If you don't want the date display,
   leave that box blank.

5. **Click the Submit button to save all your preferences.**

   Clicking Submit resets the Incoming Links module with your new settings saved.

Plugins

I cover the management and use of WordPress plugins in detail in Chapter
10; however, for the purposes of this section, I discuss the functions of the
Plugins module in the Dashboard so you know what to do with it now!

The Plugins module includes three titles of WordPress plugins that are
linked to its page within the WordPress Plugin Directory. The Plugins module
pulls information via RSS feed from the official WordPress Plugin Directory
at http://wordpress.org/extend/plugins. This module displays a

plugin from three different plugin categories in the official WordPress Plugin Directory: Most Popular, Newest Plugins, and Recently Updated.

The Plugins module doesn't have an Edit link, so you can't customize the information that it displays. Use this box to discover new plugins that can help you do fun and exciting things with your blog.

The Plugins module does have a very exciting feature that you can use to install, activate, and manage plugins on your blog. Just follow these steps to make it happen:

1. **Click the Install link next to the title of the plugin.**

   The Plugin Information popup window opens. It displays the various bits of information about the plugin you've chosen, such as title, description, version, author, date last updated, and the number of times the plugin was downloaded.

2. **Click the Install Now button.**

   This button is at the top right of the Plugin Information page.

   The Plugin Information popup window closes and the Install Plugins page in your WordPress Dashboard opens, where you see a confirmation message that the plugin has been downloaded, unpacked, and successfully installed.

3. **Specify whether to install the plugin or proceed to the Plugins page.**

   Two links are shown under the confirmation message:

   • *Activate Plugin:* Click this link to activate the plugin you just installed on your blog.

   • *Return to Plugins Page:* Click this link to go to the Manage Plugins page.

   I cover the installation, installation, and activation of WordPress plugins in further depth in Chapter 10.

4. **Click the Dashboard link to return to the Dashboard.**

   The Dashboard link is located at the top of the left menu on every page of your WordPress Dashboard.

QuickPress

The QuickPress module is a handy form that allows you to write, save, and publish a blog post right from your WordPress Dashboard. The options are similar to the ones I cover in the section on writing posts in Chapter 8.

Recent Drafts

If you're using a brand new WordPress blog and this is a new installation, the Recent Drafts module displays the message: *There are no drafts at the moment.* That is because you have not written any drafts. As time goes on, however, and you have written a few posts in your blog, you may save some of those posts as Drafts — to be edited and published at a later date. Those drafts show up in the Recent Drafts module.

WordPress displays up to five drafts and displays the title of the post, the date it was last saved, and a short excerpt. A View All link also displays; click that link to go the Manage Posts page where you can view, edit, and manage your blog posts. Check out Chapter 8 for more information.

WordPress Development Blog

When you first install WordPress, the WordPress Development Blog module is by default populated with the two most recent updates from the official WordPress development blog at `http://wordpress.org/development`. You see the title of the last post, the date it was published, and a short excerpt of the post. Click a title, and you go directly to that post on the WordPress Development Blog.

Following the updates of the WordPress Development Blog is very useful, and I highly recommend it. Why? Every single time you log in to your WordPress Dashboard, a glance at this section informs you about any news, updates, or alerts from the makers of WordPress. You can find out about any new versions of the software, security patches, or other important news regarding the software you are using to power your blog.

Although I recommend that you keep the WordPress Development Blog updates in this section, the WordPress platform lets you change this box to display posts from another blog of your choosing. You can accomplish this change by following these steps:

1. **Hover your mouse over the WordPress Development module title. Click the Configure link shown to the right of the WordPress Development Blog title.**

   The module changes to display several options to change the information contained in the box (see Figure 7-4).

2. **Type your preferred RSS feed in the Enter the RSS feed URL Here box.**

3. **Type your preferred title in the Give the Feed a Title (Optional) box.**

Figure 7-4:
Options
to change
the Feed
Title and
URL of the
WordPress
Develop-
ment Blog
module.

WordPress Development Blog	Cancel

Enter the RSS feed URL here:

http://wordpress.org/development/feed/

Give the feed a title (optional):

WordPress Development Blog

How many items would you like to display? 2 ▾

☑ Display item content?

☐ Display item author if available?

☑ Display item date?

(Submit)

4. **Specify the number of items you want to display.**

   The default number of items is 2, but you can display up to 20 by making a different choice from the drop-down menu.

5. **Specify whether you want to display the item's content.**

   Item content refers to the text content of the post. If you don't check the Display Item Content? box, WordPress doesn't display an excerpt of the post — only the post title.

6. **Specify whether you want to display the name of the person who wrote the post.**

   Leave the Display Item Author If Available? box unchecked if you don't want the author's name displayed.

7. **Specify whether you want to display the date.**

   Leave the Display Item Date? box unchecked if you don't want the date displayed.

8. **Click the Submit button to save your changes.**

   The Dashboard page refreshes with your new changes. Click the title of the box to collapse it.

If you change your mind, click the Cancel link shown to the right of the WordPress Development Blog title. Clicking Cancel discards any changes you made and keeps the original settings intact.

The title of the WordPress Development Blog module changes to the title you chose in Step 3. Figure 7-5 shows that I changed the title to Lisa's Blog.

Figure 7-5:
The
WordPress
Develop-
ment Blog
module
changes
based on
the options
you set.

Lisa's Blog

Speaking at Think Tank Live! in Milwaukee January 27, 2010
I am happy to announce that I am speaking at the Think Tank
Live Search Marketing and Social Media Summit scheduled for
February 23, 2010 in Milwaukee, WI. I will be presenting on the
topic of building a niche community web site utilizing the free
and dynamic software combination of WordPress and
BuddyPress and how business, and individuals, can leverage
the [.]

My name is Lisa and I love Brett Favre. There. I said it.
January 24, 2010
Going in to this weekend, I found myself planning my schedule
of things to do around the game on Sunday afternoon at
5:40pm between the Minnesota Vikings and New Orleans
Saints. How did I get to this place where I was scheduling
everything around a football game? It's been a long journey as
citizen of the great state of Wisconsin, and with that comes a
certa [...]

Other WordPress News

The Other WordPress News module of the Dashboard pulls in posts from a site called WordPress Planet (http://planet.wordpress.org). By keeping the default setting in this area the same, you stay in touch with several posts made by folks who are involved in WordPress development, design, and troubleshooting. You can find lots of interesting and useful tidbits if you keep this area intact. Quite often, I find great information about new plugins or themes, problem areas and support, troubleshooting, and new ideas, so I tend to stick with the default setting.

WordPress is all about user experience, however, so you can change the options to specify what displays in this area. You can change the items in this module the same way that you change the options for the WordPress Development Blog module (see the preceding section).

Arranging the Dashboard to Your Tastes

You have the ability to arrange the order of the modules in your Dashboard to suit your tastes. WordPress places a great deal of emphasis on user experience and a big part of that effort results in your ability to create a Dashboard that you find most useful. Changing the modules that are displayed, and the order they are displayed in, is very easy.

In the following steps, I show you how to move the Right Now module so that it displays on the right side of your Dashboard page:

1. **Hover your mouse over the title bar of the Right Now module.**

   When hovering over the box title, your mouse cursor changes to the Move cursor (a cross with arrows on a PC or the hand cursor on a Mac).

2. Click and hold your mouse button and drag the Right Now module to the right side of the screen.

As you drag the box, a light gray box with a dotted border appears on the right side of your screen. That gray box is a guide that shows you where you should drop the module. See Figure 7-6.

3. Release the mouse button when you have the Right Now module in place.

The Right Now module is now positioned on the right side of your Dashboard page.

The other modules on the left side of the Dashboard have now shifted down, and the Recent Comments Module is the first module shown at the top of the left side on the Dashboard page.

4. (Optional) Click once on the title bar of the Right Now module.

The module collapses. Click the title bar again, and the module expands. You can keep that module opened or closed based on your own preference.

Gray box

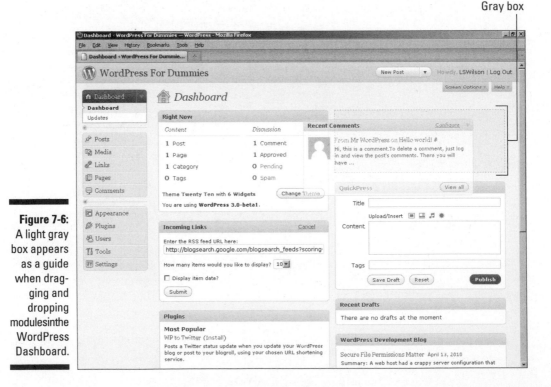

Figure 7-6:
A light gray box appears as a guide when dragging and dropping modules in the WordPress Dashboard.

Repeat these steps with each module you see on the Dashboard by dragging and dropping them so they appear in the order you prefer.

When you navigate away from the Dashboard, WordPress remembers the changes you've made. When you return, you still see your customized Dashboard and you don't need to redo these changes in the future.

If you find that your Dashboard contains a few modules you just never use, you can completely get rid of them altogether by following these steps:

1. **Click the Screen Options button at the top of the Dashboard.**

   The Screen Options menu opens, displaying the title of each module with check boxes to the left of each title.

2. **De-select the module you want to hide on your Dashboard.**

   The check mark is removed from the box, and the module disappears from your Dashboard. Figure 7-7 shows my customized Dashboard, where I've moved the QuickPress module to the top left and the Right Now module to the top right.

If you miss a module you've hidden, you can simply enable that module by selecting the module from the Screen Options menu.

Figure 7-7: My WordPress Dashboard after I customized it.

Setting Options in the Dashboard

The navigation menu is located on the left side of every page within the WordPress Dashboard. You'll find it there everywhere you go — like a loyal friend, it's always there for you when you need it!

The navigation menu is divided into ten different menus. Hover your mouse over a menu, and a down arrow appears to the right; click the down arrow to reveal the submenu. The submenus take you to areas within your Dashboard that allow you to perform tasks such as publishing a new blog post, adding a new link, or managing your comments.

When you expand a menu in the navigation menu, WordPress remembers and keeps that menu expanded as you navigate through different pages in the Dashboard. Likewise, if you collapse the menu, WordPress remembers that you've closed that menu, and the menu stays closed as you browse through your WordPress Dashboard.

The settings that allow you to personalize your blog are the first ones that I cover in the next part of this chapter. Some of the menu items, like creating and publishing new posts, are covered in detail other chapters, but they're well worth a mention here as well so that you know what you're looking at. (Each section contains a cross-reference telling you where you can find more in-depth information on that topic in this book.)

Configuring the Settings

At the very bottom of the navigation menu is the Settings menu. Click the Settings link, and a submenu drops down that contains the following links, which I discuss in the sections that follow:

- ✔ General
- ✔ Writing
- ✔ Reading
- ✔ Discussion
- ✔ Media
- ✔ Privacy
- ✔ Permalinks

General

After you install the WordPress software and log in, you can put a personal stamp on your blog by giving it a title and description, setting your contact e-mail address, and identifying yourself as the author of the blog. You take care of these and other settings on the General Settings page.

To begin personalizing your blog, start with your general settings by following these steps:

1. **Click the General link in the Settings menu.**

   The General Settings page appears (see Figure 7-8).

2. **Enter the name of your blog in the Blog Title text box.**

   The title you enter here is the one that you've given your blog to identify it as your own. In Figure 7-8, I gave my new blog the title *WordPress For Dummies,* which appears on the blog as well as in the title bar of the viewer's Web browser.

Figure 7-8: Personalize the settings of your WordPress blog on the General Settings page.

Give your blog an interesting and identifiable name. You can use *Fried Green Tomatoes,* for example, if you're blogging about the topic, the book or the movie, or even anything remotely related to the lovely Southern dish.

3. **In the Tagline text box, enter a five- to ten-word phrase that describes your blog.**

   Figure 7-8 shows that my tagline is *by Lisa Sabin-Wilson.* So my blog displays my blog title followed by the tagline: *WordPress For Dummies by Lisa Sabin-Wilson.*

   The general Internet-surfing public can view your blog title and tagline, which various search engines (such as Google, Yahoo!, and MSN) grab for indexing, so choose your words with this fact in mind. (You can find more information about search engine optimization, or SEO, in Chapter 14.)

4. **In the WordPress Address (URL) text box, enter the location where you installed your WordPress blog software.**

   Be sure to include the `http://` portion of the URL and the entire path to your WordPress installation — for example, `http://yourdomain.com`. If you installed WordPress in a folder in your directory — in a folder called `wordpress`, for example — you need to make sure to include it here. If I had installed WordPress in a folder called `wordpress`, the WordPress address would be `http://yourdomain.com/wordpress`.

5. **In the Blog Address (URL) text box, enter the Web address where people can find your blog by using their Web browsers.**

   Typically, what you enter here is the same as your domain name (`http://yourdomain.com`). If you install WordPress in a subdirectory of your site, the WordPress installation URL is different from the blog URL. If you install WordPress at `http://yourdomain.com/wordpress/` (WordPress URL), you need to tell WordPress that you want the blog to appear at `http://yourdomain.com` (the blog URL).

6. **Enter your e-mail address in the E-Mail Address text box.**

   WordPress sends messages about the details of your blog to this e-mail address. When a new user registers for your blog, for example, WordPress sends you an e-mail alert.

7. **Select a Membership option.**

   Select the Anyone Can Register box if you want to keep registration on your blog open to anyone who wants to. Keep the box unchecked if you'd rather not have open registration on your blog.

8. **From the New User Default Role drop-down menu, choose the role that you want new users to have when they register for user accounts in your blog.**

You need to understand the differences among the user roles, because each user role is assigned a different level of access to your blog, as follows:

- *Subscriber:* Subscriber is the default role. It's a good idea to maintain this role as the one assigned to new users, particularly if you don't know who is registering. Subscribers are given access to the Dashboard page, and they can view and change the options in their profiles on the Your Profile and Personal Options page. (They don't have access to your account settings, however — only to their own). Each user can change his username, e-mail address, password, bio, and other descriptors in his user profile. Subscribers' profile information is stored in the WordPress database, and your blog remembers them each time they visit, so they don't have to complete the profile information each time they leave comments on your blog.

- *Contributor:* In addition to the access Subscribers have, Contributors can upload files and write, edit, and manage their own posts. Contributors can write posts, but they can't publish the posts; the administrator reviews all Contributor posts and decides whether to publish them. This setting is a nice way to moderate content written by new authors.

- *Author:* In addition to the access Contributors have, Authors can publish and edit their own posts.

- *Editor:* In addition to the access Authors have, Editors can moderate comments, manage categories, manage links, edit pages, and edit other Authors' posts.

- *Administrator:* Administrators can edit all the options and settings in the WordPress blog.

9. **In the Timezone section, choose your UTC time from the drop-down menu.**

   This setting refers to the number of hours that your local time differs from Coordinated Universal Time (UTC). This setting ensures that all your blog posts and comments left on your blog are time-stamped with the correct time. If you're lucky enough, like me, to live on the frozen tundra of Wisconsin, which is in the Central time zone (CST), you would choose **–6** from the drop-down menu because that time zone is 6 hours off UTC.

   If you're unsure what your UTC time is, you can find it at the Greenwich Mean Time (`http://wwp.greenwichmeantime.com`) Web site. GMT is essentially the same thing as UTC.

10. **In the Date Format text box, enter the format in which you want the date to be displayed in your blog.**

This setting determines the style of the date display. The default format is already selected and displayed for you: **F j, Y** (F = the full month name; j = the two-digit day; Y = the four-digit year), which gives you the date output. This default date format displays the date like this: January 1, 2008.

Select a different format by clicking the circle to the left of the option. You can also customize the date display by selecting the Custom option and entering your preferred format in the text box provided. If you're feeling adventurous, you can found out how to customize the date format here: `http://codex.wordpress.org/Formatting_Date_and_Time`.

11. **In the Time Format text box, enter the format in which you want the time to be displayed in your blog.**

    This setting is the style of the time display. The default format is already inserted for you: **g:i a** (g = the two-digit hour; i = the two-digit minute; a = lowercase ante meridiem and post meridiem, or a.m. or p.m.), which gives you the output of 12:00 a.m.

    Select a different format by clicking the circle to the left of the option. You can also customize the date display by selecting the Custom option and entering your preferred format in the text box provided; find out how at `http://codex.wordpress.org/Formatting_Date_and_Time`.

    You can format the time and date in several ways. Go to `http://us3.php.net/date` to find potential formats at the PHP Web site.

12. **From the drop-down menu, choose the day the week starts in your calendar.**

    The display of the calendar in the sidebar of your blog is optional. If you choose to display the calendar, you can select the day of the week you want your calendar to start with.

Click the Save Changes button at the bottom of any page where you set new options. If you don't click Save Changes, your settings aren't saved, and WordPress reverts to the preceding options. Each time you click the Save Changes button, WordPress reloads the current page, displaying the new options that you just set.

Writing

Click the Writing link in the Settings menu; the Writing Settings page opens (see Figure 7-9).

This page lets you set some basic options for writing your posts. Table 7-1 gives you some information on choosing how your posts look and how WordPress handles some specific conditions.

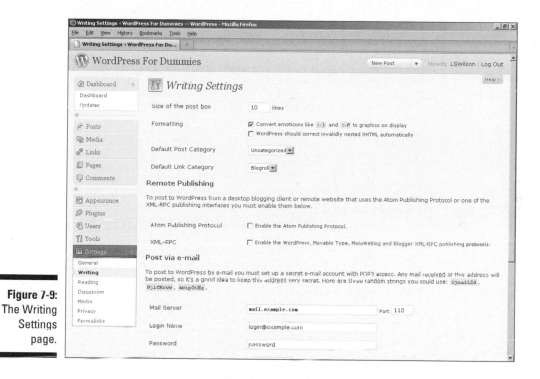

Figure 7-9:
The Writing
Settings
page.

After you set your options, be sure to click the Save Changes button; otherwise, the changes won't take effect.

Table 7-1	Writing Settings Options	
Option	*Function*	*Default*
Size of Post Box	Determines the size of the text edit box on the Write Post page. The bigger the number, the taller the box.	Ten lines
Formatting	Determines whether WordPress converts emoticons to graphics and whether WordPress corrects invalidly nested XHTML automatically. In general, I recommend selecting this option. (You can find more information about valid XHTML code at http://validator.w3.org/docs/#docs_all.)	Convert emoticons — such as :-) and :-P — to graphics and correct invalidly nested XHTML

(continued)

Table 7-1 *(continued)*

Option	Function	Default
Default Post Category	Lets you select the category that WordPress defaults to any time you forget to choose a category when you publish a post.	Uncategorized
Default Link Category	Lets you select the category that WordPress defaults to any time you forget to categorize a link.	Uncategorized
Remote Publishing	Lets you enable Atom Publishing Protocol or one of the XML-RPC publishing interfaces that enable you to post to your WordPress blog from a remote Web site or desktop publishing application.	Disabled
Post via E-Mail	Lets you publish blog posts from your e-mail account by letting you enter the e-mail and server information for the account you'll be using to send posts to your WordPress blog.	N/A
Update Services *Note:* This option is only available if your blog is made public in the Privacy settings.	Lets you indicate which ping service you want to use to notify the world that you've made updates, or new posts, to your blog. These update services include blogrolling.com and weblogs.com. The default, rpc.pingomatic.com, updates all the popular services simultaneously.	`http:// rpc.ping omatic.com`

Go to `http://codex.wordpress.org/Update_Services` for comprehensive information on update services.

Reading

The third link in the Settings menu is Reading (see Figure 7-10).

Figure 7-10:
The Reading
Settings
page.

You can set the following options in the Reading Settings page:

- **Front Page Displays:** Choose what you want to display on the front page of your blog: your latest posts or a static page. You can find detailed information about using a static page for your front page in Chapter 14.

- **Blog Pages Show at Most:** Enter the maximum number of posts you want to display on each blog page.

- **Syndication Feeds Show the Most Recent:** In the Posts box, enter the maximum number of posts you want to show in your RSS feed at any time.

- **For Each Article in a Feed, Show:** Select either Full Text or Summary. Full Text publishes the entire post to your RSS feed, whereas Summary publishes only an excerpt. (Check out Chapter 8 for more information on WordPress RSS feeds.)

- **Encoding for Pages and Feeds:** UTF-8 is the default, and recommended, character encoding for your blog. *Character encoding* is code that handles the storage and transmission of the text from your blog through the Internet connection. Your safest bet is to leave the default setting in place, because UTF-8 is the most commonly accepted character encoding and supports a wide range of languages.

Be sure to click the Save Changes button when you've set all your options in the Reading Settings page to make the changes take effect.

Discussion

Discussion is the fourth link in the Settings menu; click it to open the Discussion Settings page (see Figure 7-11). The sections on this tab let you set options for handling comments and publishing of posts to your blog.

The following sections cover the options available to you in the Discussion Settings page, which deals mainly with how comments and trackbacks are handled in your blog.

Default Article Settings

In the Default Article Settings sections, you can tell WordPress how to handle post notifications. Here are your options:

- ✔ **Attempt to Notify Any Blogs Linked to from the Article (Slows Down Posting):** Check this box, and your blog sends a notification (or *ping*) to any site you have linked to in your blog posts. This notification is also commonly referred to as a *trackback* (I discuss trackbacks in Chapter 2). Clear this box if you don't want these notifications to be sent.

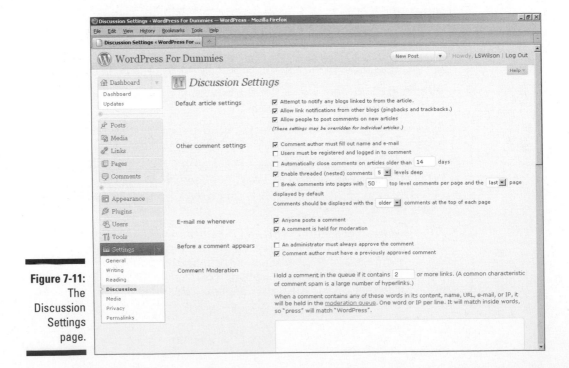

Figure 7-11:
The
Discussion
Settings
page.

✔ **Allow Link Notifications from Other Blogs (Pingbacks and Trackbacks):** By default, this box is checked, and your blog is open to be notified via a ping or trackback from another blog that has linked to yours. Any trackbacks or pings sent to your blog are listed on your site in the comments section of the blog post. If you clear this box, your blog won't accept pingbacks or trackbacks from other blogs.

✔ **Allow People to Post Comments on New Articles:** By default, this box is checked, and people can leave comments on your blog posts. If you clear this box, no one can leave comments on your blog. (You can override these settings for individual articles — more information about this is found in Chapter 8.)

Other Comment Settings

The Other Comment Settings tell WordPress how to handle comments:

✔ **Comment Author Must Fill Out Their Name and E-Mail:** Enabled by default, this option requires all commenters on your blog to fill in the Name and E-Mail field when leaving a comment. This option is very helpful in combating comment spam. (See Chapters 2 and 10 for information on comment spam.) Clear this check box to disable this option.

✔ **Users Must Be Registered and Logged in to Comment:** Not enabled by default, this option allows you to accept comments on your blog from only those people who have registered and are currently logged in as a user on your blog. If the user is not logged in, he sees a message that says: *You must be logged in in order to leave a comment.*

✔ **Automatically Close Comments on Articles Older Than *X* Days:** Check the box next to this option to tell WordPress you would like comments on older articles to be automatically closed. Fill in the text box provided with the number of days you would like to wait before WordPress closes comments on older articles.

This is a very effective anti-spam technique that many bloggers use to keep the comment and trackback spam on their blog down.

✔ **Enable Threaded (Nested) Comments *X* Levels Deep:** The drop-down menu allows you to choose the level of threaded comments you'd like to have on your blog. The default is 1; you can choose up to 10 levels. Instead of all comments being displayed on your blog in chronological order (as it is by default), nesting them allows you and your readers to reply to comments within the comment itself.

✔ **Break Comments into Pages with *X* Comments Per Page:** Fill in the text box with a number of comments you want to display on one page. This is very helpful for blogs that receive a large number of comments. It provides you with the ability to break the long string of comments into several pages, which makes it easier to read and helps speed up the load time of your site, because the page isn't loading such a large number of comments at once.

✔ **Comments Should Be Displayed with the Older/Newer comments at the Top of Each Page:** Use the drop-down menu to select Older or Newer. Selecting Older displays the comments on your blog in the order of oldest to newest. Selecting Newer does the opposite: displays the comments on your blog in the order of newest to oldest.

E-Mail Me Whenever

The two options in the E-Mail Me Whenever section are enabled by default:

✔ **Anyone Posts a Comment:** This option lets you receive an e-mail notification whenever anyone leaves a comment on your blog. Clear the box if you don't want to be notified by e-mail about every new comment.

✔ **A Comment Is Held for Moderation:** This option lets you receive an e-mail notification whenever a comment is awaiting your approval in the comment moderation queue. (See Chapter 8 for more information about the comment moderation queue.) You need to deselect this option if you don't want this notification.

Before a Comment Appears

The two options in the Before a Comment Appears section tell WordPress how you want WordPress to handle comments before they appear in your blog:

✔ **An Administrator Must Always Approve the Comment:** Disabled by default, this option keeps every single comment left on your blog in the moderation queue until you, the administrator, log in and approve it. Check this box to enable this option.

✔ **Comment Author Must Have a Previously Approved Comment:** Enabled by default, this option requires comments posted by all first-time commenters to be sent to the comment moderation queue for approval by the administrator of the blog. After comment authors have been approved for the first time, they remain approved for every comment thereafter. WordPress stores their e-mail addresses in the database, and any future comments that match any stored e-mails are approved automatically. This feature is another measure that WordPress has built in to combat comment spam.

Comment Moderation

In the Comment Moderation section, you can set options to specify what types of comments are held in the moderation queue to await your approval.

To prevent spammers from spamming your blog with a *ton* of links check the Hold a Comment in the Queue If It Contains X or More Links box. The default number of links allowed is 2. Give that setting a try, and if you find that you're getting lots of spam comments with multiple links, you may want to revisit this page and increase that number. Any comment with a higher number of links goes to the comment moderation area for approval.

The large text box in the Comment Moderation section lets you type keywords, URLs, e-mail addresses, and IP addresses in comments that you want to be held in the moderation queue for your approval.

Comment Blacklist

In this section, type a list of words, URLs, e-mail addresses, and/or IP addresses that you want to flat-out ban from your blog. Items placed here don't even make it into your comment moderation queue; the WordPress system filters them as spam. Let me just say that the words I have placed in my blacklist are not family-friendly and have no place in a nice book like this.

Avatars

The final section of the Discussion Settings page is Avatars. (See the nearby sidebar "What are avatars, and how do they relate to WordPress?" for information about avatars.) In this section, you can select different settings for the use and display of avatars on your site:

1. **In the Avatar Display section, decide how to display avatars on your site.**

   • *Don't Show Avatars:* Choose this option, and your blog won't display avatars.

   • *Show Avatars:* Choose this option to have your blog display avatars.

What are avatars, and how do they relate to WordPress?

An *avatar* is an online graphical representation of an individual. It's a small graphic icon that people use to visually represent themselves on the Web in areas they participate in conversations such as discussion forums and blog comments. *Gravatars* are globally recognized avatars; it's an avatar that you can take with you wherever you go. It appears alongside blog comments, blog posts, and discussion forums as long as the site you are interacting with is Gravatar-enabled. In October 2007, Automattic, the core group behind the WordPress platform, purchased the Gravatar service and integrated it into WordPress so that all could enjoy and benefit from the service. Gravatars are not automatic; you need to sign up for an account with Gravatar so that you can assign an avatar to you, via your e-mail address. Find out more about Gravatar by visiting http://gravatar.com.

2. **In the Maximum Rating section, set the rating for the avatars that do display on your site.**

 This feature works much like the movie rating system you're used to. You can select G, PG, R, and X ratings for the avatars that display on your site. If your site is family-friendly, you probably don't want it to display R- or X-rated avatars.

3. **Choose a default avatar in the Default Avatar section (see Figure 7-12):**

   • Mystery Man

   • Blank

   • Gravatar Logo

   • Identicon (Generated)

   • Wavatar (Generated)

   • MonsterID (Generated)

4. **Click the Save Changes button.**

Avatars

An avatar is an image that follows you from weblog to weblog appearing beside your name when you comment on avatar enabled sites. Here you can enable the display of avatars for people who comment on your blog.

Avatar Display	○ Don't show Avatars
	⊙ Show Avatars
Maximum Rating	⊙ G — Suitable for all audiences
	○ PG — Possibly offensive, usually for audiences 13 and above
	○ R — Intended for adult audiences above 17
	○ X — Even more mature than above
Default Avatar	For users without a custom avatar of their own, you can either display a generic logo or a generated one based on their e-mail address.
	⊙ Mystery Man
	○ Blank
	○ Gravatar Logo
	○ Identicon (Generated)
	○ Wavatar (Generated)
	○ MonsterID (Generated)

Figure 7-12: Default avatars you can display in your blog.

Avatars display in a couple places:

✔ **The Comments page in the Dashboard:** In Figure 7-13, the first three comments have the commenter's avatar displayed next to them.

✔ **The comments on individual blog posts to your blog:** Figure 7-14 shows a list of comments on my own personal blog.

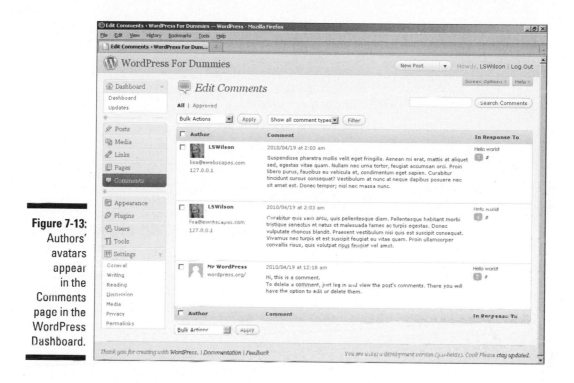

Figure 7-13:
Authors'
avatars
appear
in the
Comments
page in the
WordPress
Dashboard.

Hello world!

Posted on April 19, 2010 by LSWilson

Welcome to WordPress. This is your first post. Edit or delete it, then start blogging!

This entry was posted in Uncategorized. Bookmark the permalink. Follow any comments here with the RSS feed for this post. Edit

3 Responses to *Hello world!*

Mr WordPress *says:*

April 19, 2010 at 12:18 am (Edit)

Hi, this is a comment.
To delete a comment, just log in and view the post's comments. There you will have the option to edit or delete them.

Reply

LSWilson *says:*

April 19, 2010 at 2:03 am (Edit)

Curabitur quis sem arcu, quis pellentesque diam. Pellentesque habitant morbi tristique senectus et netus et malesuada fames ac turpis egestas. Donec vulputate rhoncus blandit. Praesent vestibulum nisi quis est suscipit consequat. Vivamus nec turpis et est suscipit feugiat eu vitae quam. Proin ullamcorper convallis risus, quis volutpat risus feugiat vel amet.

Reply

Figure 7-14:
Comments
on a post,
showing the
comment
authors'
avatars.

To enable the display of avatars in comments on your blog, the Comments Template (comments.php) in your active theme has to contain the code to display them. Hop on over to Chapter 12 to find out how to do that.

Click the Save Changes button after you've set all your options on the Discussion Settings page to make the changes take effect.

Media

The next link in the Settings menu is Media; click the Media link and the Media Settings page opens (see Figure 7-15.)

On the Media Settings page, you can configure the options for how your image files (graphics and photos) are resized for use in your blog.

The first set of options on the Media Settings page deals with images. WordPress automatically resizes your images for you in three different sizes. The dimensions are referenced in pixels by width, then height. (For example: 50 x 50 means 50 pixels in width by 50 pixels in height.)

Figure 7-15:
The Media
Settings
page.

- ✔ **Thumbnail Size:** The default is 150 x 150; enter the width and height of your choice. Select the Crop Thumbnail to Exact Dimensions box to resize the thumbnail exactly to the width and height you specified. Clear this box and WordPress resizes the image proportionally.

- ✔ **Medium Size:** The default is 300 x 300; enter the width and height numbers of your choice.

- ✔ **Large Size:** The default is 1024 x 1024; enter the width and height numbers of your choice.

The second set of options on the Media Settings page deals with embedded links and files, such as video and audio files. Check the box that says Attempt to automatically embed all plain text URLs if you want your WordPress blog to automatically attach a hyperlink to a text-based URL that you type into your posts or pages. Activating this option means you don't have to copy and paste the full code given to you by services like You Tube — instead, you simply paste the hyperlink to the video, and WordPress automatically does the video embedding for you.

Next, set the width and height for the maximum size you want embedded files to be within your post and pages. Embedded items include video players and audio players that display within your post or page.

Finally, the last set of options on the Media Settings page is the Uploading Files section. Here, you tell WordPress where to store your uploaded media files:

- ✔ **Store Uploads in This Folder:** Type the server path to the folder on your Web server where you want your file uploads to be stored. The default is `wp-content/uploads`. You can specify any folder you want. Just be sure that the folder you specify has permissions (`chmod`) set to 755 so that it is writeable. (See Chapter 6 for more information on setting file permissions.)

- ✔ **Full URL Path to Files (optional):** You can also type the full URL path to the Uploads folder as an optional setting. (The full URL path would be something like `http://yourdomain.com/wp-content/uploads`.)

- ✔ **Organize My Files into Month and Year-Based Folders:** Select this box to have WordPress organize your uploaded files in folders by month and by year. Files you upload in September 2010, for example, would be in the following folder: `/wp-content/uploads/2010/09/`. Likewise, files you upload in October 2010 would be in `/wp-content/uploads/2010/10/`.

  This box is selected by default; uncheck it if you don't want WordPress to organize your files by month and year.

Be sure to click the Save Changes button to save your configurations!

In Chapter 9, I go into much greater detail on how to insert images in your WordPress posts and pages;

Privacy

The next Settings menu option is Privacy; click it to display the Privacy Settings page.

This page contains only two options, both of which concern visibility on your blog:

- ✔ **I Would Like My Blog to Be Visible to Everyone, Including Search Engines (Like Google, Bing, Technorati) and Archivers.** This option is the default setting and means that you are freely allowing search engines to visit your blog and to list you in their search results, and letting your site be indexed in blog archive services such as Technorati.

- ✔ **I Would Like to Block Search Engines, but Allow Normal Visitors.** If you are one of those rare bloggers who *doesn't* want that type of exposure for your blog, but you do want to let normal visitors (read: no search engines) see your blog, select this option.

Generally, you want search engines to be able to find your blog. However, if you have special circumstances, you may want to enforce your privacy settings. I would block search engines, for example, because the site I'm using for the figures in this book is one that I don't want search engines to find. At the top of the site, to the right of the site title, there is a note that says *Search Engines Blocked.* This note exists only when you have your privacy settings set to block search engines. When you have Privacy On, search engines and other content bots can't find your Web site.

Be sure to click the Save Changes button after you set all your options on the Privacy Settings page to make the changes take effect.

Permalinks

The next link on the Settings menu is Permalinks. Clicking this link loads the Permalink Settings page (see Figure 7-16).

Each of the posts you create on your blog has a unique URL called a *permalink,* which is permanent link (URL) for all your blog posts, pages, and archives. I cover permalinks extensively in Chapter 8 by explaining what they are, how you can use them, and how you set the options in this page.

Figure 7-16:
The
Permalink
Settings
page.

Creating Your Personal Profile

The next place to visit to really personalize your blog is your profile page in your WordPress Dashboard.

To access your profile page, click the down arrow to the right of the Users menu; then click the Your Profile submenu link; you're taken to the Profile page (see Figure 7-17).

Here are the settings on this page:

✔ **Personal Options:** The Personal Options section is where you can set two preferences for your blog:

    • *Visual Editor:* Check this box to indicate that you want to use the Visual Editor when writing your posts. The Visual Editor refers to the formatting options you find in the Write Post page (discussed in detail in Chapter 8). By default, the box is checked, which means that the Visual Editor is on. To turn it off, clear the box.

Figure 7-17:
Establish
your profile
details here.

- *Admin Color Scheme:* These options set the colors in your Dashboard. The default is the Gray color scheme. If you have been using WordPress since before March 2007, the Blue color scheme will be familiar to you as the colors used in previous versions of the Dashboard.

- *Keyboard Shortcuts:* This enables you to use keyboard shortcuts for comment moderation. To learn more about keyboard shortcuts, click the More Information link; you're taken to the Keyboard Shortcuts page (http://codex.wordpress.org/Keyboard_Shortcuts) in the WordPress Codex with some helpful information.

✔ **Name:** This section is where you can input personal information such as your first name, last name, and nickname, and specify how you want your name to be displayed publicly. Fill in the text boxes with the requested information.

✔ **Contact Info:** In this section, you provide your e-mail address and other contact information to tell your visitors who you are and where they may contact you. Aside from e-mail, you can provide your ID for various Internet chat programs such as Yahoo! IM, AIM (AOL Instant Messenger), and Jabber/Google Talk.

Note that your e-mail address is the only required entry here. This address is the one WordPress uses to notify you when you have new comments or new user registrations on your blog. Make sure to use a real e-mail address so that you get these notifications.

✔ **About Yourself:** This section is where you can provide a little bio for yourself and change the password for your blog.

When your profile is published to your Web site, it not only can be viewed by anyone — it also gets picked up by search engines like Google and Yahoo! Always be careful with the information in your profile. Think hard about the information you want to share with the rest of the world!

- *Biographical Info:* Type a short bio in the Biographical Info text box. This information can be shown publicly if you are using a theme that displays your bio, so be creative!

- *New Password:* When you want to change the password for your blog, type your new password in the first text box in the New Password section. To confirm your new password, type it again in the second text box.

Directly below the two text boxes is a little password helper. WordPress helps you create a secure password. It alerts you if the password you've chosen is too short or not secure enough by telling you that it is Bad. When creating a new password, use a combination of letters, numbers, and symbols to make it hard for anyone to guess (for example, `aty89!#4j`). When you create a password that WordPress thinks is a good one, it lets you know by saying that the password is Strong.

Change your password frequently. I can't recommend this practice strongly enough. Some people on the Internet make it their business to attempt to hijack blogs for their own malicious purposes. If you change your password monthly, you lower your risk by keeping hackers guessing.

When you finish setting all the options on the Profile page, don't forget to click the Update Profile button to save your changes.

Setting Your Blog's Format

In addition to setting your personal settings in the Dashboard, you can manage the day-to-day maintenance of your blog. This next section takes you through the links to these sections in the navigation menu, directly underneath the Dashboard link.

Posts

Click the down arrow to the right of the Pages menu and a submenu drops down with four links: Edit, Add New, Tags, and Categories. Each link gives you the tools you need to publish content to your blog:

- **Edit:** This link opens the Edit Posts page where you see a listing of all the saved posts you've written on your blog. On this page, you can search for posts by date, category, or keyword. You can view all posts, only posts that have been published, or just those posts that have been saved, but not yet published (*drafts*). You can also edit and delete posts from this page. Check out Chapter 8 for more information on editing posts on your blog.

- **Add New:** This link opens the Add New Post page, which is where you compose your blog posts, set the options for each post (such as assigning a post to a category, making it a private or public post), and publish the post to your blog. You can find more information on posts, post options, and publishing in Chapter 8.

  You can also get to the Add New Post page by clicking the Posts menu.

- **Categories:** This link opens the Categories page, where you can view, edit, add, and delete categories on your blog. Find more information on categories in Chapter 8.

- **Post Tags:** This link opens the Tags page in your WordPress Dashboard where you can view, add, edit, and delete tags on your blog. Chapter 8 provides you with more information about what tags are and why you use them on your blog.

Media

Click the Media menu to expand the submenu of links for this section:

- **Library:** This link opens the Media Library page. On this page, you view, search, and manage all the media files you've ever uploaded to your WordPress blog.

- **Add New:** This link opens the Upload New Media page where you can use the built-in uploader to transfer media files from your computer to the media directory in WordPress. Chapter 9 takes you through the details of how to upload images, videos, audio, and other media files (such as Microsoft Word or PowerPoint documents) using the WordPress upload feature.

  You can also get to the Upload New Media page by clicking the Media menu.

Links

The next menu header in the navigation menu is Links. Expand the Links submenu by clicking the down arrow to the right of the Links menu:

- **Edit:** This link opens the Edit Links page, where you can view, search, edit, and delete existing links in your WordPress blog. Chapter 8 gives you detailed information about links, link lists, and blogrolls.

- **Add New:** This link opens the Add New Link page, where you can add new links to your link lists. (You can find more information about creating and managing link lists in Chapter 8.)

  You can also get to the Add New Link page by clicking the Links menu.

- **Link Categories:** This link opens the Link Categories page where you can add new, view, edit, and delete existing link categories (see Chapter 8).

Pages

People use this feature to create pages on their sites such as an About Me or Contact Me page. Flip to Chapter 8 for more information on pages. Click the Pages menu to reveal the submenu links:

- **Edit:** This link opens the Edit Pages page where you have the ability to search, view, edit, and delete pages in your WordPress blog.

- **Add New:** This link opens the Add New Page page where you can compose, save, and publish a new page on your blog. Table 7-2 describes the difference between a post and a page — it's subtle, but posts and pages are very different from one another!

  You can also get to the Add New Page page by clicking the Pages menu.

Table 7-2	The Differences between a Post and a Page	
WordPress Options	*Page*	*Post*
Appears in blog post listings	No	Yes
Appears as a static page	Yes	No
Appears in category archives	No	Yes
Appears in monthly archives	No	Yes
Appears in Recent Posts listings	No	Yes
Appears in site RSS feed	No	Yes
Appears in search results	Yes	Yes

Comments

The Comments menu doesn't have a menu of links. You simply click the Comments menu title to open the Edit Comments page, where WordPress gives you the options to view:

- ✔ **All:** This setting shows all comments that currently exist on your blog. This includes approved, pending, and spam comments.

- ✔ **Awaiting Moderation:** This setting shows comments that are not yet approved by you but are pending in the moderation queue.

- ✔ **Approved:** This setting shows all comments that have been previously approved by you.

- ✔ **Spam:** This setting shows all of the comments that are marked as spam.

- ✔ **Trash:** This setting shows comments that you have marked as Trash, but have not yet been deleted permanently from your blog.

You can find information in Chapter 2 about the purpose of comments. In Chapter 8, I give you details on how to use the Manage Comments section of your WordPress Dashboard.

Appearance

When you click the Appearance menu in the navigation menu, a submenu drops down with the following links:

- ✔ **Themes:** Click this link to open the Manage Themes page where you can manage the themes available on your blog. Check out Chapter 11 to learn about using themes on your WordPress blog, and how to manage those themes on this page.

  You can also navigate to this page by clicking the Themes menu.

- ✔ **Widgets:** This link opens the Widgets page where you can add, delete, edit, and manage the widgets you use on your blog.

- ✔ **Editor:** This link opens the Theme Editor page where you can edit your theme templates. Chapters 11, 12, and 13 have extensive information on themes and templates.

- ✔ **Add New Themes:** This link opens the Install Themes page, where you can browse the official Themes Directory from within your WordPress Dashboard. You can find, preview, and install new themes to your blog on the Install Themes page.

✔ **Custom Menus:** This link opens the Menus page, where you can build navigation menus to display on your site. Chapter 13 provides information on creating menus using this feature.

✔ **Custom Header:** This link opens the Your Header Image page, where you can upload an image to use in the header (or top) of your WordPress blog; however this menu item and page exist only if you have the Twenty Ten theme activated. The Twenty Ten theme is activated by default on all new WordPress blogs, which is why I've included this menu item in this list. Not all WordPress themes use the Customize Header feature, so you don't see this menu item if your theme doesn't take advantage of that feature.

✔ **Custom Background:** This link opens the Custom Background page, where you can upload an image to use as the background of your WordPress blog design; as with the Custom Header option above, the Custom Background option only exists in the Appearances menu if you have the default Twenty Ten theme activated. Not all WordPress themes use the Custom Background feature.

Uploading custom header and background images helps you individualize the visual design of your blog or Web site. More information on tweaking and customizing your WordPress theme can be found in Chapter 13. Chapter 11 gives you a great deal of information about how to use WordPress themes (including where to find, install, and activate them in your WordPress blog), as well as detailed information on using WordPress widgets to display the content you want.

Part V provides information about WordPress themes and templates. You can dig deep into WordPress template tags and tweak an existing WordPress theme by using Cascading Style Sheets (CSS) to customize your theme a bit more to your liking.

Plugins

The next menu in the navigation menu is Plugins. Click the Plugins menu to expand the submenu of links:

✔ **Installed:** Click this link and open the Manage Plugins page where you can view all the plugins currently installed on your blog. On this page, you also have the ability to activate, deactivate, and delete plugins on your blog (see Chapter 10). If you click the Plugins menu, you also go to the Manage Plugins page.

✔ **Add New:** This link opens the Install Plugins page where can search for plugins from the official WordPress Plugin Directory by keyword, author, or tag. You can also install plugins directly to your blog from the

WordPress Plugin Directory — you find out all about this exciting feature in Chapter 10!

✔ **Editor:** This link opens the Edit Plugins page where you can edit the plugin files in a text editor. I very strongly advise against editing plugin files unless you know what you are doing (Read: You are familiar with PHP and WordPress functions). Head over to Chapter 10 to read more information on editing plugin files.

Users

The Users menu has three links:

✔ **Authors & Users:** Click this link to go to the Users page where you can view, edit, and delete on your WordPress blog. Each user has a unique login name and password as well as having an e-mail address assigned to his or her account. You can view and edit their information on the Users page.

✔ **Add New:** This link opens the Add New User page, where you can add new users to your WordPress blog. Simply type the user's username, First Name, Last Name, E-Mail (required), Website, and a password in the fields provided and click the Add User button. You can also select whether you want WordPress to send login information to the new user by e-mail. If you like, you can also assign a new role for the new user. Turn to the earlier section, "Configuring the Settings," for more info about user roles.

✔ **Your Profile:** Turn to the "Creating Your Personal Profile" section, earlier in this chapter, for more information about creating a profile page.

Tools

The last menu item in the navigation menu (and subsequently in this chapter!) is Tools. Click the Tools menu to drop down the submenu of links that includes:

✔ **Tools:** WordPress comes packaged with two extra features that you can use on your blog, if needed. They are Press This and Category/Tag Conversion.

✔ **Import:** WordPress gives you the ability to import from a different blog platform. This feature is covered in depth in Appendix A.

✔ **Export:** WordPress also allows you to export your content from WordPress so you can import it into a different platform, or to another WordPress blog. This information is also covered in Appendix A.

Chapter 8

Establishing Your Blog Routine

In This Chapter

▶ Setting up categories

▶ Building your blogroll

▶ Exploring permalinks

▶ Writing and editing posts and pages

▶ Managing and moderating comments

*W*ordPress is a powerful publishing tool, especially when you use the full range of options available. With the basic settings configured (which you do in Chapter 7), now is the time to go forth and blog! You can, at this point, skip to the "Blog It!: Writing Your First Entry" section in this chapter and jump right in to creating new posts for your blog. Or you can stay right here with me and discover some of the options you can set to make your blog a bit more organized and logical from the get-go.

A blog can become unwieldy and disorganized, requiring you to revisit these next few features sometime in the near future so that you can get the beast under control. So why not do a little planning and get the work over with now? I promise it won't take that long, and you'll thank me for it later.

Staying on Topic with Categories

In WordPress, a *category* is what you determine to be the main topic of a blog post. Through the use of categories, you can file your blog posts into topics, by subject. To improve your readers' experiences in navigating through your blog, WordPress organizes posts by the categories you assign to them. Visitors can click the categories they're interested in to see the blog posts you've written on those particular topics. You should know ahead of time that the list of categories you set up is displayed on your blog in a few different places, including the following:

✔ **Body of the post:** In most WordPress themes, you see the title followed by a statement such as Filed In: *Category 1*, *Category 2*. The reader can click the category name to go to a page that lists all the posts you've made in that particular category. You can assign a single post to more than one category.

✔ **Sidebar of your blog theme:** You can place a full list of category titles in the sidebar. A reader can click any category and get taken to a page on your site that lists the posts you've made within that particular category.

Subcategories (also known as *category children*) can further refine the main category topic by listing specific topics related to the main (parent) category. In your WordPress Dashboard, on the Manage Categories page, subcategories are listed directly below the main category. Here's an example:

> Books I Enjoy (main category)
>
> > Fiction (subcategory)
> >
> > Nonfiction (subcategory)
> >
> > Trashy romance (subcategory)
> >
> > Biographies (subcategory)
> >
> > *For Dummies* (subcategory)

Changing the name of a category

Upon installation, WordPress gives you one default category called Uncategorized (see the Categories page shown in Figure 8-1). That category name is pretty generic, so you'll definitely want to change it to one that's more specific to you. (On my blog, I changed it to Life in General. Although that name's still a bit on the generic side, it doesn't sound quite so . . . well, uncategorized.)

The default category also serves as kind of a fail-safe. If you publish a post to your blog and don't assign that post to a category, the post automatically gets assigned to the default category, no matter what you name the category.

So how do you change the name of that default category? When you're logged in to your WordPress Dashboard, just follow these steps:

1. **Click the down arrow to the right of the Posts menu, and then click the Categories link.**

   The Categories page opens, containing all the tools you need to set up and edit category titles for your blog.

2. **Click the title of the category you would like to edit.**

   If you want to change the Uncategorized category, click the word Uncategorized, and you go to the Edit Category page (see Figure 8-2).

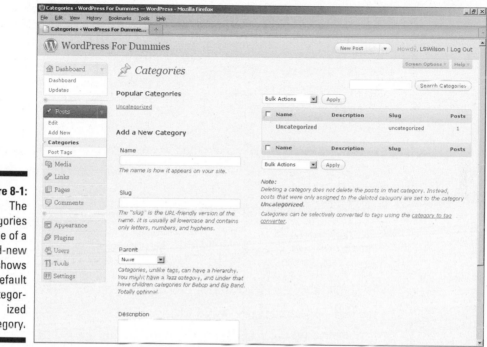

Figure 8-1:
The
Categories
page of a
brand-new
blog shows
the default
Uncategor-
ized
category.

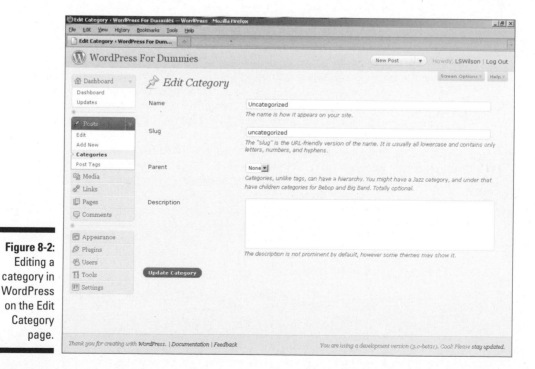

Figure 8-2:
Editing a
category in
WordPress
on the Edit
Category
page.

3. **Type the new name for the category in the Category Name text box.**

4. **Type the new slug in the Category Slug text box.**

   The term slug refers to the word(s) used in the Web address for the specific category. For example, the category of Books has a Web address of `http://yourdomain.com/category/books`; if you change the Category Slug to Books I Like, then the Web address is `http://yourdomain.com/category/books-i-like` (WordPress automatically inserts a dash between the slug words in the Web address).

5. **Choose a parent category from the Category Parent drop-down menu.**

   If you want this category to be a main category, not a subcategory, choose None.

6. **(Optional) Type a description of the category in the Description text box.**

   Use this description to remind yourself what your category is about. Some WordPress themes display the category description right on your site, too, which can be helpful for your visitors. (See Chapter 12 for more about themes.) You'll know if your theme is coded in this way if your site displays the category description on the category page(s).

7. **Click the Update Category button.**

   The information you just edited is saved, and the Categories page reloads, showing your new category name.

Creating new categories

Today, tomorrow, next month, next year — as your blog grows in size and age, you will continue adding new categories to further define and archive the history of your blog posts. You aren't limited in the number of categories and subcategories you can create in your blog.

Creating a new category is as easy as following these steps:

1. **Click the down arrow to the right of the Posts menu, and then click the Categories link.**

   The Categories page opens.

2. **The left side of the Categories page displays the Add a New Category section.**

   See Figure 8-3.

3. **Type the name of your new category in the Name text box.**

   Suppose that you want to create a category in which you file all your posts about the books you read. In the Name text box, type something like **Books I Enjoy**.

Add a New Category

Name

The name is how it appears on your site.

Slug

_The "slug" is the URL-friendly version of the
name. It is usually all lowercase and contains
only letters, numbers, and hyphens._

Parent

None

_Categories, unlike tags, can have a hierarchy.
You might have a Jazz category, and under that
have children categories for Bebop and Big Band.
Totally optional._

Description

_The description is not prominent by default;
however, some themes may show it._

Add Category

Figure 8-3:
Create
a new
category
on your
blog.

4. **Type a name in the Slug text box.**

   The slug creates the link to the category page that lists all the posts
   you've made in this category. If you leave this field blank, WordPress
   automatically creates a slug based on the category name. If the category
   is Books I Enjoy, WordPress automatically creates a category slug like
   this: `http://yourdomain.com/category/books-i-enjoy`. If you
   want to shorten it, however, you can! Type **books** in the Category
   Slug text box, and the link to the category becomes this: `http://
   yourdomain.com/category/books`.

5. **Choose the category's parent from the Parent drop-down menu.**

   Choose None if you want this new category to be a parent (or top level)
   category. If you'd like this category to be a subcategory of another category, choose the category you want to be the parent of this one.

6. **(Optional) Type a description of the category in the Description
   text box.**

   Some WordPress templates are set up to actually display the category
   description directly beneath the category name (see Chapter 12).
   Providing a description helps you to further define the category intent
   for your readers. The description can be as short or as long as you like.

What are tags, and how/why do I use them?

Tags are not to be confused with categories, but a lot of people do confuse them. *Tags* are clickable, comma-separated keywords that help you microcategorize a post by defining the topics in it. Unlike WordPress categories, tags do not have a hierarchy; there are no parent tags and child tags. If you write a post about your dog, for example, you can put that post in the Pets category — but you can also add some specific tags that let you get a whole lot more specific, such as poodle, small dogs. If someone clicks

your poodle tag, he finds all the posts you've ever made that contain the poodle tag.

Another reason to use tags: Search-engine spiders harvest tags when they crawl your site, so tags help other people find your site when they search for specific words.

You can manage your tags in the WordPress Dashboard by clicking the Tags link on the Pages menu. The Tags page opens where you can view, edit, delete, and add new tags.

7. **Click the Add Category button.**

That's it! You've added a new category to your blog. Armed with this information, you can add an unlimited number of categories to your blog.

You can delete a category on your blog by hovering the pointer over the title of the category you want to delete. Then click the Delete link that appears below the category title.

Deleting a category doesn't delete the posts and links in that category. Instead, posts in the deleted category are assigned to the Uncategorized category (or whatever you've named the default category).

If you have an established WordPress blog with categories already created, you can convert some or all of your categories to tags. To do so, look for the Category to Tag Converter link on the right side of the Category page in your WordPress Dashboard. Click it to convert your categories to tags. (See the nearby sidebar "What are tags, and how/why do I use them?" for more information on tags.)

Link Lists: Sharing Your Favorite Sites

A *link list,* commonly referred to as a *blogroll,* is a list of links to other Web sites and blogs that you've collected and want to share with your readers. The link list is displayed in your blog, usually in the sidebar, through the use of widgets, or on a dedicated page of links, if your theme has a links page template (see Chapter 12 to find out how to create a template).

You can use a link list in various ways:

- ✔ Share links with other blogs that have linked to your blog.
- ✔ Provide additional resources that you think your readers will find useful.
- ✔ Provide links to other sites you own.

Organizing your links

As with posts, you can create multiple categories for your links in the WordPress Dashboard if you want to have more than one link list. Sometimes, having a large list of links below the heading Blogroll is just too generic, and you may want to display groups of links with different headings that further define them.

By default, WordPress provides one link category called Blogroll. You can keep this name as is or change it in the same way that you change a post category name (refer to "Changing the name of a category," earlier in this chapter). Just click the name of the category and edit the details as you need to.

You can define your links by creating link categories in the Dashboard and then assigning links to the appropriate categories. To create link categories, follow these steps:

1. **Click the down arrow to the right of the Links menu, and then click the Link Categories link.**

   The Link Categories page opens, as shown in Figure 8-4. The left side of the Link Categories page displays the Add Category section.

2. **Type the name of the link category in the Link Category Name box.**

3. **Type the slug of the link category in the Link Category Slug box.**

   This entry is the same as the category slug described previously in the "Changing the name of a category" section in this chapter.

4. **(Optional) Type a description of the link category in the Category Description box.**

   Providing a description helps you further define the category intent for your readers. The description can be as short or as long as you like. Some WordPress themes are set up to actually display the category description directly beneath the category name (check out Chapter 12 for information on template tags that will allow you to add category descriptions).

5. **Click the Add Category button.**

   The Link Categories page refreshes and displays your new link category.

Figure 8-4:
The Link
Categories
page.

Revisit the Link Categories page any time you want to add, edit, or delete a link. To edit or delete a link category, you would follow the same steps as you did in the previous section for post categories. You can create an unlimited amount of link categories to sort your link lists by topics. (I know one blogger who has 50 categories for his links.)

In Chapter 5, I show you how to display your link lists by using WordPress widgets, and in Chapter 12, I provide information about different ways you can display your link lists by using template tags.

Adding new link loves

You've created your link categories; now you just need to add some new links! To add a new link, follow these steps:

1. **Click the Add New link on the Links menu.**

   The Add New Link page opens, as shown in Figure 8-5.

2. **Type the name of the link in the Name text box.**

   This is the actual name of the site that you are adding to your link list.

Figure 8-5:
Add a new
link with the
Add New
Link page.

3. Type the URL of the link in the Web Address box.

This is the destination you want your visitors to go to when they click
the name of the site. Don't forget to include the http:// part of the
Web address; for example, http://lisasabin-wilson.com.

4. (Optional) Type a description of the site in the Description box.

Providing a description helps further define the site for your readers.
Some WordPress templates are coded to display the link description
directly below the link name through the use of a specific WordPress
template tag.

5. (Optional) Select a category.

Assign your new link to a category by checking the box to the left of the
category you've chosen in the Categories module. If you don't select a
category for your new link, it's automatically assigned to the default category. Figure 8-6 shows the list of link categories I have in my blog.

If you find that the Link Category is not an option you use regularly, you
can collapse (close) this module by clicking anywhere in the Categories
title bar. You can also move the Categories module to a different position on the Add New Link page by dragging and dropping it to a new
location.

Figure 8-6:
You can
assign a
link to an
existing
category or
add a new
category
here.

6. **(Optional) Select a target for your new link.**

   Click one of the following radio buttons in the Target section:

   - *_blank:* Loads the link in a new browser window

   - *_top:* Loads the link in the top frame (if your site is designed with frames)

   - *_none:* Loads the link in the same browser window

   The third option — None — is my personal preference and recommendation. I like to let my visitors decide whether they want a bunch of new browser windows opening every time they click a link on my site.

   You can reposition the Target module by dragging and dropping it to a new location on the Add New Link page. You can also collapse this module.

7. **Set the Link Relationship (XFN) options (Optional).**

   XFN stands for XHTML Friends Network and allows you to indicate the relationship you have with the people you are linking to by defining how you know, or are associated with, them. Table 8-1 lists the different relationships you can assign to your links. Link Relationship (XFN) is kind of a silly bookmark-type assignment that indicates how well you know the person whose site or blog you're linking to by defining your relationship with her. You can find more information on XFN at `http://gmpg.org/xfn`.

   You can reposition the Link Relationship module by dragging and dropping it to a new location on the Add New Link page. You can also collapse (close) this module.

Table 8-1	Link Relationships Defined
Link Relationship	*Description*
Identity	Check this box if the link is to a Web site you own.
Friendship	Choose the option (Contact, Acquaintance, Friend, or None) that most closely identifies the friendship, if any.
Physical	Check this box if you've met the person you're linking to face to face. Sharing pictures over the Internet doesn't count; this selection identifies a person you've physically met.
Professional	Check one of these boxes if the person you're linking to is a co-worker or colleague.
Geographical	Choose Co-Resident if the person you're linking to lives with you, or choose Neighbor or None, depending on which option applies to your relationship with the person you're linking to.
Family	If the blogger you're linking to is a family member, choose the option that tells how the person is related to you.
Romantic	Choose the option that applies to the type of romantic relationship, if any, you have with the person you're linking to. Do you have a crush on him? Is she your creative muse or someone you consider to be a sweetheart?

 8. **Set the advanced options for your new link (see Figure 8-7).**

   You have four options in the Advanced module:

   • *Image Address:* Type the URL of the picture that you want to appear next to the link in your link list.

     This option associates an image with the link. To use it, you need to know the direct URL to the image source (such as `http://yourdomain.com/images/image.jpg`).

     To find the URL for an image displayed on a Web site, right-click the image and choose Properties from the shortcut menu. Copy and paste all the text from the Address (URL) field to the Image Address box in the WordPress options box.

   • *RSS Address:* Add the site's RSS feed alongside the link that appears on your site. (Not all WordPress themes accommodate this feature.)

     To find the RSS URL of the site you're linking to, visit that site, and locate the RSS link. (It's usually listed in the sidebar or footer of the site.) Right-click the link, and from the shortcut menu, choose Copy Shortcut (in Internet Explorer) or Copy Link Location (in Firefox). Then, in WordPress, paste the link in the RSS Address field.

Figure 8-7:
Advanced
link options
give you
settings
to further
manage the
individual
links in your
blogroll.

- *Notes:* Type your notes in the Notes field.

  These notes aren't displayed on your site, so feel free to enter whatever notes you need to further define the details of this link. A month from now, you may not remember who this person is or why you linked to her, so here is where you can add notes to remind yourself.

- *Rating:* Use the Rating drop-down menu to rate the link from 0–10, 0 being the worst and 10 being the best. Some WordPress themes display your link list in the order in which you've rated your links, from best to worst.

You can reposition the Advanced module by dragging and dropping it to a new location on the Add New Link page. You can also collapse (close) this module.

9. **To save your changes, scroll up to the top of the Add New Links page and click the Add Link button. Choose whether to make the link public or private.**

To keep the link private, select the Keep This Link Private box. No one you can see the link. If you want the link to be publicly displayed on your blog, leave that box unchecked.

You can reposition the Save module by dragging and dropping it to a new location on the Add New Link page. You can also collapse (close) this module.

A blank Add New Links page opens, ready for you to add another new link!

Editing existing links

You can edit the links in your blog by clicking the Edit link on the Links menu; the Edit Links page opens.

When you first view the Edit Links page, some links are already assigned to your blog. By default, WordPress provides seven links in your link list. These links go to some helpful Web sites that contain information and resources for the WordPress software. You can delete these links, but I recommend saving them for future reference.

Here's what you can do with your links:

- **Edit an existing link:** Click the name of the link you'd like to edit. The Edit Link page opens. Edit the fields you need to change; click the Save button at the top right of the page.

- **Sort the links:** You can sort by Link ID, Name, Address, or Rating by using the Order by Name drop-down menu. Likewise, you can sort your links by category by using the View All Categories drop-down menu and selecting the Link Category you'd like to filter your links by.

- **Search for specific links using keywords and phrases:** Enter your keyword in the text box at the top right hand side of the Edit Links page and click the Search Links button. If any links match the keywords and/or phrase you typed, they display on the page.

Examining a Blog Post's Address: Permalinks

Each WordPress blog post is assigned its own Web page, and the address (or URL) of that page is called a *permalink*. Posts that you see in WordPress blogs usually have the post permalink in four typical areas:

- The title of the blog post
- The Comments link below the post
- A Permalink link that appears (in most themes) below the post
- The titles of posts appearing in a Recent Posts sidebar

Permalinks are meant to be permanent links to your blog posts (which is where the *perma* part of that word comes from, in case you're wondering).

Other bloggers can use a post permalink to refer to that particular blog post. So ideally, the permalink of a post never changes. WordPress creates the permalink automatically when you publish a new post.

By default, a blog post permalink in WordPress looks like this:

```
http://yourdomain.com/?p=100/
```

The p stands for *post,* and 100 is the ID assigned to the individual post. You can leave the permalinks in this format, if you don't mind letting WordPress associate each post with an ID number.

WordPress, however, lets you take your permalinks to the beauty salon for a bit of makeover so you can create pretty permalinks. I'll bet you didn't know that permalinks could be pretty, did you? They certainly can. Allow me to explain.

Making your post links pretty

Pretty permalinks are links that are more pleasing to the eye than standard links and, ultimately, more pleasing to search-engine spiders. (See Chapter 14 for an explanation of why search engines like pretty permalinks.) Pretty permalinks look something like this:

```
http://yourdomain.com/2008/01/01/pretty-permalinks/
```

Break down that URL, and you see the date when the post was made, in year/month/day format. You also see the topic of the post.

To choose how your permalinks look, click Permalinks in the Settings menu. The Permalink Settings page opens (see Figure 8-8).

In this page, you find several options for creating permalinks:

- ✔ **Default** (ugly permalinks): WordPress assigns an ID number to each blog post and creates the URL in this format: http://yourdomain.com/?p=100.
- ✔ **Day and Name** (pretty permalinks): For each post, WordPress generates a permalink URL that includes the year, month, day, and post slug/title: http://yourdomain.com/2008/01/01/sample-post/.
- ✔ **Month and Name** (also pretty permalinks): For each post, WordPress generates a permalink URL that includes the year, month, and post slug/title: http://yourdomain.com/2008/01/sample-post/.
- ✔ **Numeric** (not so pretty): WordPress assigns a numerical value to the permalink. The URL is created in this format: http://yourdomain.com/archives/123.

Figure 8-8:
Make your
permalinks
pretty.

✓ **Custom Structure:** WordPress creates permalinks in the format you
   choose. You can create a custom permalink structure by using tags or
   variables, as I discuss in the next section.

To create the pretty-permalink structure, select the Day and Name radio
button; then click the Save Changes button at the bottom of the page.

Customizing your permalinks

A *custom permalink structure* is one that lets you define which variables you
want to see in your permalinks by using the tags in Table 8-2.

If you want your permalink to show the year, month, day, category, and
post name, you'd select the Custom Structure radio button in the Customize
Permalink Structure page and type the following tags in the Custom Structure
text box:

```
/%year%/%monthnum%/%day%/%category%/%postname%/
```

Table 8-2	Custom Permalinks
Permalink Tag	**Results**
`%year%`	4-digit year (such as `2007`)
`%monthnum%`	2-digit month (such as `02` for February)
`%day%`	2-digit day (such as `30`)
`%hour%`	2-digit hour of the day (such as `15` for 3 p.m.)
`%minute%`	2-digit minute (such as `45`)
`%second%`	2-digit second (such as `10`)
`%postname%`	Text — usually, the post name — separated by hyphens (such as `making-pretty-permalinks`)
`%post_id%`	The unique numerical ID of the post (such as `344`)
`%category%`	The text of the category name that you filed the post in (such as `books-i-read`)
`%author%`	The text of the post author's name (such as `lisa-sabin-wilson`)

Under this permalink format, the link for a post made on February 1, 2008, called WordPress For Dummies and filed in the Books I Read category, would look like this:

```
http://yourdomain.com/2008/01/01/books-i-read/wordpress-for-dummies/
```

Be sure to include the slashes before tags, between tags, and at the very end of the string of tags. This format ensures that WordPress creates correct, working permalinks by using the correct `re_write` rules located in the `.htaccess` file for your site. (See the following section for more information on `re_write` rules and `.htaccess` files.)

Changing the structure of your permalinks in the future affects the permalinks for all the posts on your blog . . . new and old. Keep this fact in mind if you ever decide to change the permalink structure. An especially important reason: Search engines (such as Google and Yahoo!) index the posts on your site by their permalinks, so changing the permalink structure makes all those indexed links obsolete.

Don't forget to click the Save Changes button at the bottom of the Customize Permalink Structure page; otherwise your permalink changes aren't saved!

Making sure that your permalinks work with your server

After you set the format for the permalinks for your site by using any options other than the default, WordPress writes specific rules, or directives, to the .htaccess file on your Web sever. The .htaccess file in turn communicates to your Web server how it should serve up the permalinks, according to the permalink structure you've chosen to use.

To use an htaccess file, you need to know the answers to two questions:

✔ Does your Web server configuration use and give you access to the .htaccess file?

✔ Does your Web server run Apache with the mod_rewrite module?

If you don't know the answers, contact your hosting provider to find out.

If the answer to both questions is yes, proceed to the next section. If the answer is no, skip to the "Working with servers that don't use Apache mod_rewrite" section, later in this chapter.

Creating .htaccess files

You and WordPress work together in glorious harmony to create the .htaccess file that lets you use a pretty permalink structure in your blog. The file works like this:

1. Using a plain-text editor (such as Notepad for Windows or TextEdit for a Mac), create a blank file; name it htaccess.txt; and upload it to your Web server via FTP. (See Chapter 6 for more information about FTP.) When the file is on your Web server, rename the file .htaccess (notice the period at the beginning), and make sure that it is writable by the server by changing permissions to either 755 or 777. (See Chapter 6 for information on changing permissions on server files.)

   If .htaccess already exists, you can find it in the root of your directory on your Web server — that is, the same directory where you find your wp-config.php file. If you don't see it in the root directory, try changing the options of your FTP client to show hidden files. (Because the .htaccess file starts with a period [.], it may not be visible until you configure your FTP client to show hidden files.)

2. Create the permalink structure in the Customize Permalink Structure page in your WordPress Dashboard.

3. Click the Save Changes button at the bottom of the Customize Permalink Structure page.

   WordPress inserts into the .htaccess file the specific rules necessary for making the permalink structure functional in your blog.

If you followed these steps correctly, you have an .htaccess file on your Web server that has the correct permissions set so that WordPress can write the correct rules to it. Your pretty permalink structure works flawlessly. Kudos!

If you open the .htaccess file and look at it now, you'll see that it's no longer blank. It should have a set of code in it called *rewrite rules,* which looks something like this:

```
# BEGIN WordPress
<IfModule mod_rewrite.c>
RewriteEngine On
RewriteBase /
RewriteCond %{REQUEST_FILENAME} !-f
RewriteCond %{REQUEST_FILENAME} !-d
RewriteRule . /index.php [L]
</IfModule>

# END WordPress
```

I could delve deeply into .htaccess and all the things you can do with this file, but I'm restricting this section to how it applies to WordPress permalink structures. If you'd like to unlock more mysteries about .htaccess, check out "Comprehensive Guide to .htaccess" at http://javascriptkit.com/howto/htaccess.shtml.

Working with servers that don't use Apache mod_rewrite

Using permalink structures requires that your Web hosting provider has a specific Apache module option called mod_rewrite activated on its servers. If your Web hosting provider doesn't have this item activated on its servers, or if you're hosting your site on a Windows server, the custom permalinks work only if you type **index.php** in front of any custom permalink tags.

For example, create the custom permalink tags like this:

```
/index.php/%year%/%month%/%date%/%postname%/
```

This format creates a permalink like this:

```
http://yourdomain.com/index.php/2008/02/01/wordpress-for-dummies
```

You don't need an .htaccess file to use this permalink structure.

Through my experiences over the years, I have discovered that Yahoo! Hosting doesn't allow users access to the .htaccess file on their server, and it doesn't use mod_rewrite. So if you're hosting your domain on Yahoo!, you will need to use the custom permalink technique that I describe elsewhere in this chapter in the section "Working with servers that don't use Apache mod_ rewrite."

Discovering the Many WordPress RSS Options

In Chapter 2, you can read about RSS feed technology and why it's an important part of publishing your blog. Allow me to quote myself from that chapter: For your blog readers to stay updated with the latest and greatest content you post to your site, they need to subscribe to your RSS feed.

RSS feeds come in different flavors, including RSS 0.92, RDF/RSS 1.0, RSS 2.0, and Atom. The differences among them lie within the base code that makes up the functionality of the syndication feed. What's important is that WordPress supports all versions of RSS — which means that anyone can subscribe to your RSS feed with any type of feed reader available.

I mention many times throughout this book that WordPress is very intuitive, and this section on RSS feeds is a shining example of a feature that WordPress automates. WordPress has a built-in feed generator that works behind the scenes to create feeds for you. This feed generator creates feeds from your posts, comments, and even categories.

The RSS feed for your blog posts is *autodiscoverable,* which means that almost all RSS feed readers and even some browsers (Firefox, Internet Explorer 7, and Safari, for example) automatically detect the RSS feed URL for a WordPress blog. Table 8-3 gives you some good guidelines on how to find the RSS feed URLs for the different sections of your blog.

Table 8-3	URLs for Built-In WordPress Feeds
Feed Type	*Example Feed URL*
RSS 0.92	http://*yourdomain*.com/wp-rss.php or
	http://*yourdomain*.com/?feed=rss
RDF/RSS 1.0	http://*yourdomain*.com/wp-rss2.php or
	http://*yourdomain*.com/?feed=rdf

(continued)

Table 8-3 *(continued)*

Feed Type	Example Feed URL
RSS 2.0	`http://yourdomain.com/wp-rss2.php` or `http://yourdomain.com/?feed=rss2`
Atom	`http://yourdomain.com/wp-atom.php` or `http://yourdomain.com/?feed=atom`
Comments RSS	`http://yourdomain.com/?feed=rss&p=50` `p` stands for *post,* and 50 is the post ID. You can find the post ID in the Dashboard by clicking the Manage tab. The post ID is listed immediately to the left of the post title.
Category RSS	`http://yourdomain.com/wp-rss2.php?cat=50` `cat` stands for *category,* and 50 is the category ID. You can find the category ID in the Dashboard by clicking the Manage tab and then the Categories subtab. The category ID is listed immediately to the left of the category title.

If you're using custom permalinks (see "Making your post links pretty," earlier in this chapter), you can simply add `/feed` to the end of any URL on your blog to find the RSS feed. Some of your links will look similar to these:

- `http://yourdomain.com/feed` — your main RSS feed

- `http://yourdomain.com/comments/feed` — your comments RSS feed

- `http://yourdomain.com/category/cat-name/feed` — RSS feed for a category

Try it with any URL on your site. Add `/feed` at the end, and you'll have the RSS feed for that page.

RSS feeds are important parts of delivering content from your blog to your readers. RSS feeds are expected these days, so the fact that WordPress has taken care of the feeds for you, is compliant with all RSS formats, and offers so many internal feeds gives the software a huge advantage over any of the other blog-software platforms.

If you intend to use the Atom publishing protocol, you need to enable it manually because it is disabled by default. Click the Writing link on the Settings menu, and then check the two boxes in the Remote Publishing section to enable Atom publishing in WordPress.

Blog It!: Writing Your First Entry

It's finally time to write your first post in your new WordPress blog! The topic you choose to write about and the writing techniques you use to get your message across are all on you; I have my hands full writing this book! I *can* tell you, however, how to write the wonderful passages that can bring you blog fame. Ready?

Composing your blog post

Composing a blog post is a lot like typing an e-mail: You give it a title, you write the message, and you click a button to send your words into the world.

 You can collapse or reposition all the modules on the Add New Posts page to suit your needs. The only section on the Add New Posts page that cannot be collapsed and repositioned is the actual title and post box (where you write your blog post).

Follow these steps to write a basic blog post:

1. **Click the Add New link on the Posts menu.**

   The Add New Post page opens, as shown in Figure 8-9.

2. **Type the title of your post in the text box at the top of the Add New Post page.**

3. **Type the content of your post in the text box.**

   You can use the Visual Text Editor to format the text in your post. I explain the Visual Text Editor and the buttons and options after these steps.

4. **Click the Save Draft button in the Publish module, located at the top right side of the Add New Post page.**

   The page refreshed with your post title and content saved, but not yet published to your blog.

By default, the area in which you write your post is in Visual Editing mode, as indicated by the Visual tab that appears above the text. Visual Editing mode is how WordPress provides WYSIWYG (What You See Is What You Get) options for formatting. Rather than have to embed HTML code in your post, you can simply type your post, highlight the text you want to format, and click the buttons (shown in Figure 8-9) that appear above the box in which you type your post.

Figure 8-9:
This page is where you give your blog post a title and write your post body.

If you've ever used a word processing program, such as Microsoft Word, you'll recognize many of these buttons:

✔ **Bold:** Embeds the `<strong> </strong>` HTML tag to emphasize the text in bold. Example: **Bold Text.**

✔ **Italic:** Embeds the `<em> </em>` HTML tag to emphasize the text in italics. Example: *Italic Text.*

✔ **Strikethrough:** Embeds the `<strike> </strike>` HTML tag that puts a line through your text. Example: ~~Strikethrough Text~~.

✔ **Unordered List:** Embeds the `<ul><li> </li></ul>` HTML tags that create an unordered, or bulleted, list.

✔ **Ordered List:** Embeds the `<ol><li> </li></ol>` HTML tags that create an ordered, or numbered, list.

✔ **Blockquote:** Inserts the `<blockquote> </blockquote>` HTML tag that indents the paragraph or section of text you've selected.

✔ **Align Left:** Inserts the `<p align="left"> </p>` HTML tag that lines up the paragraph or section of text you've selected against the left margin.

✔ **Align Center:** Inserts the `<p align="center"> </p>` HTML tag that positions the paragraph or section of text you've selected in the center of the page.

✔ **Align Right:** Inserts the `<p align="right">` `</p>` HTML tag that lines up the paragraph or section of text you've selected against the right margin.

✔ **Insert/Edit Link:** Inserts the `<a href=" ">` `</a>` HTML tag around the text you've selected to create a hyperlink.

✔ **Unlink:** Removes the hyperlink from the selected text, if it was previously linked.

✔ **Insert More Tag:** Inserts the `<!--more-->` tag, which lets you split the display on your blog page. It publishes the text written above this tag with a Read More link, which takes the user to a page with the full post. This feature is good for really long posts.

✔ **Toggle Spellchecker:** Perfect for typo enthusiasts! Checking your spelling before you post is always a good idea.

✔ **Toggle Full Screen Mode:** Lets you focus purely on writing, without the distraction of all the other options on the page. Click this button, and the Post text box expands to fill the full height and width of your browser screen. To bring the Post text box back to its normal state, click the Toggle Full Screen button again. Voilà — it's back to normal!

✔ **Show/Hide Kitchen Sink:** I saw this button and thought, "Wow! WordPress does my dishes, too!" Unfortunately, the button's name is a metaphor that describes the advanced formatting options available with the Visual Text Editor. Click this button, and a new formatting menu drops down, providing options for underlining, font color, custom characters, undo and redo, and so on — a veritable kitchen sink full of options!

You can turn off the Visual Text Editor by clicking the Your Profile link on the Users menu. Uncheck the Use the Visual Editor When Writing box to turn off this editor if you'd rather insert the HTML code yourself in your posts.

If you'd rather embed your own HTML code and skip the Visual Text Editor, click the HTML tab that appears to the right of the Visual tab. If you're planning to type HTML code in your post — for a table or video files, for example, — you have to click the HTML tab before you insert that code. If you don't, the Visual Text Editor formats your code, and it most likely will look nothing like you intended it to.

At this point, you can skip to the "Publishing your post" section of this chapter for information on publishing your post to your blog, or continue with the following sections to discover how to refine the options for your post.

WordPress has a nifty, built-in autosave feature that saves your work while you're typing and editing a new post. If your browser crashes or you accidentally close your browser window before you've saved your post, it will be there for you when you get back. Those WordPress folks are so thoughtful!

Dressing up your posts with images, video, and audio

Directly above and to the left of the Visual Text Editor row of buttons is an Add Media area with a row of four icons. These icons let you insert images/photos, photo galleries, videos, and audio files into your posts. WordPress has an entire Media Library capability, which I describe in great detail in Chapter 9.

Refining your post options

After you write the post, you can choose a few extra options before you publish it for the entire world to see. These settings apply to the post you're currently working on — not to any future or past posts. You can find these options below and to the right of the Post text box (see Figure 8-10). Click the title of each option — the settings for that specific option expand.

You can reposition the different post option modules on the Add New Post page to fit the way you use this page.

Excerpt

Excerpts are optional hand-crafted summaries of your content that can be used in your theme. Learn more about manual excerpts.

Send Trackbacks

Send trackbacks to:

(Separate multiple URLs with spaces)

Trackbacks are a way to notify legacy blog systems that you've linked to them. If you link other WordPress blogs they'll be notified automatically using pingbacks, no other action necessary.

Custom Fields

Add New Custom Field:

Name	Value

Add Custom Field

Custom fields can be used to add extra metadata to a post that you can use in your theme.

Discussion

☑ Allow Comments.
☑ Allow trackbacks and pingbacks on this page.

Figure 8-10: Several options are available for your blog post.

Here are the options found underneath the Post text box:

- ✓ **Excerpt:** Excerpts are short summaries of your posts. Many bloggers use snippets to show teasers of their blog posts, thereby encouraging the reader to click the Read More links to read the posts in their entirety. Type your short summary in the Excerpt box. Excerpts can be any length, in terms of words; however, the point is to keep it short and sweet and tease your readers into clicking the Read More link.

- ✓ **Send Trackbacks:** I discuss trackbacks in Chapter 2, if you'd like to refresh your memory banks on what they are. If you want to send a trackback to another blog, enter the blog's trackback URL in the Send Trackbacks To box. You can send trackbacks to more than one blog; just be sure to separate trackback URLs with spaces.

- ✓ **Custom Fields:** Custom fields add extra data to your posts and are fully configurable by you.

- ✓ **Discussion:** Decide whether to let readers submit comments through the comment system by checking Allow Comments on this Post box. By default, the box is checked; uncheck it to disallow comments on this post.

Here are the options found to the right of the Post text box:

- ✓ **Publish:** These are the publishing and privacy options for your post, which I covered in the "Publishing your post" section.

- ✓ **Categories:** You can file your posts in different categories to organize them by subject. (See more about organizing your posts by category in "Staying on Topic with Categories," earlier in this chapter.) Check the box to the left of the category you want to use. You can toggle between listing all categories, or seeing just the categories you use the most by clicking the All Categories or Most Used links, respectively. Don't see the category you need listed here? Click the + Add New Category link, and you can add a category right there on the Add New Post page!

- ✓ **Post Tags:** Type your desired tags in the Add New Tag text box. Be sure to separate each tag with a comma so that WordPress knows where each tag begins and ends. Cats, Kittens, Feline represents three different tags, for example, but without the commas, WordPress would consider those three words to be one tag. See the sidebar "What are tags, and how/why do I use them?" earlier in this chapter for more information on tags.

- ✓ **Featured Image:** Some WordPress themes are configured to use an image (photo) to represent each post that you have on your blog. The image can display on the home/front page, blog page, archives, or anywhere within the content display on your Web site. If you're using a theme that has this option, you can easily define the post thumbnail by clicking the Set Featured Image link under the Featured Image module on the Add New Post page. Then you can assign an image that you've uploaded to your site as the featured image for a particular post.

When you finish setting the options for your post, don't navigate away from this page; your options have not yet been fully saved. The next section on publishing your post covers all the options you need for saving your post settings!

Publishing your post

You have given your new post a title and written the content of your new blog post. Maybe you've even added an image or other type of media file to your blog post (see Chapter 9), and have configured the tags, categories, and other options. Now the question is: Publish? Or not to publish (yet)?

WordPress gives you three options for saving or publishing your post when you're done writing it. The Publish box is located on the right side of the Add New (or Edit) Post page. Just click the title of the Publish box to expand the settings you need. Figure 8-11 shows the available options in the Publish box.

Figure 8-11:
The publish status for your blog posts.

> **Publish**
>
> (Save Draft)   (Preview)
>
> Status: **Draft**
> [Draft ▾] (OK) Cancel
>
> Visibility: **Public**
> ⦿ Public
>   ☐ Stick this post to the front page
> ○ Password protected
> ○ Private
> (OK) Cancel
>
> 🗓 Publish **immediately**
> [Feb ▾] 21 , 2010 @ 21 : 47
> (OK) Cancel
>
>   (Publish)

The Publish module has several options:

- ✔ **Save Draft:** Choose this option to save your post as a draft. The Edit Post page reloads with all your post contents and options saved; you can continue editing it now, tomorrow, or the next day. To access your draft posts, click the Edit link on the Posts menu.

- ✔ **Preview:** Click the Preview button to view your post in a new window, as it would appear on your live blog if you had published it. Previewing the post doesn't publish it to your site yet. It gives you the opportunity to view it on your site and check it for any formatting or content changes you'd like to make.

✔ **Status:** Click the Edit link to open the settings for this option. A drop-down menu appears and you can select Draft or Pending Review:

> • Select *Draft* to save the post, but not publish it to your blog.
>
> • Select *Pending Review,* and the post shows up in your list of drafts next to a Pending Review header. This option lets the administrator of the blog know that contributors have entered posts that are waiting for administrator review and approval (helpful for blogs with multiple authors).

Click the OK button to save your settings.

✔ **Stick This Post to the Front Page:** Select this box to have WordPress publish the post to your blog and keep it at the very top of all blog posts until you edit this post and change this setting.

This is otherwise known as a *sticky post.* Typically, posts are displayed in a chronological order on your blog, displaying the most recent post on top. If you make a post sticky, it remains at the very top no matter how many other posts you make after it. When you want to un-stick the post, deselect the Stick This Post to the Front Page box.

✔ **Password Protected:** By assigning a password to a post, you can publish a post to your blog that only you can see. You can also share the post password with a friend, who can see the content of the post after entering the password. But why would anyone want to do this? Imagine that you just ate dinner at your mother-in-law's house and she made the *worst* pot roast you've ever eaten. You can write all about it! Protect it with a password and give the password to your trusted friends so that they can read all about it without offending your mother-in-law.

✔ **Private:** Publish this post to your blog so that only you can see it — no one else will be able to see it, ever. You may want to do this for posts that are personal and private only to yourself (if you're keeping a personal diary, for example).

✔ **Publish Immediately:** Click the Edit link, and you can set the timestamp for your post. If you want the post have the current time and date, ignore this setting altogether.

If you'd like to future-publish this post, you can set the time and date for anytime in the future. This feature has come in handy for me many times. For example, when I have a vacation planned and I don't want my blog to go without updates while I'm gone, I'll sit down and write a few posts and set the date for a time in the future. They're published to my blog while I was somewhere tropical, diving with the fishes.

✔ **Publish:** This button wastes no time! It bypasses all the previous draft, pending review and sticky settings and publishes the post directly to your blog immediately.

After you choose an option from the drop-down menu, click the Save button. The Write Post page saves your publishing-status option.

If you want to publish your post right away, skip all the other options in the Publish module, and just click the Publish button. This method eliminates the fuss with the Publish Status options and sends your new post to your blog in all its glory.

If you click Publish and for some reason don't see the post you just published on the front page of your blog, you probably left the Publish Status drop-down menu set to Unpublished. You'll find your new post in the draft posts, which you'll find by clicking the Edit link on the Posts menu.

You are your own editor

While I write this book, I have editors looking over my shoulder, making recommendations, correcting my typos and grammatical errors, and helping me by telling me when I get too long-winded. You, on the other hand, are not so lucky! You are your own editor and have full control of what you write, when you write it, and how you write it. You can always go back and edit previous posts to correct typos, grammatical errors, and other mistakes by following these steps:

1. **Find the post that you want to edit by clicking the Edit link on the Posts menu.**

   The Edit Posts page opens and lists the 20 most recent posts you've made to your blog.

   You can filter that listing of posts by date by choosing a date from the Show All Dates drop-down menu at the top of the Edit Posts page. For example, if you choose April 2010, the Edit Posts page reloads, displaying only those posts that were published in the month of April 2010.

   You can also filter the post listing by category. Select your desired category from the View All Categories drop-down menu.

2. **When you find the post you need, click its title.**

   The Edit Post window opens. In this window, you can edit the post and/or any of its options.

   You can also click the Edit link that appears beneath the post title on the Edit Posts page.

   If you only need to edit the post options, click the Quick Edit link. The post options open, and you can configure post options like the title, status, password, categories, tags, comments, and timestamp. Click the Save button to save your changes.

3. **Edit your post; then click the Update Post button.**

   The Edit Post window refreshes with all of your changes saved.

Look Who's Talking on Your Blog

The feature that really catapulted blogging into the limelight is the comments feature, which lets visitors interact with the authors of blogs. I cover the concept of blog comments and trackbacks in Chapter 2. They provide a great way for readers to interact with site owners, and vice versa.

Managing comments and trackbacks

To find your comments, click the Comments link on the Comments menu; the Edit Comments page opens (see Figure 8-12).

When you hover over the comment with your mouse, several links appear that give you the opportunity to manage those comments:

✔ **Unapprove:** This link only appears if you have comment moderation turned on and appear with approved comments only. The comment is placed in the moderation queue, which you get to by clicking the Awaiting Moderation link that appears below the Manage Comments

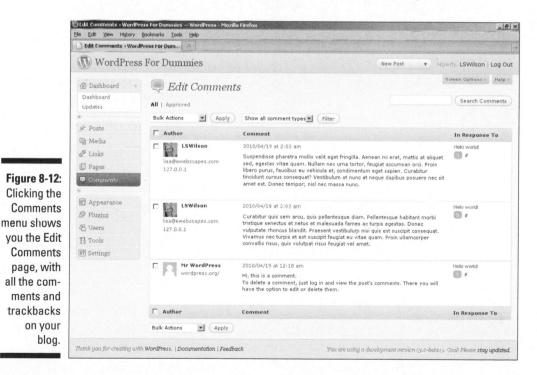

Figure 8-12: Clicking the Comments menu shows you the Edit Comments page, with all the comments and trackbacks on your blog.

header. The moderation queue is kind of a holding area for comments that haven't yet been published to your blog. (See the following section for more on the moderation queue.)

✔ **Reply:** Click this link, and a text box drops down, where you can type and submit your reply to this person. This feature eliminates the need to have to load your live site in order to reply to a comment.

✔ **Quick Edit:** Click this link and, without ever leaving the Edit Comments page, the comment options open, and you can configure the post options like name, e-mail, URL, and comment content. Click the Save button to save your changes.

✔ **Edit:** Click this link to open the Edit Comment page where you can edit the different fields, such as name, e-mail, URL, and comment content (see Figure 8-13).

✔ **Spam:** Click this link to mark the comment as spam and toss it into the spam bin where it will never be heard from again!

✔ **Trash:** This link does exactly what it says; it sends the comment to the trash can and deletes it from your blog.

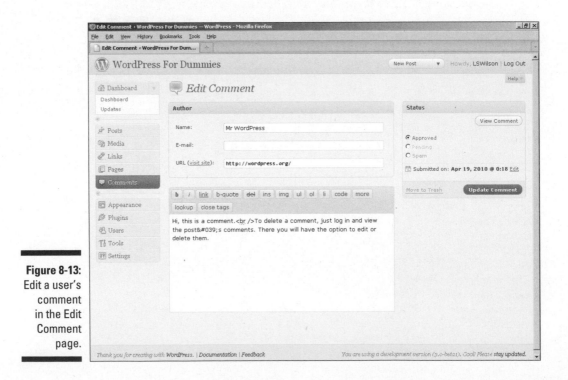

Figure 8-13:
Edit a user's
comment
in the Edit
Comment
page.

If you have a lot of comments listed in this page and want to bulk-edit them, check the boxes to the left of all the comments you want to manage; then select one of the following from the Actions drop-down menu at the top left of the Edit Comments page: Approve, Mark As Spam, Unapprove, or Delete.

Moderating comments and trackbacks

If you have your options set so that comments aren't published to your blog until you approve them, you can approve comments from the Edit Comments page as well. Just click the Pending link, and you go to the Edit Comments page. If you have comments and/or trackbacks awaiting moderation, you see them on this page, and you can approve them, mark them as spam, or delete them.

A nice feature of WordPress is that it immediately notifies you of any comments sitting in the moderation queue, awaiting your action. This notification, which appears on every single page, is a small orange conversation bubble that appears in the left navigation menu, to the right of the Comments menu. Figure 8-14 shows that I have 10 comments awaiting moderation. I'd better get busy and deal with those comments!

Figure 8-14:
A small conversation bubble telling me that I have a comment awaiting moderation.

Tackling spam with Akismet

I touch on Akismet a few times throughout this book. Why do I discuss it so much? Only because it's my humble opinion that Akismet is the mother of all plugins and that no WordPress blog is complete without a fully activated version of Akismet running in it.

Apparently WordPress agrees, because the plugin is packaged in every WordPress software release beginning with version 2.0. Akismet was created by the folks at Automattic, the same folks who brought you the WordPress.com-hosted version (discussed in Part II of this book). Automattic also works with of some of the original developers of the WordPress software platform.

Akismet is the answer to combatting comment and trackback spam. Matt Mullenweg of Automattic says Akismet is a "collaborative effort to make comment and trackback spam a non-issue and restore innocence to blogging, so you never have to worry about spam again" (from the Akismet Web site at `http://akismet.com`).

I've been blogging since 2002. I started blogging with the Movable Type blogging platform and moved to WordPress in 2003. As blogging became more and more popular, comment and trackback spam became more and more of a nuisance. One morning in 2004, I found that 2,300 pieces of disgusting comment spam had been published to my blog. Something had to be done! The folks at Automattic did a fine thing with Akismet. Since the emergence of Akismet, I've barely had to think about comment or trackback spam except for the few times a month I check my Akismet spam queue.

I talk in greater detail about plugin use in WordPress in Chapter 10, where you find out how to activate Akismet and make sure that it is protecting your blog from trackback and comment spam.

Part IV
Flexing and Extending WordPress

The 5th Wave   By Rich Tennant

FREELANCER NED WILLIS CONSULTS WITH A MEMBER OF HIS TECHNICAL STAFF

"...and that's pretty much all there is to migrating your blog to WordPress."

In this part . . .

Ready? Set? Action! This part of the book starts by showing you how to add media files — images, video, and audio — to your site to create a fun interactive experience for your readers. This part also covers using WordPress plugins to extend the capabilities of your blog, and finding and using free WordPress themes to change the look of your blog.

Chapter 9

Media Management: Images, Audio, and Video

In This Chapter

▶ Adding images, photo galleries, and videos to your blog posts

▶ Uploading audio files

▶ Exploring the WordPress Media Library

*A*dding images and photos to your posts can really dress up the content. By using images and photos, you give your content a dimension that you can't express in plain text. Through visual imagery, you can call attention to your post and add depth to it.

The same goes for adding video and audio files to your posts and blog. Video lets you provide entertainment through moving, talking (or singing!) streaming video. Audio files let you talk to your visitors and add a personal touch. Many bloggers use video and audio to report news and to broadcast Internet radio and television shows. The possibilities are endless!

In this chapter, you discover how to add some special touches to your blog posts by adding images, video, and audio to posts, and even find out how to run a full-fledged photo gallery on your site, all through the WordPress.org software and its integrated Media Library.

This chapter is pertinent to the WordPress.org platform only. If you're using the hosted WordPress.com version, check out Chapter 4 for information on adding images, video, and audio to your blog.

You add these extras to your blog posts in the Add Media area of the Write Post page. You can add them as you're writing your post, or come back and add them later. The choice is yours!

Inserting Images into Your Blog Posts

Adding images to a post is pretty easy with the WordPress image uploader. Jump right in and give it a go by clicking the Upload an Image icon on the Add New Post page. The Add an Image window lets you choose images from your hard drive or from a location on the Web (see Figure 9-1).

Figure 9-1:
The
WordPress
Add an
Image
window.

Add an Image   ✕

From Computer | From URL | Media Library

Add media files from your computer

Choose files to upload   **Select Files**   Cancel Upload

You are using the Flash uploader. Problems? Try the Browser uploader instead.

After a file has been uploaded, you can add titles and descriptions.

The interface that WordPress uses for file uploads is based on Adobe Flash. Flash is a specific set of multimedia technologies programmed to handle media files on the Web. Some browsers and operating systems are not configured to handle Flash-based applications. If you experience difficulties with the image uploader, WordPress gives you an easy alternative. Click the Browser Uploader link in the image uploader, and you can use a non-Flash based uploader to transfer your files.

To add an image from the Web after you click the Add an Image icon, follow these steps:

1. **Click the From URL tab in the Add an Image window.**

   The Add Media File from URL window opens.

2. **Type the URL (Internet address) of the image in the Image URL text box.**

   Type the full URL, including the http and www portion of the address. You can easily find the URL of any image on the Web by right-clicking (PC) or Control-clicking (Mac) and selecting Properties from the menu.

3. **Type a title for the image in the Image Title text box.**

4. **Type a description of the image in the Alternate Text textbox.**

   The alternative text is what shows in a browser for visually impaired people who use text readers or, if, for some reason, the image does not load properly. While alternate text gives the visitors to your site a description of what the image is, it's also good to add for SEO (search engine optimization). Search engines read the alternative text (also called ALT tags) and give search engines additional descriptive text to further categorize and define your site in listings and directories.

5. **(Optional) Type the caption of the image in the Image Caption text box.**

   The words you type here display underneath the image on your blog as a caption.

6. **Choose an alignment option by selecting the None, Left, Center, or Right radio button.**

7. **Type the URL you want the image linked to.**

   Whatever option you choose determines where your readers go when they click the image you've uploaded:

   - *None:* You don't want the image to be clickable.

   - *Link to Image:* Readers can click through to the direct image itself.

8. **Click the Insert into Post button.**

To add an image from your own hard drive after you click the Add an Image icon, follow these steps:

1. **Click the From Computer tab and then click the Select Files button.**

   A dialog box opens from which you can select an image (or multiple images) from your hard drive.

2. **Select your image(s); then click Open.**

   The image is uploaded from your computer to your Web server. WordPress displays a progress bar on the upload and displays an image options box when the upload is finished.

3. **Edit the details for the image(s) by clicking the Show link that appears to the right of the image thumbnail.**

   Clicking Show drops down a box (see Figure 9-2) that contains several image options:

   - *Title:* Type a title for the image.

   - *Alternate Text:* Type the alternate text (see previous section) for the image.

   - *Caption:* Type a caption for the image (such as **This is a flower from my garden**).

   - *Description:* Type a description of the image.

   - *Link URL:* Type the URL you want the image linked to. Whatever option you choose determines where your readers go when they click the image you've uploaded:

None: You don't want the image to be clickable.

File URL: Readers can click through to the direct image itself.

Post URL: Readers can click through to the post that the image appears in. You can type your own URL in the Link URL text box.

- *Alignment:* Choose None, Left, Center, or Right. (See Table 9-1, in the following section, for styling information regarding image alignment.)

- *Size:* Choose Thumbnail, Medium, Large, or Full Size.

TIP

WordPress automatically creates small and medium-size versions of the images you upload through the built-in image uploader. A *thumbnail* is a smaller version of the original file. You can edit the size of the thumbnail by clicking the Settings link and then clicking Miscellaneous. In the Image Sizes section, designate your desired height and width of the small and medium thumbnail images generated by WordPress.

Figure 9-2:
You can set several options for your images after you upload them.

Add an Image	✕

File name: wp4d.2e.lg_.png
File type: image/png
Upload date: April 19, 2010
Dimensions: 218 × 274

Edit Image

Title   *   WordPress For Dummies by Lisa Sabin-Wilson

Alternate Text   WordPress For Dummies by Lisa Sabin-Wilson
Alt text for the image, e.g. "The Mona Lisa"

Caption   WordPress For Dummies by Lisa Sabin-Wilson

Description

Link URL   http://yourdomain.com/wp-content/uploads/2010/04/wp4d.2e.lg_.png
   [None] [File URL] [Post URL]
   Enter a link URL or click above for presets.

Alignment   ◉ ▪ None   ○ ▪ Left   ○ ▪ Center   ○ ▪ Right

Size   ○ Thumbnail   ○ Medium   ○ Large   ◉ Full Size
   (150 × 150)   *(218 × 274)*

Use as featured image   Delete

Save all changes

If you're uploading more than one image, skip to the "Inserting a photo gallery" section, later in this chapter.

4. **Click the Edit Image button (as shown in Figure 9-2) to edit the appearance of the image.**

The image editor (as seen in Figure 9-3) options include:

- **Crop:** Click this button to cut the image down to a smaller size.

- **Rotate counter-clockwise:** Click this button to rotate the image to the left.

- **Rotate clockwise:** Click this button to rotate the image to the right.

- **Flip vertically:** Click this button to flip the image upside down, and back again

- **Flip horizontally:** Click this button to flip the image from right to left, and back again.

- **Undo:** Click this button to undo any changes you've made.

- **Redo:** Click this button to redo images edits that you've undone.

- **Scale Image**: Click this link to drop down the option menu that gives you the ability to set a specific width and height for the image.

5. **Click the Insert into Post button.**

Figure 9-3:
The
WordPress
Image Editor
options.

The image uploader window closes, and you return to the Add New Post page (or the Add New Page page, if you're writing a page). WordPress has inserted the HTML to display the image in your post, as shown in Figure 9-4; you can continue editing your post, save it, or publish it.

To see the actual image and not the code, click the Visual tab that's just above the Post text box.

Figure 9-4:
WordPress
inserts the
correct
HTML code
for your
uploaded
image into
your post.

Aligning your images

When you upload your image, you can set the alignment for your image as None, Left, Center, or Right. The WordPress theme you're using, however, may not have these alignment styles accounted for in its stylesheet. If you set the alignment to Left, for example, but the image on your blog doesn't appear to be aligned at all, you may need to add a few styles to your theme's stylesheet.

I discuss themes and templates in great detail in Part V. For purposes of making sure that you have the correct image alignment for your newly uploaded images, however, here is a quick-and-dirty method:

1. **Click the Editor link in the Appearance menu.**

   The Edit Themes page opens. All the template files for your active theme are listed on the right side of the page.

2. **Click the Stylesheet template.**

   The Stylesheet (`style.css`) template opens in the text box on the left side of the page.

3. **Add your desired styles to the stylesheet.**

Table 9-1 shows the styles you can add to your stylesheet to make sure that image-alignment styling is present and accounted for in your theme.

Table 9-1	Styling Techniques for Image Alignment
Image Alignment	*Add This to Your Stylesheet (style.css)*
None	`img.alignnone {float:none; margin: 5px 0 5px 0;}`
Left	`img.alignleft {float:left; margin: 5px 10px 5px 0px;}`
Center	`img.aligncenter {display:block; float:none; margin: 5px auto;}`
Right	`img.alignright {float:right; margin: 5px 0 5px 10px;}`

These styles are just examples of what you can do. Get creative with your own styling. You find more information about using CSS (Cascading Style Sheets) to add style to your theme(s) in Chapter 13.

Inserting a photo gallery

You can also use the WordPress image uploader to insert a full photo gallery into your posts. Upload your images; then, instead of clicking the Insert into Post button, click the Gallery tab at the top of the image uploader window (refer to Figure 9-1). This tab displays thumbnails of all the images you have uploaded for your post.

Follow these steps to insert a photo gallery into a blog post:

1. **(Optional) On the Gallery tab, under the Options column, type the order that you want the images to appear in the gallery.**

   Type the number of the sequence in which you want this image displayed. (If you want this image displayed first, for example, type the number 1.)

2. **Set different options for your gallery:**

   - *Link Thumbnails To:* Select Image File or Attachment Page.
   - *Order Images By:* Select Menu Order, Name, or Date/Time.
   - *Order:* Select Ascending or Descending.
   - *Gallery Columns:* Select how many columns of images you'd like to display in your gallery.

3. **Click the Save All Changes button.**

   All the changes you made to each individual image listed in the gallery are saved.

4. **Click the Insert Gallery button.**

   WordPress inserts into your post a piece of short code that looks like this: `[gallery]`.

   Table 9-2 shows some gallery short codes that you can use to manually set the display settings for your photo gallery.

5. **(Optional) Change the order of appearance of the images in the gallery, as well as the markup (HTML tags or CSS selectors):**

   • `captiontag`: Change the markup that surrounds the image caption by altering the gallery short code. Here are some examples: `[gallery captiontag="div"]` places `<div></div>` tags around the image caption (the `<div>` tag is considered a block level element and creates a separate container for the content); to have the gallery appear on a line of its own, the `[gallery captiontag="p"]` code places `<p class="gallery-caption"></p>` tags around the image caption. The default markup for the `captiontag` option is `dd`.

   • `icontag`: Defines the HTML markup around each individual thumbnail image in your gallery. Change the markup around the `icontag` (thumbnail icon) of the image by altering the gallery short code to something like `[gallery icontag="p"]`, which places `<p class="gallery-icon"></p>` tags around each thumbnail icon. The default markup for `icontag` is `dt`.

   • `itemtag`: Defines the HTML markup around each item in your gallery. Change the markup around the `itemtag` (each item) in the gallery by altering the gallery short code to something like `[gallery itemtag="span"]`, which places `<span class="gallery-item"></span>` tags around each item in the gallery. The default markup for the `itemtag` is `dl`.

   • `captiontag`: Define the HTML markup around the image caption for each image in your gallery. Change the markup around the `captiontag` (caption) for each image by altering the gallery short code to something like `[gallery captiontag="p"]`, which places `<p></p>` tags around the image caption. The default markup for `captiontag` is `dd`.

   • `orderby`: Defines the order that the images are displayed within your gallery. Change the order used to display the thumbnails in the gallery by altering the gallery short code to something like `[gallery orderby="menu_order ASC"]`, which displays the thumbnails in ascending menu order. Another parameter you can use is `ID_order ASC`, which displays the thumbnails in ascending order according to their IDs.

Table 9-2	Gallery Short Code Examples
Gallery Short Code	Output
`[gallery columns="4" size="medium"]`	A four-column gallery containing medium-size images
`[gallery columns="10" id="215" size="thumbnail"]`	A ten-column gallery containing thumbnail images pulled from the blog post with the ID 215.
`[gallery captiontag="p" icontag="span"]`	A three-column (default) gallery in which each image is surrounded by `<span></span>` tags and the image caption is surrounded by `<p></p>` tags.

6. **Define the style of the `<span>` tags in your CSS stylesheet.**

   The `<span>` tags create an inline element; an element contained within a `<span>` tag stays on the same line as the element before it; there is no line break. You need a little knowledge of CSS to alter the `<span>` tags. Click the Design tab in your WordPress Dashboard, and then click the Theme Editor subtab to edit the stylesheet for your theme. Here's an example of what you can add to the stylesheet (`style.css`) for your current theme:

```
span.gallery-icon img {
padding: 3px;
background: white;
border: 1px solid black;
margin: 0 5px;
}
```

   Placing this bit of CSS in the stylesheet (`style.css`) of your active theme automatically places a 1-pixel black border around each thumbnail, with 3 pixels of padding and a white background. The left and right margins are 5 pixels wide, creating nice spacing between images in the gallery.

7. **Click the Update File button to save changes to your Stylesheet (style. css) template.**

Figure 9-5 shows my post with my photo gallery displayed, using the preceding steps and CSS example in the default WordPress theme: Twenty Ten. This code is the gallery short code that I used for the gallery shown in Figure 9-5 — `[gallery icontag="span" size="thumbnail"]`.

Matt Mullenweg, co-founder of the WordPress platform, created a very extensive photo gallery by using the built-in gallery options in WordPress. Check out the fabulous photo gallery at `http://ma.tt/category/gallery/`.

Figure 9-5:
A photo gallery inserted into my post with gallery short codes and CSS examples.

Some great WordPress plugins work in tandem with the WordPress gallery feature. Check out Chapter 10 for information on how to install and use WordPress plugins in your blog.

WordPress gallery plugins

Here are a handful of great plugins:

✔ **NextGEN Gallery by Alex Rabe** (`http://wordpress.org/extend/plugins/nextgen-gallery`): Creates sortable photo galleries and more.

✔ **Organizer by Imthiaz** (`http://wordpress.org/extend/plugins/organizer`): Organizes, renames, resizes, and manages image files.

✔ **Random Image widget by Marcel Proulx** (`http://wordpress.org/extend/plugins/random-image-widget`): Display images at random from your image-upload folder.

✔ **Mini-Slides by Roland Rust** (`http://wordpress.org/extend/plugins/mini-slides`): Create inline slideshows.

Inserting Video Files into Your Blog Posts

Whether you're producing your own videos for publication or want to embed other people's videos that you find interesting, placing a video file in a blog post has never been easier with WordPress.

Check out a good example of a video blog at `http://1938media.com`. Loren Feldman and his team produce video for the Web and for mobile devices.

Several video galleries on the Web today allow you to add videos to blog posts; Google's YouTube service (`http://youtube.com`) is a good example of a third party video service that allows you to share videos from their service. To add video from the Web, click the Add Video icon, then click the From URL tab and follow these steps:

1. **Type the URL (Internet address) of the video in the Video URL text box.**

   Type the full URL, including the `http` and www portion of the address. Video providers, such as YouTube, usually list the direct link for the video file on their sites; you can copy and paste it into the Video URL text box.

2. **(Optional) Type the title of the video in the Title text box.**

   Giving a title to the video allows you to provide a bit of a description of the video. It's a good idea to provide a title if you can, so that your readers know what the video is about.

3. **Click the Insert into Post button.**

   A link to the video is inserted into your post. WordPress doesn't embed the actual video in the post; it inserts only a link to the video. Your blog visitors click the link to load another page where the video can be played.

The previous steps give you the ability to insert a hyperlink that your readers can click and view the video on another web site (like YouTube.com). WordPress also has a nifty feature called Auto-Embed that automatically embeds videos within your posts and pages by simply typing the URL for the video into the body of your post, or page.

WordPress will automatically detect that a URL you typed in your post is a video from YouTube (for example) and it will automatically wrap the correct HTML embed code around that URL to make sure the video player displays in your post (in a standards, XHTML compliant way).

You do need to enable the Auto-Embed feature on the Media Settings page:

1. **Click the Media link under the Settings menu in your WordPress Dashboard.**

   The Media Settings page loads in the Dashboard.

2. **Place a checkmark in the box labeled Attempt to automatically embed all plain text URLs.**

   The Auto-Embed feature is now enabled.

3. **Set the dimensions you want the (video) to display in the Maximum embed size box.**

   Enter your preferred size (width and height) that you want the videos to appear in your posts and pages.

4. **Be sure to click the Save Changes button!**

   You're ready to automatically embed links into your WordPress posts.

Currently, WordPress will automatically embed videos from YouTube, Vimeo, DailyMotion, blip.tv, Flickr, Hulu, Viddler, Qik, Revision3, Scibd, PhotoBucket, PollDaddy, Google Videom, and VideoPress-type videos from WordPress.tv.

To upload and post to your blog a video from your computer, click the Add Video icon on the Edit Post or Add New Post page. Then follow these steps:

1. **Click the Choose Files to Upload button.**

   An Open dialog box opens.

2. **Select the video file you want to upload, and click Open (or double-click the file).**

   You return to the file uploader window in WordPress, which shows a progress bar while your video uploads. When the upload is complete, a box containing several options drops down.

3. **Type a title for the file in the Title text box.**

4. **Type a caption for the file in the Caption text box.**

5. **Type a description of the file in the Description text box.**

6. **Click the File URL button.**

   It provides a direct link in your post to the video file itself.

7. **Click Insert into Post.**

   WordPress doesn't embed a video player in the post; it inserts only a link to the video.

Inserting Audio Files into Your Blog Posts

Audio files can be music files or a recording of you speaking to your readers; it adds a nice personal touch to your blog, and you can easily share audio files on your blog through the use of the Upload Audio feature in WordPress. After you've inserted an audio file in your blog posts, your readers can listen to it on their computers or download it onto an MP3 player and listen to it on their drives to work, if they want.

Click the Add Audio icon on the Edit Post or Add New Post page, and follow these steps to upload an audio file to your blog post:

1. **Click the Choose Files to Upload button.**

   An Open dialog box opens.

2. **Choose the file you want to upload, and click Open (or double-click the file).**

   You return to the file uploader window in WordPress, which shows a progress bar while your audio file uploads. When the upload is complete, a box containing several options drops down.

3. **Type a title for the file in the Title text box.**

4. **Type a caption for the file in the Caption text box.**

5. **Type a description of the file in the Description text box.**

6. **Click the File URL button.**

   You can provide a direct link in your post to the video file itself.

7. **Click Insert into Post.**

   A link to the audio file is inserted into your post. WordPress doesn't embed an actual audio player in the post; it only inserts a link to the audio file. Visitors click the link to open another page where the audio file can be played.

Some great WordPress plugins for audio handling can enhance the functionality of the file uploader and help you manage audio files in your blog posts. Check out Chapter 10 for information on how to install and use WordPress plugins in your blog.

Keeping Media Files Organized

If you've been running your blog for any length of time, you can easily forget what files you've uploaded with the WordPress uploader. I used to have to log in to my Web server via FTP and view the uploads folder to see what I had in there.

Now, the WordPress Media Library makes it very convenient and easy to discover which files are in your uploads folder.

To find an image, video, or audio file that you've already uploaded using the file uploader and use that file in a new post, follow these steps:

1. **Click the Upload Media icon to open the file uploader window.**

2. **Click the Media Library link at the top.**

   You see all the files you've ever uploaded to your blog with the file uploader feature (see Figure 9-6). Files you've uploaded through other methods, like FTP, are not displayed in the Media Library.

Figure 9-6:
The Media Library shows all the files you've ever uploaded to your blog.

3. **Select the file you want to reuse, and click the Show link.**

4. **Set the options for that image: Title, Caption, Description, Link URL, Order, Alignment, and Size.**

5. **Click the Insert into Post button.**

   The correct HTML code is inserted into the Post text box.

If you only want to view the files you've uploaded and don't need a particular image or file for a new post, click the Edit link in the Media menu, which opens the Media Library page.

The Media Library page lists all the files you've ever uploaded to your WordPress blog. By default, the page displays all types of files, but you can click the Images, Audio, or Video link to specify which file type you want to see (see Figure 9-7).

Figure 9-7:
The
WordPress
Media
Library
page.

You can do the following tasks on the Media Library page:

- **Filter media files by date.** If you want to view all media files that were uploaded in July 2010 choose that date from the drop-down menu and click the Filter button; the page reloads and displays only the media files uploaded in the month of July 2010.

- **Search media files using a specific keyword.** If you want to search your Media Library for all files that reference kittens, then you type the word **kittens** in the Search box in the upper right side of the Media Library page. Then click the Search Media button; the page reloads and displays only media files that contain the keyword or tag of kittens.

- **Delete media files.** Click the small white box that appears to the left of every thumbnail on the Manage Media page; then click the Delete button that shows at the top left of the page. The page reloads, and the media file you've just deleted is now gone.

- **View media files.** On the Manage Media page, click the thumbnail of the file you'd like to view. The actual file opens in your Web browser. If necessary, you can copy the permalink of the file from your browser's address bar.

WordPress video and audio plugins

There are some great WordPress plugins for audio and video handling. Check out Chapter 10 for information on how to install and use WordPress plugins.

Here are a handful of great plugins for audio:

✔ **Audio Player by Martin Laine** (`http://wordpress.org/extend/plugins/audio-player`): Embeds a Flash MP3 player in your blog posts without any special HTML.

✔ **1 Bit Audio Player by Mark Wheeler** (`http://wordpress.org/extend/plugins/1-bit-audio-player`): Autodetects MP3 files on your site and inserts a stylish player.

✔ **Podcasting by Ronald Heft, Jr.** (`http://wordpress.org/extend/plugins/podcasting`): Supports several media formats and automatically creates a podcast RSS feed.

Here are a handful of great plugins for video:

✔ **wordTube by Alex Rabe** (`http://wordpress.org/extend/plugins/wordtube`): Creates a YouTube-like player when you insert video files within your posts without any special HTML.

✔ **Smart YouTube by Vladimir Prelovacn** (`http://wordpress.org/extend/plugins/smart-youtube`): Inserts YouTube videos into blog posts, comments, and RSS feeds.

✔ **WP-Vidavee by Vidavee Labs** (`http://wordpress.org/extend/plugins/wp-vidavee-film-manager`): Uploads, manages, organizes, and displays video in your blog.

✔ **Video Embedder by Kristoffer Forsgren** (`http://wordpress.org/extend/plugins/video-embedder`): Embeds video from various sources.

Chapter 10

Making the Most of WordPress Plugins

In This Chapter

▶ Plugging in to plugins

▶ Finding, downloading, and unpacking plugin files

▶ Uploading and installing plugins

▶ Activating and managing plugins

▶ Using the plugins that come with WordPress

▶ Exploring open source plugins

*H*alf the fun of running a WordPress–powered blog is playing with the hundreds of plugins that you can install to extend your blog's functions and options. WordPress plugins are like those really cool custom rims you put on your car: Although they don't come with the car, they're awesome accessories that make your car better than all the rest.

In this chapter, you find out what plugins are, how to find and install them, and how they enhance your blog in a way that makes your blog unique. Using plugins can also greatly improve your readers' experiences by providing them various tools they can use to interact and participate — just the way you want them to!

This chapter assumes that you already have WordPress installed on your Web server. Installing plugins pertains only to the WordPress.org software. If you're skipping around in the book and haven't yet installed WordPress on your Web server, you can find instructions in Chapter 6.

WordPress.com users can't install or configure plugins on their hosted blogs. I don't make the rules, so please don't kill the messenger.

Finding Out What Plugins Are

A *plugin* is a small program that, when added to WordPress, interacts with the software to provide some extensibility to the software. Plugins aren't part of the core software; they aren't software programs either. They typically don't function as stand-alone software. They do require the host program (WordPress, in this case) to function.

Plugin developers are the people who write these gems and share them with the rest of us — usually, for free. Like WordPress, plugins are free to anyone who wants to further tailor and customize his site to his own needs.

Although plugins are written and developed by people who have the set of skills required to do so, I would say that the WordPress user community is also largely responsible for the ongoing development of plugins. Ultimately, the end users are the ones who put those plugins to the true test of the real world in their own blogs. Those same users are also the first to speak up and let the developers know when something isn't working right, helping the developers troubleshoot and fine-tune their plugins. The most popular plugins are created by developers who encourage open communication with the user base. Overall, WordPress is one of those great open source projects in which the relationship between developers and users fosters a creative environment that keeps the project fresh and exciting every step of the way.

Literally thousands of plugins are available for WordPress — certainly way too many for me to list in this chapter alone. I could, but then you'd need heavy machinery to lift this book off the shelf! So here are just a few examples of things that plugins let you add to your WordPress blog:

- ✔ **E-mail notification:** Your biggest fans can sign up to have an e-mail notification sent to them every time you update your blog.

- ✔ **Submit your blog to social networking services:** Allow your readers to submit your blog posts to some of the most popular social networking services, such as Digg, Technorati, and Del.icio.us.

- ✔ **Stats program:** Keep track of where your traffic is coming from; which posts on your blog are the most popular; and how much traffic is coming through your blog on a daily, monthly, and yearly basis.

Chapter 17 gives you a peek at some of the most popular plugins on the scene today. In the meantime, this chapter takes you through the process of finding plugins, installing them in your WordPress blog, and managing and troubleshooting them.

Exploring Manage Plugin page

Before you start installing plugins for your blog, it's important for you to explore the Manage Plugins page in your WordPress Dashboard and understand how to manage the plugins after you install them. Click the title of the Plugins menu on your WordPress Dashboard to view the Manage Plugins page (shown in Figure 10-1).

The Manage Plugins page is where you manage all the plugins you install in your WordPress blog. By default, the Manage Plugins page displays a full listing of all the WordPress plugins you currently have installed. You can filter the listing of plugins using the three links shown directly below the Manage Plugins page title:

- ✔ **All:** This is the default view for the Manage Plugins page and shows a listing of all plugins currently installed on your WordPress Web site, whether they are active or not.

- ✔ **Active:** Clicking this link shows a list of the plugins that are currently activated and in use on your WordPress Web site.

Figure 10-1:
The Manage Plugins page in the WordPress Dashboard.

✔ **Inactive:** Clicking this link changes the display and shows list of plugins that are installed but not currently active. (*Note:* This link only displays on the Manage Plugins page if you have inactive plugins.)

With a quick glance at the Manage Plugins page, you can easily tell which plugins are active — and which aren't — by the shade of the background color of each plugin listed. A grey background means the plugin is *not* active. A white background means the plugin *is* active. In Figure 10-1, the background of the Akismet plugin is gray, and the background of the Hello Dolly plugin is white. Akismet isn't active, but Hello Dolly is.

You can mass manage your plugins on the Manage Plugins page. You can deactivate all your plugins at once by selecting the box to the left of each plugin name, and then selecting Deactivate in the Bulk Actions drop-down menu at the top of the page (as shown in Figure 10-1). Then click the Apply button. Likewise, you can activate, upgrade, or delete the plugins listed by selecting Activate or the Delete item in the Bulk Actions drop-down menu. To quickly select all your plugins with one click, select the box to the left of the Plugin heading on the Manage Plugins page.

The Manage Plugins page displays plugins in two columns, which give details for each plugin:

✔ **Plugin:** This column lists the plugin name so that you can find it easily when browsing the Manage Plugins page. Directly beneath the plugin name, you see a few links for easy plugin management:

- **Activate:** This link only appears below the title of plugins that aren't active. Click the link to activate a plugin.

- **Deactivate:** This link only appears below the title of plugins that are active. Click the link to deactivate a plugin.

- **Delete:** This link only appears below the title of plugins that aren't active. Click the link to delete the plugin from your site (see more about this topic in the "Uninstalling Plugins" section later in this chapter).

- **Edit:** This link appears below all listed plugins, whether they are active or not. Click the link to visit the Edit Plugins page. If you feel comfortable doing so, you can edit the individual plugin files.

✔ **Description:** This column lists a description for the plugin. Depending on the plugin, you may also see brief instructions on using the plugin. Directly below the description are the version number of the plugin, the plugin author's name, and a link to the Web site where you can read more information about the plugin.

Discovering the one-click plugin upgrade

For a lot of reasons, mainly security reasons and feature updates, you really want to make sure that you always use the most up-to-date versions of the plugins in your blog. With everything you have to do every day, how can you possibly keep up with knowing whether the plugins you're using have been updated?

You don't have to. WordPress does it for you.

Figure 10-2 shows an out-of-date version (2.2.1) of Akismet installed and activated. WordPress notifies you when there is a new update available for a plugin in three different ways, as seen in Figure 10-2:

✔ **Dashboard:** The Updates link below the Dashboard menu displays a red circle with a white number. The number indicates how many plugins have updates available. In Figure 10-2, you see that there is currently one plugin with an update available on my site. Click the Update link to see which plugins have updates available.

Figure 10-2: WordPress tells you when a new plugin version is available.

✓ **Plugins:** The Plugins menu title displays a light grey circle with a number. Like the Updates link, the number indicates how many plugins have updates available, as seen in Figure 10-2.

✓ **Manage Plugins page:** Figure 10-2 shows the Manage Plugins page. Below the Akismet plugin you see a message that says, *"There is a new version of Akismet available. View version 2.2.7 Details or Upgrade automatically."*

WordPress not only gives you a message that a new version of the plugin is available, but also gives you a link to a page where you can download the new version or a link that you can click to upgrade the plugin right there and then — WordPress's one-click plugin upgrade.

Click the *Upgrade Automatically* link, and WordPress grabs the new files off the WordPress.org server, uploads them to your plugins directory, deletes the old plugin, and activates the new one. Figure 10-3 shows the Upgrade Plugin page that displays while the plugin is being upgraded.

WordPress notifies you of an out-of-date plugin and provides you with the one-click upgrade function *only* for plugins that are in the official WordPress Plugin Directory (`http://wordpress.org/extend/plugins`). If a plugin you are using is not listed in the directory, then the notification and one-click upgrade function won't be present for that plugin.

Figure 10-3:
Upgrade
Plugin page.

Another way that WordPress alerts you that you have out-of-date plugins is in the left navigation menu. When you have an out-of-date plugin, a number appears next to the Updates link in the Dashboard menu, indicating that you have a plugin, or plugins, that need to be upgraded. Figure 10-4 shows my Dashboard telling me that I have one plugin that needs to be upgraded. After you upgrade the plugin, the number disappears.

Whatever you do, do *not* ignore the plugin update messages that WordPress gives you. Plugin developers usually release new upgrades because of security problems or vulnerabilities that require an upgrade. If you notice that there's an upgrade available for a plugin you're using, stop what you're doing and upgrade it — it only takes a few seconds.

For the automatic plugin upgrade to work, your plugin directory (/wp-content/plugins) must be writable on your Web server, which means that you should have set permissions of 755 or 777 (depending on your Web-server configuration). See Chapter 6 for information about changing file permissions on your Web server, or contact your Web hosting provider for assistance.

Figure 10-4:
Bubble
next to the
Updates
link alerts
you that
you have
out-of-date
plugins.

Getting the Most out of the Plugins Included with WordPress

At this writing, WordPress packages two plugins with the installation files:

- ✔ **Akismet:** This plugin is essential.
- ✔ **Hello Dolly:** This plugin isn't necessary to make your blog run smoothly, but it adds some extra fun.

Akismet

I touch on Akismet a few times throughout this book. Why so much? It's my humble opinion that Akismet is the mother of all plugins and that no WordPress blog is complete without a fully activated version of Akismet.

Apparently WordPress agrees, because the plugin has been packaged in every WordPress software release since version 2.0. Akismet was created by the folks at Automattic — the same folks who bring you the Sidebar Widgets plugin.Akismet is the answer to comment and trackback spam. Matt Mullenweg of Automattic says Akismet is a "collaborative effort to make comment and trackback spam a non-issue and restore innocence to blogging, so you never have to worry about spam again" (from the Akismet Web site at `http://akismet.com`).

To use the plugin, follow these steps:

1. **On the Manage Plugins page, click the Activate link to the right of the Akismet plugin name and description.**

   A yellow box appears at the top of the page, saying: "Akismet is almost ready. You must enter your WordPress.com API key for it to work" (see Figure 10-5). An API key is a string of numbers and letters and functions like a unique password given to you by WordPress.com; it's the key that allows your WordPress.org application to communicate with your WordPress.com account.

2. **Click the link in the yellow box to obtain your WordPress.com API key.**

   Clicking this link takes you the WordPress.com Web site. If you have an account already, log in to it. If you don't have an account on WordPress. com, you need to create a WordPress.com account to get an API key. (See Chapter 3 to find out how to create your own WordPress.com account.) Although you have to create a WordPress.com account, you don't need to use it; you just need to get the API key.

Figure 10-5:
After you activate Akismet, WordPress tells you that the plugin isn't quite ready to use yet.

3. **Log in to your WordPress.com account, click the Personal Settings link in the Users menu.**

   Personal Settings page opens, and you find your WordPress.com API key at the top of that page, as shown in Figure 10-6. (I have blacked out my own API key because — shhhh — it's a secret, and I'm not supposed to share it!)

4. **When you have your API key, go to the Akismet Configuration page by clicking the Akismet Configuration link in the Plugins menu in your WordPress Dashboard.**

5. **Enter the API key in the WordPress.com API Key box, and click the Update Options button to fully activate the Akismet plugin.**

Akismet catches spam and throws it into a queue, holding the spam for 15 days and then deleting it from your database. It's probably worth your while to check the Akismet Spam page once a week to make sure that the plugin hasn't captured any legitimate comments or trackbacks.

You can rescue those nonspam captured comments and trackbacks by doing the following (after you've logged in to your WordPress Dashboard):

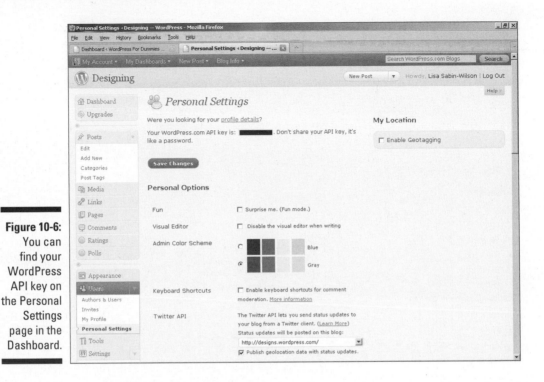

Figure 10-6:
You can
find your
WordPress
API key on
the Personal
Settings
page in the
Dashboard.

1. **Click the Comments menu.**

   The Edit Comments page appears, displaying a list of the most recent comments on your blog.

2. **Click the Spam link.**

   The Edit Comments page now displays all spam comments that the plugin caught.

3. **Browse through the list of spam comments, looking for any comments or trackbacks that are legitimate.**

4. **If you locate one that's legitimate, select the Approve link box directly below the entry.**

   The comment is marked as legitimate. In other words, you don't consider this comment to be spam. The comment is then approved and published on your blog.

Check your spam filter often. I just found four legitimate comments caught in my spam filter and was able to de-spam them, releasing them from the binds of Akismet and unleashing them upon the world.

The folks at Automattic did a fine thing with Akismet. Since the emergence of Akismet, I've barely had to think about comment or trackback spam, except for the few times a month I check my Akismet spam queue.

Hello Dolly

Matt Mullenweg, co-founder of WordPress, developed the Hello Dolly plugin. Anyone who follows the development of WordPress knows that he is a huge jazz fan. How do we know this? Every single release of WordPress is named after some jazz great. One of the most recent releases of the software, for example, is named Ella — after jazz great Ella Fitzgerald; another release was named Coltrane after the late American jazz saxophonist and composer, John Coltrane.

So, knowing this, it isn't surprising that Mullenweg developed a plugin named Hello Dolly. Here's the description of it that you see in the Plugin Management page in your Dashboard:

> This is not just a plugin, it symbolizes the hope and enthusiasm of an entire generation summed up in two words sung most famously by Louis Armstrong: Hello, Dolly. When activated, you will randomly see a lyric from Hello, Dolly in the upper right of your admin screen on every page.

> Is it necessary? No. Is it fun? Sure!

Activate the Hello Dolly plugin on the Manage Plugins page in your WordPress Dashboard. When you've activated it, your WordPress blog greets you with a different lyric from the song "Hello, Dolly!" each time.

If you want to change the lyrics in this plugin, you can edit them by clicking the Edit link to the right of the Hello Dolly plugin on the Manage Plugins page. The Plugin Editor opens and lets you edit the file in a text editor. Make sure that each line of the lyric has its own line in the plugin file.

Using Plugins: Just the Basics

In this section, I show you how to install a plugin in your WordPress blog, using the built-in plugins feature. The auto-installation of plugins from within your WordPress Dashboard only works for plugins that are included in the official WordPress Plugin Directory. You can manually install plugins on your WordPress blog, which I cover in the next section.

WordPress makes it super easy to find, install, and then activate plugins for use on your blog — just follow these simple steps:

1. **Click the Add New link in the Plugins menu.**

   The Install Plugins page opens where you can browse the official WordPress Plugins Directory from your WordPress Dashboard.

2. **Select a plugin to install on your blog:**

   • *Term*: If you want to search for plugins that allow you to add additional features for comments on your site, select Term in the drop-down menu and then enter the word **Comments** in the Search text box on the Install Plugins page. Click the Search button, and a list of plugins returns that deal specifically with comments.

   • *Author or Tag:* Select Author or Tag in the drop-down menu and then enter the author or tag name in the Search box and click the Search button.

You can also search by tag by clicking any of the tag names that appear at the bottom of the Install Plugins page under the Popular Tags heading.

I want to install a very popular plugin called Subscribe to Comments by Mark Jaquith (see the next section in this chapter for a description of this plugin). Enter the words **Subscribe to Comments** in the Search text box on the Install Plugins page.

Figure 10-7 shows the results page for the Subscribe to Comments, which is listed as the first plugin on the Search Results page.

3. **Click the Install link below the plugin name.**

   A Description window opens, giving you information about the Subscribe to Comments plugin, including a description of the plugin, version number, author name, and an Install Now button.

Figure 10-7: Finding a plugin to install using the built-in Plugin Directory search.

4. **Click the Install Now button.**

   You go to the Installing Plugins page within your WordPress Dashboard, where you find a confirmation message that the plugin has been downloaded, unpacked, and successfully installed.

5. **Specify whether to install the plugin or proceed to the Plugins page.**

   Two links are shown below the confirmation message:

   - *Activate Plugin:* Click this link to activate the plugin you just installed on your blog.

   - *Return to Plugin Installer:* Click this link to go to the Install Plugins page.

The auto-installation of plugins from your WordPress Dashboard works on most Web-hosting configurations. However, some Web hosting services don't allow the kind of access that WordPress needs to complete the auto-installation. If you get any errors, or find that you are unable to use the plugin auto-installation feature, I recommend getting in touch with your Web hosting provider to find out if it can assist you.

Installing Plugins Manually

In the following sections, I show you how to find, upload, and install the very popular Subscribe to Comments plugin, developed by Mark Jaquith. I'm using the Subscribe to Comments plugin as a real-world example to take you through the mechanics involved in downloading, unpacking, uploading, activating, and using a plugin in WordPress.

Subscribe to Comments gives your readers the opportunity to subscribe to individual comment threads on your site so that they receive a notification, via e-mail, when a new comment has been left on the comment thread (or blog post) that they have chosen to subscribe to. This plugin helps keep lively discussions active in your blog.

Installing the Subscribe to Comments plugin takes you through the process, but keep in mind that every plugin is different. Reading the description and installation instructions for each plugin you want to install is very important.

Finding and downloading the files

The first step in using plugins is locating the one you want to install. The absolute best place to find WordPress plugins is the official WordPress Plugins Directory found at `http://wordpress.org/extend/plugins` where, at the time of this writing, you will find almost 9,000 plugins available for download.

To find Mark Jaquith's Subscribe to Comments plugin, follow these steps:

1. **Go to the official WordPress Plugin Directory, located at** `http://wordpress.org/extend/plugins`.

   The home page opens; see Figure 10-8.

2. **In the search box at the top of the page, enter the keywords** Subscribe to Comments **and then click the Search Plugins button.**

3. **Locate the Subscribe to Comments plugin on the search results page, and click the plugin name.**

   The Subscribe to Comments page opens in the WordPress Plugin Directory, where you find a description of the plugin, as well as other information about the plugin (see Figure 10-9). For example, take note of the important information in the FYI box:

   • *Version:* The number shown in this area is the most recent version of the plugin.

   • *Other Versions:* This link takes you to a page that displays all the previous versions of the plugin. This is helpful if you have to revert to an older version of the plugin if the new version fails on your individual WordPress installation.

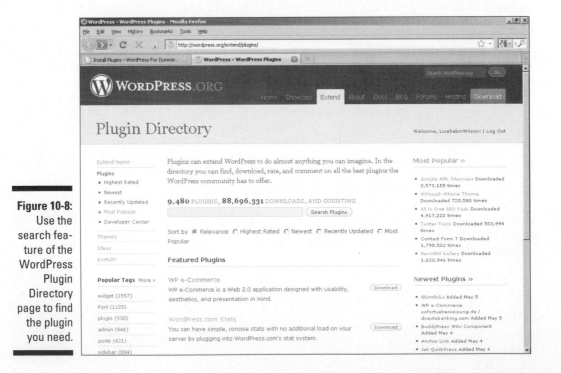

Figure 10-8:
Use the search feature of the WordPress Plugin Directory page to find the plugin you need.

- *Last Updated:* This displays the date that the plugin was last updated by the author.

- *Requires WordPress Version:* This tells you what version of WordPress you need to successfully use this plugin. For example, Figure 10-9 shows that the Subscribe to Comments plugin requires WordPress version 2.0.6 or higher; that means that this plugin doesn't work with versions lower than 2.0.6. Helpful!

- *Compatible Up To:* This tells you what version of WordPress this plugin is compatible up to. For example, if this section tells you the plugin is compatible up to version 2.3 — that means you can't use the plugin with versions higher than 2.3. I say usually because the plugin developer may not update the information in this section — especially if there have been no changes to the plugin files themselves. The best way to check is to download the plugin and install it and see if it works! (Figure 10-9 shows that Mark Jaquith's Subscribe to Comments plugin is compatible up to WordPress version 2.3.1 — however, I can verify that it does work in all versions up to the most recent, 2.6.1.)

- *Author Homepage:* This link takes you to the plugin author's main Web site.

- *Plugin Homepage:* This link takes you to the specific Web site for the plugin. Often, this is a page within the plugin author's Web site.

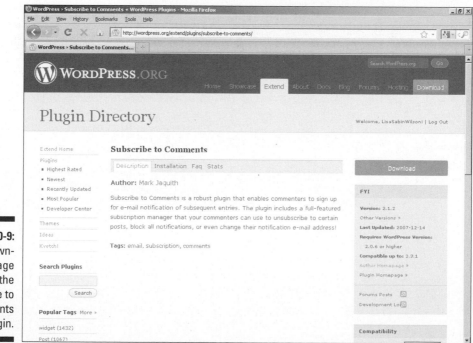

Figure 10-9: The download page for the Subscribe to Comments plugin.

4. **Click the Download button to download the files.**

   If you're using Internet Explorer, click the Download button, and a dialog box opens, asking whether you want to open or save the file. Click Save to save the zip file to your hard drive, and *remember where you saved it.*

   If you're using Mozilla Firefox, click the Download button, and a dialog box opens, asking what Firefox should do with the file. Select the Save File radio button and then click OK to save it to your hard drive. Again, *remember where you saved it.*

   For other browsers, follow the download instructions in the corresponding dialog box.

5. **Locate the file on your hard drive, and open it with your favorite decompression program.**

   If you're unsure how to use a decompression program, refer to the documentation available with the program.

6. **Unpack the plugin files you downloaded for the Subscribe to Comments plugin.**

Reading the instructions

Frequently, the plugin developer includes a `readme` file inside the zip file. Do what the title of the file says: Read it. Many times, it contains the exact documentation and instructions that you will find on the plugin developer's page.

Make sure that you read the instructions carefully and follow them correctly. Ninety-nine percent of WordPress plugins have great documentation and instructions from the plugin developer. If you don't follow the instructions correctly, at best, the plugin just won't work on your blog. At worst, the plugin creates all sorts of ugly errors, requiring you to start over from step one.

You can open `readme.txt` files in any text-editor program, such as Notepad or WordPad on a PC, or TextEdit on a Mac.

In the case of Mark Jaquith's Subscribe to Comments plugin, the `readme.txt` file contains instructions on how to upload and use the plugin, as well as some answers to frequently asked questions on troubleshooting the installation and use.

Every plugin is different in terms of where the plugin files are uploaded and in terms of the configurations and setup necessary to make the plugin work on your site. Read the installation instructions very carefully and follow those instructions to the letter to install the plugin correctly on your site.

Uploading and Activating Plugins

Now you're ready to upload the plugin files to your Web server. Connect to your Web server via FTP. Locate the plugin files you just unpacked on your hard drive. In the event that the plugin developer didn't include a `readme.txt` file with instructions, check the plugin developer's page for specific instructions on how to install the plugin in your WordPress blog. Specifically, the documentation in the `readme.txt` file and/or on the plugin's Web site should address the following points:

- ✔ What directory on your Web server you upload the plugin files to.

- ✔ What to do if you need to change permissions for any of the plugin files after you upload them to your Web server. (See Chapter 6 if you need information on changing file permissions.)

- ✔ What to do if you need to set specific configurations in the plugin file to make it work.

- ✔ What to do if you need to modify your theme template files to include the plugin's functions in your blog.

Uploading the files

Mark Jaquith left some nice instructions for you in the plugin zip file. Look for the `readme.txt` file inside the zip files you download from his site.

To install the Subscribe to Comments plugin, follow these easy steps:

1. **Double-click the** `subscribe-to-comments` **folder in the files you downloaded and unpacked on your computer.**

   A folder opens, containing two files: `subscribe-to-comments.php` and `readme.txt`. (You also see another folder called `extras`. This folder contains the plugin installation instructions in two additional formats: HTML [`readme.html`] and Microsoft PowerPoint [`subscribe-to-comments.pot`].)

   Figure 10-10 shows all the files and folders contained in the Subscribe to Comments plugin.

2. **Close the folder after you've determined that it contains all the necessary files.**

3. **Connect to your Web server via FTP, and open the** `/wp-content/plugins/` **folder.**

   This folder contains all the plugins that are currently installed in your WordPress blog.

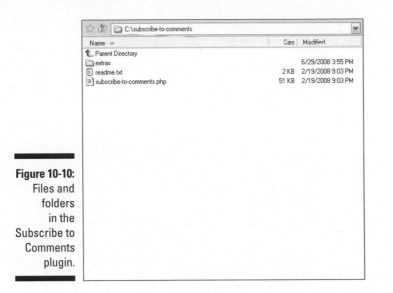

Figure 10-10:
Files and
folders
in the
Subscribe to
Comments
plugin.

4. **Upload the entire** `subscribe-to-comments` **folder into the** `/wp-content/plugins/` **folder on your Web server.**

   Figure 10-11 shows the plugin files and where they should be located on your Web server. *Note:* The plugins on my Web server may differ from the ones you've chosen to install on yours; however, you can see where I placed the `subscribe-to-comments` folder.

Figure 10-11:
Correct
location
for the
Subscribe to
Comments
plugin on
your Web
server.

Activating the plugin

When you have the plugin files uploaded to the correct location on your Web server, open your browser, and log in to your WordPress Dashboard. After you log in, head to the Manage Plugins page to activate the Subscribe to Comments plugin:

1. **Click the Installed link on the Plugins menu.**

   The Mange Plugins page opens, listing all the plugins installed in your WordPress blog.

2. **Locate the Subscribe to Comments plugin.**

   If you have a lot of plugins installed on your WordPress Web site, you can narrow down your search by clicking the Inactive link, which lists the currently inactive plugins.

3. **Click the Activate link below the plugin name.**

   The Manage Plugins page refreshes, and the Subscribe to Comments plugin is now displayed as an active plugin on the Manage Plugins page.

If you've followed all these steps in your own blog, congratulations — you now have Subscribe to Comments installed. Great job!

Setting Plugin Options

Some, but not all, WordPress plugins provide an administration page where you can set options that are specific to that particular plugin. You can find the plugin administration page in any of these places:

- The Settings page (click the Settings menu)
- The Tools menu (located in the navigation menu)
- The Plugins menu (located in the navigation menu)

You can find the Subscribe to Comments Options page by clicking the Subscribe to Comments link in the Settings menu. The Subscribe to Comments Options page opens (see Figure 10-12).

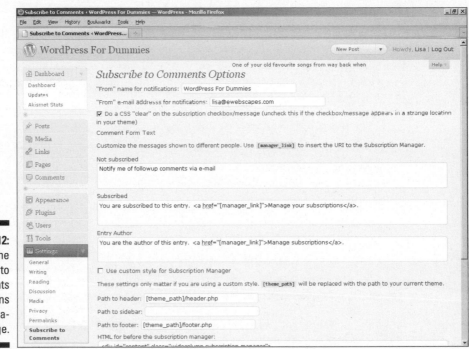

Figure 10-12:
The
Subscribe to
Comments
Options
administra-
tion page.

Uninstalling Plugins

After all this talk about installing and activating plugins, what happens if you install and activate a plugin, and then at some point decide that it just isn't what you want? Don't worry — you aren't stuck forever with a plugin that you don't want. WordPress lets you be fickle and finicky in your plugin choices!

To uninstall a plugin from your WordPress blog:

1. **Click the Installed link on the Plugins menu.**

   The Manage Plugins page opens.

2. **Locate the plugin you want to uninstall.**

3. **Click the Deactivate link below the plugin.**

   The Manage Plugins page refreshes, and the plugin now displays as deactivated (or inactive).

4. Select the plugin.

Place a checkmark in the box to the left of the plugin name.

5. Select Delete in the Bulk Actions drop down menu and then click the Apply button.

The Delete Plugin(s) page opens, and a confirmation message displays asking you if you're sure you want to delete this plugin. (See Figure 10-13.)

6. Click the Yes, Delete These Files button.

The Manage Plugins page refreshes, and the plugin you just deleted is gone from the lists of plugins.

Bang! You're done. That's all it takes.

Don't forget to remove any bits of code that you may have added to your theme templates for that particular plugin; otherwise, it may cause ugly error messages to display in your blog.

Figure 10-13:
Confirm-
ation
question on
the Delete
Plugin(s)
page.

Understanding the Open Source Environment

The WordPress software was built on an existing platform called b2. Matt Mullenweg, co-founder of WordPress, was using b2 as a blogging platform at the time the developer of that program abandoned it. What did this mean for its users? It meant no more development unless someone somewhere picked up the ball and continued with the platform. Enter Mullenweg and WordPress.

Apply this same concept to plugin development, and you'll understand that plugins sometimes fall by the wayside and drop off the face of the Earth. Unless someone takes over when the original developer loses interest, future development of that plugin ceases. It's important to understand that most plugins are developed in an open source environment, which means a few things for you, the end user:

✔ The developers who created your favorite plugin aren't obligated to continue development. If they find a new hobby or simply tire of the work, they can give it up completely. If no one picks up where they left off, you can kiss that plugin goodbye if it doesn't work with the latest WordPress release.

✔ Developers of popular plugins generally are extremely good about updating them when new versions of WordPress are released, or when a security bug or flaw is discovered. Keep in mind, however, that no timetable exists for these developers to hold to. Many of these folks have day jobs, classes, or families that can keep them from devoting as much time to the project as you want them to.

✔ Beware of the pitfalls of falling in love with any particular WordPress plugin, because in the world of plugin development, it's easy come, easy go. Try not to let your Web site become dependent on a plugin, and don't be surprised if a plugin you love doesn't exist tomorrow. You can use the plugin for as long as it continues to work for you, but when it stops working (such as with a new WordPress release or a security exploit that makes it unusable), you have a rough decision to make. You can

  • Stop using the plugin, and try to find a suitable alternative.

  • Hope that another developer takes over the project when the original developer discontinues his involvement.

  • Try to find someone to provide a fix for you (in which case, you'll more than likely have to pay that someone for her time).

I don't want to make the world of WordPress plugins sound like gloom and doom, but I do think it's very important for you to understand the dynamics in play. Consider this section food for thought.

Getting premium plugins

Not all plugins were created equally. In 2010, the WordPress community saw the emergence of premium, or paid, plugins. These plugins are slightly different from the plugins you find in the official WordPress Plugin Directory, mainly because they have a nominal fee associated with them. Most of the premiums plugins also provide great value and support. Here are two examples of premium plugin directories available today:

✔ **Plugin Buddy** (`http://pluginbuddy.com`): Run by WordPress experts and veterans from the team at iThemes (`http://ithemes.com`), Plugin Buddy is a repository of quality premium plugins like BackUp Buddy and Billboard.

✔ **WPPlugins** (`http://wpplugins.com`): This app store has several premium plugins to use on your WordPress Web site. Visit and browse through its selection to see what WPPlugins has in store for you.

Chapter 11

Finding and Installing WordPress Themes

In This Chapter

▶ Distinguishing between safe and unsafe WordPress themes

▶ Finding free WordPress themes

▶ Downloading, installing, and activating themes

▶ Browsing and installing themes from your Dashboard

In previous chapters, I cover how to use the WordPress platform to publish your posts and pages. In those chapters, you discover how to categorize your posts, build your link lists, and set the publishing and profile options in the WordPress Dashboard. In this chapter, I focus on the visual look and format of your blog — in other words, how other people see your blog after you start publishing your content.

In Chapter 10, I introduce WordPress plugins and discuss some of the thousands of free plugins you can use to add functionality to your blog. Similarly, thousands of free themes are available for you to download and use. This chapter shows you where to find them and takes you through the processes of downloading, installing, and using them.

Getting Started with Free Themes

WordPress comes packaged with one very useful default theme called Twenty Ten (named after the year it was first released in version 3.0 of WordPress). Most bloggers who use WordPress usually don't waste any time at all in finding a theme that they like better than the default WordPress theme. The Twenty Ten theme is meant to get you started. While you're not limited to the default theme, it's a very functional theme for a basic blog. Feel free to use it to get you started on your way.

Are all WordPress themes free?

Not all WordPress themes are created equal, and it's important for you, the user, to know the difference between free and premium themes:

✓ **Free:** These themes are free, period. You can download and use them on your Web site at absolutely no cost. It's a courtesy to include a link to the designer in the footer of your blog — but you can even remove that link if you want to.

✓ **Premium:** These themes cost money. You usually find premium themes available for download only after you've paid anywhere from $10 to $500. The designer feels that these themes are a cut above the rest and, therefore, are worth the money you spend for them. Generally, you're not allowed to remove any designer-credit links that appear in these themes, and you're not allowed to redistribute the themes. (***Note:*** You *won't* find premium themes in the official WordPress Theme Directory.) I provide information on where to find premium themes at the end of this chapter.

Free WordPress themes, such as those I discuss in Chapter 18, are popular because of their appealing designs and their ease of installation and use. They're great tools to use when you launch your new blog, and if you dabble a bit in graphic design and CSS (Cascading Style Sheets), you can customize one of the free WordPress themes to fit your own needs. (See Chapter 13 for some resources and tools for templates and template tags, as well as a few great CSS references.) Also see the nearby sidebar "Are all WordPress themes free?" for information about free versus premium themes.

By using free themes, you can have your blog up and running with a new design — without the help of a professional — pretty fast. And with thousands of themes available, you can change your theme as often as you want. Chapter 15 presents information on hiring blog professionals, if you decide later that you want a more customized theme for your blog.

Finding free themes

Finding the theme that fits you best may take some time, but with thousands available, you'll eventually find one that suits you. Trying out several free themes is like trying on different "outfits" for your blog. You can change outfits as needed until you find just the right theme.

In July 2008, WordPress launched the official WordPress Free Themes Directory at `http://wordpress.org/extend/themes` (see Figure 11-1).

The WordPress Theme Directory isn't the only place on the Web to find free WordPress themes, but it's the place to find the most functional and *safe* themes available. Safe themes contain clean code and basic WordPress functions that are considered fundamental requirements in a theme to ensure that your WordPress blog functions with the minimum requirements. The WordPress.org Web site lists the basic requirements that theme designers have to meet before their theme is accepted into the themes directory; you can find that listing of requirements at `http://wordpress.org/extend/themes/about`.

Unsafe themes, on the other hand, are developed by people who are looking to take advantage of the blog owners who use them. These particular themes are not allowed in the official WordPress Free Themes Directory. They contain elements such as the following:

✔ **Spam links:** These links usually appear in the footer of the theme and can link to some pretty unsavory places. The designers of these themes hope to benefit from traffic from your site. They count on the idea that most blog owners won't notice the links or know how to remove them.

✔ **Malicious code:** Unscrupulous theme designers can, and do, place code in theme files that inserts hidden malware and/or virus links and spam. Sometimes, you see a line or two of encrypted code that looks like it's just part of the theme code, and unless you have a great deal of knowledge of PHP, you may not know that the theme is infected with dangerous code.

The results of these unsafe theme elements can range from simply annoying to downright dangerous, affecting the integrity and security of your computer and/or hosting account. For this reason, the official WordPress Theme Directory is considered to be a safe place from which to download free themes. WordPress designers develop these themes and upload them to the theme directory, and each theme gets vetted by the folks behind the WordPress platform. In the official directory, themes that contain unsafe elements are simply not allowed to play.

My strong recommendation for finding free themes is to stick with the official WordPress Theme Directory. That way, you know you're getting a clean, quality theme for your blog. You can rest assured that themes from the official directory are safe, and free of spam and malicious code.

Previewing themes

While you're visiting the WordPress Theme Directory, you can easily browse the various themes by using the following features:

✔ **Search:** Type a keyword in the Search box at the top of the page (refer to Figure 11-1) and then click the Search Themes button. A new page opens, displaying themes related to the keyword you searched for.

✔ **Featured Themes:** These themes are listed in the center of the themes directory, randomly. WordPress changes the featured themes listing regularly.

✔ **Most Popular:** These themes have been downloaded most often.

✔ **Newest Themes:** These themes are the latest to be added to the directory.

✔ **Recently Updated:** These themes have been updated most recently by their designers.

When you find a theme in the directory that you want to take a closer look at, click its name to open a page that describes that theme (see Figure 11-2):

✔ **Download:** Click this button to download the theme to your computer.

✔ **Preview:** Click this button to open a new window that shows what the theme looks like in a live blog.

Figure 11-2:
Download
or preview
a particu-
lar theme
from the
WordPress
Free
Themes
Directory.

Downloading themes

To download the theme you want, follow these steps:

1. **Click the Download button on the theme page (refer to Figure 11-2).**

   The theme files are compressed in a .zip file.

2. **Use your favorite decompression program to unpack the files to your own computer.**

3. **Connect to your Web server via FTP, and upload the entire theme folder to the** /wp-content/themes/ **directory of your Web server.**

   The left side of Figure 11-3 shows that I saved the Hybrid theme files on my computer. The right side of Figure 11-3 shows that I uploaded the Hybrid theme folder to the /wp-content/themes/ directory of my Web server (read more about the Hybrid theme by Justin Tadlock in Chapter 16).

Figure 11-3:
The direc-
tory for your
theme files,
shown in
an FTP
window.

Activating a New Theme

When you have the theme uploaded to your Web server, you can activate it by logging in to your WordPress Dashboard and following these simple steps:

1. **Click the Appearance menu.**

   The Manage Themes page opens, listing all the themes currently installed in your `themes` directory. The active theme is shown in the Current Theme section at the top of the page. All available themes you may have uploaded to your Web server are shown in the Available Themes section (see Figure 11-4).

   Available themes appear on the Manage Themes page in alphabetical order. If you have a lot of themes in your `themes` directory, they're displayed ten on a page, with Next and Previous links to help you navigate all the themes available for your blog.

2. **Click the name or thumbnail image of the theme you want to use.**

   A preview window opens, showing you what your blog will look like with this new theme applied (see Figure 11-5).

   Click the X in the top-left corner of the preview window to close the theme without activating it.

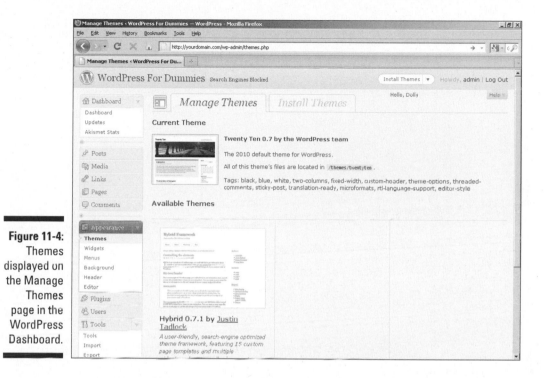

Figure 11-4:
Themes
displayed on
the Manage
Themes
page in the
WordPress
Dashboard.

3. **Click the Activate Theme link.**

   This link, located in the top-right corner of the preview window, is labeled with the theme name. Figure 11-5 shows an Activate Hybrid link, because that's the name of the theme I want to use.

   WordPress applies the theme you chose to your blog.

Using sidebar widgets

Most free WordPress themes come with built-in code that lets you take advantage of sidebar widgets for your blog. WordPress widgets are wonderful! (Say *that* ten times fast, why don't you?) Widgets are so wonderful because they let you arrange the display of content in your blog sidebar, such as your blogroll(s), recent posts, and monthly and category archive listings. With widgets, you can accomplish this arranging without needing to know a single bit of code.

In Chapter 5, I cover how to use sidebar widgets. Although that chapter pertains to the hosted WordPress.com platform, WordPress.org users can follow the same steps. One difference for WordPress.org users is the use of plugins (see Chapter 10). Some plugins have a built-in feature that enables you to include that plugin's functions in your sidebar through the use of a widget. (WordPress.com doesn't have this feature because it doesn't allow uploading and activating various plugins.)

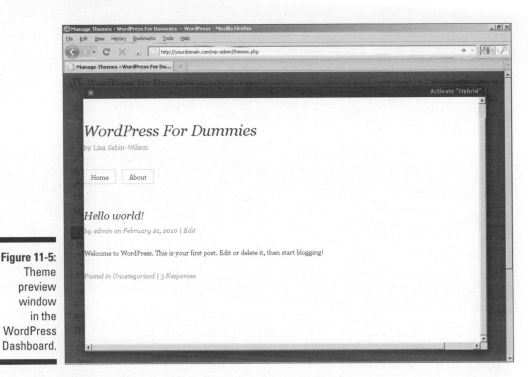

Figure 11-5:
Theme
preview
window
in the
WordPress
Dashboard.

Browsing and Installing Themes from the Dashboard

Earlier in this chapter, I covered how to find and install a new theme on your WordPress blog by downloading them from the WordPress Free Themes Directory, uploading them to your Web server via FTP and activating the theme within your WordPress Dashboard. The WordPress platform does give you a much easier way to browse the Free Themes Directory to find, preview, and install themes on your site without ever leaving the comfort of the WordPress Dashboard. The following steps show you how to do it:

1. **Click the Themes link in the Appearances menu in your WordPress Dashboard.**

   The Install Themes page opens, where you can find a new theme by browsing the Free WordPress Themes Directory directly from your WordPress Dashboard.

2. **Click the Install Themes tab at the top of the Manage Themes page.**

   This opens the Install Themes page.

3. **Search for a new theme.**

   On the Install Themes page you can search for a new theme by keyword, author, or tag. You can also further filter the results by using the Feature Filter check boxes that allow you to filter theme results by color, columns, width, features, and subjects. The Install Themes page is shown in Figure 11-6.

4. **Preview a new theme.**

   After searching for a new theme, the search results page displays a list of themes for you to choose from. Click the Preview link underneath the theme of your choice to view a sample of how the theme looks. Figure 11-7 shows a preview of a theme called Blossom, which I found by searching for the keyword *Pink* on the Install Themes page.

5. **Install a new theme on your blog.**

   After you've found a theme you like, click the Install link underneath the theme name to install the theme on your blog. This pops open a new window with a button labeled Install New — click that button to complete the installation.

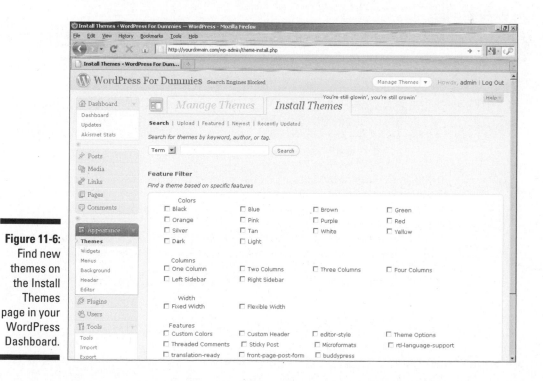

Figure 11-6: Find new themes on the Install Themes page in your WordPress Dashboard.

6. **Activate the new theme.**

    After you click the Install New button, the pop-up window closes, and the Installing theme page appears in your WordPress Dashboard. Click the Activate link shown on the Installing Theme page to activate and display the new theme on your site.

At the beginning of this chapter, I mentioned that the only themes found in the official WordPress Free Themes Directory are free and have been vetted by the WordPress folks, so are sure to be free of any virus or malicious code. The same holds true for the themes you find by using the Add New Themes feature in your WordPress Dashboard. This feature hooks into the official WordPress Free Themes directory, so you are sure to find only those themes that are free and safe.

Deciding to Use Premium Themes

As WordPress becomes more and more popular, I've seen many different business models crop up around the Web that focus on providing WordPress users with premium services and support, such as custom design, consulting, and development, for example. (See Chapter 15 for information on hiring professional services for your blog.)

Premium WordPress themes have become a very popular way for talented designers to provide a service they are very passionate about (designing themes) while making a little money for their efforts, at the same time. There are many schools of thought as to what makes a theme *premium* as opposed to a free theme. Actually, the topic of what is considered premium and what is not, in regards to WordPress themes, is guaranteed to spark passionate debate among designers and theme users, alike. Almost everyone agrees there are indicators of premium themes, however:

✔ Very high-quality graphic design and CSS development.

✔ A theme structure with functions that make it very easy for the user to customize and adjust the theme to suit their own needs. This includes, but is not limited to, altering the header graphic/logo and color scheme and changing images and icons.

✔ Comprehensive documentation, providing the user with extensive instructions on how to use the theme, especially if the theme has multiple features and customization options.

✔ Premium themes are fully supported by the designer who created them. Typically, when you buy a premium theme, you should expect full support on the use of that theme for as long as you're using it.

✔ Premium themes are not free. I've seen pricing on premium themes in the range of $10 to $500.

This is not to say that some free themes don't have some, or all, the features I just listed — it's just that, for the most part, they don't. Keep in mind that just because a designer calls a theme premium doesn't mean that the theme has passed through any kind of official quality review. One designer's view of what constitutes a premium theme can, and will, differ from the next.

Fully investigate any theme before you put money down on it. Some things to check out before you pay:

✔ E-mail the designer who is selling the premium theme and ask about a support policy.

✔ Find people who have purchased the theme and contact them to find out their experiences with the theme and the designer.

✔ Carefully read any terms that the designer has published on his site to find out any restrictions that exist with licensing.

✔ If the premium theme designer has a support forum, ask whether you can browse through the forum to find out how actively the designer answers questions and provides support. Are users waiting weeks to get their questions answered? Or does the designer seem to be on top of support requests?

✔ Do a search in Google for the theme and the designer. Often, users of premium themes post about their experiences with the theme and the designer. You can find out a lot of positive, and potentially, negative information about the theme and the designer before you buy it.

While premium themes are cropping up all over the Web, a handful really stand out with quality products and services. The following three premium themes are tried and true, with a very stable and successful following of clients who use them.

✔ **iThemes:** Cory Miller and his team of designers and code wranglers provide a total of 30 premium themes available for purchase, with prices ranging from $79.95 to $199.95 each. You can also purchase an all-in-one package that includes all themes for $499.95. All theme purchases at iThemes include full support on the use of the theme(s) for the lifetime of your membership at iThemes. The iThemes premium themes can be found at `http://ithemes.com`.

✔ **StudioPress:** Created by long-time WordPress user, expert and veteran, Brian Gardner, StudioPress offers a variety of high-quality premium WordPress themes that you are able to purchase with a starting price of $59.95 — you may also purchase an all-inclusive themes package starting at $249.95. Theme purchases at StudioPress include a complete support package with access to a support forum staffed by people who are ready to assist you with your most burning questions. You can find StudioPress, and browse through its premium theme offerings at `http://studiopress.com`.

✔ **Theme Garden:** Jason Schuller is the creative genius behind the Theme Garden and is a nicely inexpensive option for those looking for quality, premium WordPress themes. You can purchase a subscription starting at $50 for three months. Annual theme subscriptions cost $100–$275. Theme subscriptions provide you with access to any theme on Theme Garden, as well as access to newly released themes for the duration membership. Find the Theme Garden at `http://themegarden.com`.

You can't find, preview, or install Premium Themes using the Add New Themes feature on your WordPress Dashboard (covered in the previous section of this chapter). You can only find, purchase, and download Premium themes at an official third-party Web site. Once you find a premium theme you like, you need to install it via the FTP method I cover in the "Downloading themes" section in this chapter. You can find a very nice selection of premium themes on the WordPress Web site: `http://wordpress.org/extend/themes/commercial`.

Part V
Customizing WordPress

The 5th Wave   By Rich Tennant

DENISE AND JERRY LEVIN — AUTHORS OF "LOST IN THE MALL PARKING LOT," "THE MISPLACED GALLERY INVITATION," AND, "THE BAD HAIRCUT — WHY ME?"

Truthfully? If it weren't for WordPress, many of our adventures would have remained untold.

In this part . . .

This part of the book is about digging into WordPress themes and templates, discovering how to tweak template code so you can change the appearance of your blog. A walk-through on essential WordPress template tags and functions, basic HTML, and CSS helps you put together a nice theme to suit your individual style and flair. This part also touches on the use of WordPress as a full-blown content management system (CMS), as well as how you can use WordPress to run a network that includes multiple sites on one single installation.

Chapter 12

Understanding Themes and Templates

In This Chapter

▶ Looking at the basic blog structure

▶ Exploring the required templates

▶ Understanding The Loop and Main Index template

▶ Putting together a basic theme

▶ Using common template tags

*T*here are those who like to get their hands dirty (present company included!). If you're one of them, you need to read this chapter. WordPress users who create their own themes do so in the interest of:

▶ **Individuality:** Having a theme that no one else has. (If you use one of the free themes, you can pretty much count on the fact that at *least* a dozen other WordPress blogs will have the same look as yours.)

▶ **Creativity:** Displaying your own personal flair and style.

▶ **Control:** Having full control of how the blog looks, acts, and delivers your content.

Many of you aren't at all interested in creating your own templates for your WordPress blog, however. Sometimes, it's just easier to leave matters to the professionals and to hire an experienced WordPress theme developer to create a custom look for your WordPress Web site or to use one of the thousands of free themes provided by WordPress designers (see Chapter 11). Chapter 18 also tells you where you can get ten free WordPress themes.

Creating themes does require you to step into the code of the templates, which can be a scary place sometimes — especially if you don't really know what you're looking at. A good place to start is understanding the structure of a WordPress blog. Separately, the parts won't do you any good. But when you put them together, the real magic begins! This chapter covers the basics of doing just that, and near the end of the chapter, you find specific steps to put your own theme together.

You don't need to know HTML to use WordPress. If you plan to create and design WordPress themes, however, you need some basic knowledge of HTML and Cascading Style Sheets (CSS). For assistance with HTML, check out *HTML 4 For Dummies,* 5th Edition, by Ed Tittel and Mary Burmeister, or *HTML, XML, and CSS Bible,* 3rd Edition, by Bryan Pfaffenberger, Steven M. Schafer, Chuck White, and Bill Karow (both published by Wiley).

Using WordPress Themes: The Basics

A WordPress theme is a collection of WordPress templates made up of WordPress template tags. When I refer to a WordPress *theme,* I'm talking about the group of templates that makes up the theme. When I talk about a WordPress *template,* I'm referring to only one of the template files that contain WordPress template tags. WordPress template tags make all the templates work together as a theme (more about this topic later in the chapter).

Understanding theme structure

The rest of this chapter provides important information about the steps to take when building a WordPress theme, but here is a brief overview of the templates that make up a WordPress theme and where you find them, both on your server and within your WordPress Dashboard. Follow these steps:

1. **Connect to your Web server via FTP, and have a look at the existing WordPress themes on your server.**

   The correct location is /wp-content/themes/ (see Figure 12-1). When you open this folder, you find the /twentyten theme folder.

   If a theme is uploaded to any folder other than /wp-content/themes, it won't work.

2. **Open the folder for the Twenty Ten theme (/wp-content/themes/twentyten), and look at the template files inside.**

   When you open the Twenty Ten theme folder, you see several files. At minimum, you find these five templates in the default theme:

   - *Stylesheet* (style.css)
   - *Header template* (header.php)
   - *Main Index* (index.php)

- *Sidebar template* (`sidebar.php`)

- *Footer template* (`footer.php`)

Figure 12-1:
WordPress
themes in
the `/wp-`
`content/`
`themes`
folder on
your Web
server.

These files are the main WordPress template files, and I discuss them in more detail in this chapter. There are several template files, however, and you should try to explore all if you can. Take a peek inside and see the different template functions they contain. These filenames are the same in every WordPress theme. See the "Contemplating the Structure of a WordPress Blog" section, later in this chapter, for more information about these template files.

3. **Click the Editor link on the Appearance menu to look at the template files within a theme.**

   This page lists the various templates available within the active theme. (Figure 12-2 shows the templates in the default Twenty Ten theme.) A text box on the left side of the screen displays the contents of each template, and this box is also where you can edit the template file(s). To view and edit a template file, click the template name in the list on the right side of the page.

The Edit Themes page also shows the template tags within the template file. These tags make all the magic happen in your blog; they connect all the templates to form a theme. The next section of this chapter discusses these

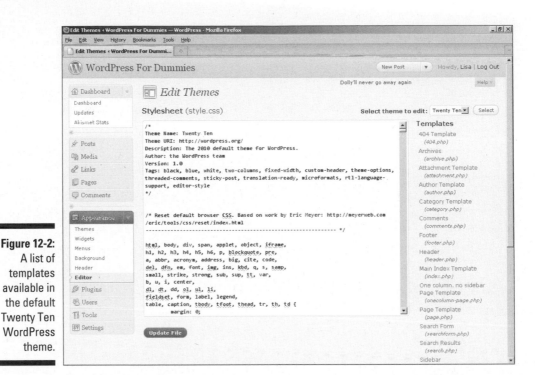

Figure 12-2:
A list of
templates
available in
the default
Twenty Ten
WordPress
theme.

template tags in detail, showing you what they mean and how they function.
A later section provides steps for putting them all together to create your
own theme (or edit an existing theme).

Below the text box on the Edit Themes page is a drop-down menu labeled
Documentation. Click the arrow on the right side of the menu, and a list drops
down that contains all of the template tags used in the template you are currently viewing. This list is helpful when you edit templates, and it gives you
some insight into some of the different template tags used to create functions
and features within your WordPress theme.

Connecting templates

The template files don't work alone; for the theme to function, the files need
one another. To tie these files together as one working entity, you use template tags to pull the information from each template — Header, Sidebar, and
Footer — into the Main Index. I refer to this procedure as *calling* one template
into another. (You can find more information in the "Getting Familiar with the
Four Main Templates," section, later in this chapter.)

Contemplating the Structure of a WordPress Blog

A WordPress blog, in its very basic form, has four main areas (labeled in Figure 12-3).

These four main areas appear in the default theme that comes in every version of WordPress:

- ✔ **Header:** This area usually contains the name of the site along with the site tagline or slogan. Sometimes, the header also contains a graphic or image.
- ✔ **Body:** This area is where your blog posts appear in chronological order.
- ✔ **Sidebar:** This area is where you find lists of blog-related elements, such as the blogroll, the archives, and a list of recent posts.

Header

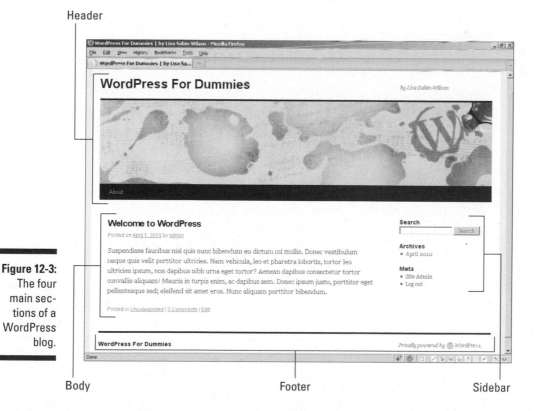

Figure 12-3:
The four main sections of a WordPress blog.

Body   Footer   Sidebar

✔ **Footer:** This area, at the bottom of the page, often contains links to further information about the blog, such as who designed it, which company provides hosting for the blog, and copyright information.

These four areas are the absolute bare bones of a *basic* WordPress blog template. You can extend these areas and create new sections that carry more information, of course, but for the purpose of this chapter, I'm focusing on the basics.

The default WordPress theme is called Twenty Ten, and in my opinion, it's a pretty doggone wonderful starting point for you, especially if you're just getting your feet wet in the blogosphere. I don't cover all the tags and templates that the Twenty Ten theme includes; rather, I touch on the basics to get you on your way to understanding templates and template tags for WordPress.

Many themes developed for WordPress are free for public use; I strongly recommend finding one that you like and downloading it. Use the free themes as a jumping-off place to get started in theme development. Really, why reinvent the wheel? With the free themes available today, most of the work has already been completed for you, and you may find it easier to use one of these themes than to start a theme from scratch.

Each free theme that is available for download is different, depending on what the developer included (such as CSS styling, display options, format, and layout). So experimenting with a few themes is fun and is a great way to learn more about the development of WordPress themes. A great place to find free WordPress themes is the official WordPress Theme Directory at `http://wordpress.org/extend/themes`.

To build a *basic* WordPress theme that covers the four basic areas of a blog, you need these five templates:

✔ `header.php`

✔ `index.php`

✔ `sidebar.php`

✔ `footer.php`

✔ `style.css`

Each WordPress theme comes with a stylesheet (`style.css`), which drives the formatting and layout of your blog template in terms of where the elements are positioned on the page, what the font looks like, what colors your hyperlinks will be, and so on. As you may have already figured out, you don't use CSS to put content on your site; rather, you use CSS to style the content that's already there.

Chapter 13 provides information on tweaking the design of your theme by combining the template tags presented in this chapter with some CSS adjustments in your theme files.

Right now, I'm covering only the basics; at the end of this chapter, however, I provide some ideas on how you can use various templates to further extend your blog functionality — using templates for categories, archives, static pages, multiple sidebars, and so on. After you build the basics, you can spread your wings and step into more advanced themes.

Examining the Anatomy of a Template Tag

Before starting to play around with template tags in your WordPress templates, it's important to understand what makes up a template tag and why.

WordPress is based in PHP (a scripting language for creating Web pages) and uses PHP commands to pull information from the MySQL database. Every tag begins with the function to start PHP and ends with a function to stop PHP. In the middle of those two commands lives the request to the database that tells WordPress to grab the data and display it.

A typical template tag looks like this:

```
<?php get_info(); ?>
```

This entire example tells WordPress to do three things:

- Start PHP (<?php).
- Use PHP to get information from the MySQL database and deliver it to your blog (get_info();).
- Stop PHP (?>).

In this case, get_info is the actual tag function, which grabs information from the database to deliver it to your blog. What information is retrieved depends on what tag function appears between the two PHP commands. As you may notice, there's a lot of starting and stopping of PHP throughout the WordPress templates. The process seems as though it would be resource intensive, if not exhaustive — but it really isn't.

For every PHP command you start, you need a stop command. Every time a command begins with <?php, somewhere later in the code is the closing ?> command. PHP commands that aren't structured properly cause really ugly errors on your site, and they've been known to send programmers, developers, and hosting providers into loud screaming fits.

Getting Familiar with the Four Main Templates

In the following sections, I cover some of the template tags that pull in the information you want to include in your blog. To keep this chapter shorter than 1,000 pages, I focus on the four main templates that get you going with creating your own theme or with editing the template tags in the theme you're currently using. Here are those four main templates:

- ✔ Header
- ✔ Main Index
- ✔ Sidebar
- ✔ Footer

The Header template

The Header template for your WordPress themes is the starting point for every WordPress theme, because it tells Web browsers the following:

- ✔ The title of your blog
- ✔ The location of the CSS
- ✔ The RSS feed URL
- ✔ The blog URL
- ✔ The tagline (or description) of the blog

Every page on the Web has to start with a few pieces of code. In every `header.php` file in any WordPress theme, you'll find these bits of code at the top:

- ✔ The `DOCTYPE` (which stands for *document type declaration*) tells the browser which type of XHTML standards you're using. The Twenty Ten theme uses `<!DOCTYPE html>`, which is a declaration for W3C standards compliance mode and covers all major browser systems.
- ✔ The `<html>` tag (*HTML* stands for *Hypertext Markup Language*) tells the browser which language you're using to write your Web pages.
- ✔ The `<head>` tag tells the browser that the information contained within the tag shouldn't be displayed on the site; rather, it's information about the document.

In the header template of the Twenty Ten, these bits of code look like the following example, and you should leave them intact:

```
<!DOCTYPE html>
<html <?php language_attributes(); ?>>
<head>
```

On the Edit Themes page, click the Header template link to display the template code in the text box. Look closely, and you see that the `<!DOCTYPE html>` declaration, `<html>` tag, and `<head>` tag show up in the template.

The `<head>` tag needs to be closed at the end of the Header template, which looks like this: `</head>`. You also need to include a fourth tag, the `<body>` tag, which tells the browser where the information you want to display begins. Both the `<body>` and `<html>` tags need to be closed at the end of the template, like this: `</body></html>`.

Using bloginfo parameters

The Header template makes much use of one WordPress template tag in particular: `bloginfo();`.

What differentiates the type of information that a tag pulls in is a *parameter*. Parameters are placed inside the parentheses of the tag, enclosed in single quotes. For the most part, these parameters pull information from the settings in your WordPress Dashboard. The template tag to get your blog title, for example, looks like this:

```
<?php bloginfo('name'); ?>
```

Table 12-1 lists the various parameters you need for the `bloginfo();` tag and shows you what the template tag looks like. The parameters in Table 12-1 are listed in the order of their appearance in the Twenty Ten `header.php` template file, and pertain to the `bloginfo();` template tag only.

Table 12-1	Tag Values for bloginfo(); in the Default Twenty Ten Template Header	
Parameter	**Information**	**Tag**
charset	Character settings set in Settings/General	`<?php bloginfo ('charset'); ?>`
name	Blog title, set in Settings/General	`<?php bloginfo ('name'); ?>`
description	Tagline for your blog, set in Settings/General	`<?php bloginfo ('description'); ?>`

(continued)

Table 12-1 *(continued)*

Parameter	Information	Tag
url	Your blog's Web address, set in Settings/General	`<?php bloginfo ('url'); ?>`
stylesheet_url	URL of primary CSS file	`<?php bloginfo ('stylesheet url'); ?>`
pingback_url	Displays the track-back URL for your blog on single post pages	`<?php bloginfo ('pingback_url'); ?>`

Creating title tags

Here's a useful tip about your blog's `<title>` tag: Search engines pick up the words used in the `<title>` tag as keywords to categorize your site in their search engine directories.

The `<title></title>` tags are HTML tags that tell the browser to display the title of your Web site in the title bar of a visitor's browser. Figure 12-4 shows how the title of my personal blog sits in the title bar of the browser window. (The *title bar* is the top bar in your browser. In Figure 12-4, it says Lisa Sabin-Wilson — Designer, Author: WordPress For Dummies.)

Search engines love the title bar. The more you can tweak that title to provide detailed descriptions of your site (otherwise known as search engine optimization or SEO), the more the search engines will love your Blog site. Browsers will show that love by giving your site higher rankings in their results. For more information and tips on SEO with WordPress, see Chapter 14.

The blog `<title>` tag is the code that lives in the Header template between these two tag markers: `<title></title>`. In the default Twenty Ten theme, this bit of code looks like this (don't let this code scare you! I promise I'll break it down for you!):

```
<title><?php
// Returns the title based on the type of page being
        viewed
if ( is_single() ) { single_post_title(); echo ' | ';
        bloginfo( 'name' );
```

```
} elseif ( is_home() || is_front_page() ) {bloginfo(
        'name' ); echo ' | '; bloginfo( 'description'
        ); twentyten_the_page_number();


} elseif ( is_page() ) {single_post_title( '' ); echo ' |
        '; bloginfo( 'name' );

} elseif ( is_search() ) {printf( __( 'Search results
        for "%s"', 'twentyten' ), esc_html( $s )
        ); twentyten_the_page_number(); echo ' | ';
        bloginfo( 'name' );

} elseif ( is_404() ) {    _e( 'Not Found', 'twentyten' );
        echo ' | '; bloginfo( 'name' );

} else {wp_title( '' ); echo ' | '; bloginfo( 'name' );
        twentyten_the_page_number();
}
?></title>
```

The title bar displays your site name.

Figure 12-4:
The title
bar of a
browser.

It may help for me to put this example into plain English. The way the Twenty Ten Header template displays the title is based on the type of page that is being displayed — and it shrewdly uses SEO to help you with the browser powers that be. Table 12-2 breaks down what's happening.

Table 12-2	Title Tags and What They Do	
Title Tags and Parameters	*Tags Used*	*What Is Displayed in the Title Bar*

`if ( is_single() ) { single_post_ title(); echo ' │ '; bloginfo ( 'name' ); }`	`is_single();`
	
	`single_post_ title();`
	
	`bloginfo('name');`
		If the reader is viewing a single post, the post title and blog name are displayed.

`elseif ( is_home() || is_front_page() ) {bloginfo( 'name' ); echo ' │ '; bloginfo ( 'description' ); twentyten_the_ page_number();}`	`is_home();`
	
	`is_front_page();`
	
	`bloginfo('name')`
	
	`bloginfo ('description');`
	
	`twentyten_the_ page_number();`
		If the reader is viewing the home page or the front page, the blog name and description are displayed. Also displays the page number if the reader is visiting a page.

`elseif ( is_page() ) {single_post_ title( '' ); echo ' │ '; bloginfo ( 'name' ); }`	`is_page();`
	
	`single_post_ title();`
	
	`bloginfo('name');`
		If the reader is viewing a page, the post title and the blog name are displayed.

`elseif ( is_ search() ) {printf( __( 'Search results for "%s"', 'twentyten' ), esc_html( $s ) ); twentyten_the_ page_number(); echo ' │ '; bloginfo ( 'name' ); }`	`is_search();`
	
	`twentyten_the_ page_number();`
	
	`bloginfo('name');`
		If the reader is viewing the search results page, the words 'Search results for', are displayed, as well as the search phrase and the name of the blog. It also displays the page number of the page the reader is viewing.

Title Tags and Parameters	Tags Used	What Is Displayed in the Title Bar
`elseif ( is_404()` `) {` `_e( 'Not Found',` `'twentyten' );` `echo '	';` `bloginfo('name');`	`is_404();` `bloginfo('name');`	If the page is not found and a 404 error page is visible, the words "Not Found" followed by the blog name are displayed.
`} else {wp_title(` `''); echo '	';` `bloginfo('name'` `); twentyten_the_` `page_number(); }`	`wp_title();` `bloginfo('name');` `twentyten_the_` `page_number();`	If the reader is viewing any other page within the site other than what has already been defined in the previous tags, the title of the page, followed by the blog name, are displayed. Also displays the page number.

The title bar of the browser window always displays your blog name unless you're on a single post page. In that case, it displays your blog title plus the title of the post on that page.

Within some of the WordPress template tags, such as the `<title>` tag in the earlier example, you may notice some weird characters that look like a foreign language. You may wonder what `&raquo;` is, for example. It isn't part of any PHP function or CSS style. Rather, it's a *character entity* — a kind of code that enables you to display a special character in your blog. The `&raquo;` character entity displays a double right-angle quotation mark. See Table 12-2 for examples of common character entities.

Displaying your blog name and tagline

The default Twenty Ten theme header displays your blog name and tagline. My blog name and tagline are

- **Blog name:** WordPress For Dummies
- **Blog tagline:** by Lisa Sabin-Wilson

Refer to Figure 12-4 to see these two elements in the header of the site.

You can use the `bloginfo();` tag plus a little HTML code to display your blog name and tagline. Most blogs have a clickable title, which is a site title that takes you back to the main page when it's clicked. No matter where your visitors are on your site, they can always go back home by clicking the title of your site in the header.

To create a clickable title, use the following code:

```
<a href="<?php bloginfo('url'); ?>"><?php
          bloginfo('name'); ?></a>
```

The `bloginfo('url');` tag is your main blog Internet address, and the `bloginfo('name');` tag is the name of your blog (refer to Table 12-1). So the code creates a link that looks something like this:

```
<a href="http://yourdomain.com">Your Blog Name</a>
```

The tagline generally isn't linked back home. You can display it by using the following tag:

```
<?php bloginfo('description'); ?>
```

This tag pulls the tagline directly from the one that you've set up on the General Settings page in your WordPress Dashboard.

This example shows how WordPress is intuitive and user-friendly; you can do things such as changing the blog name and tagline with a few keystrokes in the Dashboard. Changing your options in the Dashboard creates the change on every page of your site — no coding experience required. Beautiful, isn't it?

In the Twenty Ten templates, these tags are surrounded by tags that look like these: `<h1></h1>` or `<h4></h4>`. These tags are `<header>` tags, which define the look and layout of the blog name and tagline in the CSS of your theme. I cover CSS further in Chapter 13.

The Main Index template

The Main Index template drags your blog posts out of the MySQL database and inserts them into your blog. This template is to your blog what the dance floor is to a nightclub — where all the action happens.

The filename of the Main Index template is `index.php`. You can find it in the `/wp-content/themes/twentyten/` folder.

The first template tag in the Main Index template calls in the Header template, meaning that it pulls the information from the Header template into the Main Index template, as follows:

```
<?php get_header(); ?>
```

Figure 12-5:
A WordPress
blog missing
the call to
the header.
It's naked!

Your theme can work without calling in the Header template, but it'll be missing several essential pieces — the CSS and the blog name and tagline, for starters. Without the call to the Header template, your blog will resemble the image shown in Figure 12-5.

The Main Index template in the Twenty Ten theme calls in three other files in a similar fashion:

- ✔ `get_template_part( 'loop', 'index' );` — this function calls in the template file named: `loop.php`.

- ✔ `get_sidebar();` — this function calls in the template file named: `sidebar.php`.

- ✔ `get_footer();` — this function calls in the template file named: `footer.php`.

Each of these three functions and template files is covered in upcoming sections of this chapter.

Earlier in this chapter, in the "Connecting Templates" section, I explain the concept of *calling in* a template file using a function or template tag. That is exactly what the Main Index template does with the four functions for the header, loop, sidebar, and footer templates explained in this section.

The Loop

I'm not talking about America's second-largest downtown business district, originating at the corner of State and Madison streets in Chicago. I could write about some interesting experiences I've had there . . . but that would be a different book.

The Loop in this case is a function that WordPress uses to display the posts on your blog. The Loop has a starting point and an ending point; anything placed in between is used to display each post, including any HTML, PHP, or CSS tags and codes.

In your travels as a WordPress user, you may run across plugins or scripts with instructions that say something like this: "This must be placed within The Loop." That's The Loop that I discuss in this section, so pay particular attention. Understanding The Loop arms you with the knowledge you need for tackling and understanding your WordPress themes.

Quite a few variations of the WordPress Loop are available, but I cover the most common use in this section. When you understand the common use, you can begin to push the envelope a bit further and use variations to suit your needs. This common use displays your posts in chronological order, starting with your most recent post and followed by less recent posts, ordered by date.

The basic and most common use of the Loop in WordPress is to pull blog posts from the database and display them on your Web site. In the default Twenty Ten theme, you find the loop in a template called: loop.php. The beginning, or first line, of the Loop looks like this:

```
<?php while ( have_posts() ) : the_post(); ?>
```

At the bottom of the template, the Loop ends with one line of code:

```
<?php endwhile; ?>
```

The Loop is no different from any other template tag; it must begin with a function to start PHP, and it must end with a function to stop PHP. The Loop begins with PHP and then makes a request: "While there are posts in my blog, display them on this page." This PHP function tells WordPress to grab the blog post information from the database and return it to the blog page. The end of The Loop is like a traffic cop with a big red stop sign telling WordPress to stop the function completely.

REMEMBER

You can set the number of posts displayed per page in the Reading Settings page in the WordPress Dashboard. The Loop abides by this rule and displays only the number of posts per page that you've set.

The big if

PHP functions in a pretty simple, logical manner. It functions by doing what you and I do on a daily basis — making decisions based on questions and answers. PHP deals with three basic variables:

- if
- then
- else

The basic idea is this: IF this, THEN that, or ELSE this.

If your blog has posts (and most do, even when you first install it), WordPress proceeds with The Loop, starting with the piece of code that looks like this:

```php
<?php while (have_posts()) : the_post(); ?>
```

This code tells WordPress to grab the posts from the MySQL database and display them on your blog page.

Then The Loop closes with this tag:

```php
<?php endwhile; ?>
```

Near the beginning of the Loop template, there is a template tag that looks like this:

```php
<?php if ( ! have_posts() ) : ?>
```

The '!' prior to the function: `have_posts()` means does not. So to read that template tag in plain English, it says: `If [this blog] does not have posts`.

If, then, and else

In our daily lives, we deal with if, then, else situations every day, as in these examples:

- **IF** I have a dollar, **THEN** I'll buy coffee, or **ELSE** I'll drink water.

- **IF** it's warm outside, **THEN** I'll take a walk, or **ELSE** I'll stay in.

- **IF** I understand this code, **THEN** I'll be happy, or **ELSE** I'll rip my hair out.

If your blog meets that condition (that is, if it doesn't have any posts), WordPress skips The Loop and displays a message that no posts exist:

```
<div id="post-0" class="post error404 not-found">
<h1 class="entry-title"><?php _e( 'Not Found', 'twentyten'
        ); ?></h1>
<div class="entry-content">
<p><?php _e( 'Apologies, but no results were found for the
        requested Archive. Perhaps searching will help
        find a related post.', 'twentyten' ); ?></p>
<?php get_search_form(); ?>
</div><!-- .entry-content -->
</div><!-- #post-0 -->
```

With the PHP, WordPress displays the title *Not Found,* followed by the statement *Apologies, but no results were found for the requested Archive. Perhaps searching will help find a related post,* followed by the template tag to include a search box that lets users search your blog for more information.

Mixed within the template tags and functions explained in these sections of this chapter, you find basic HTML mark up. For example

```
<div id="">
```

```
<h1>
```

and

```
<div class="">
```

HTML, along with CSS (Cascading Style Sheets), are explained in Chapter 13. HTML and CSS drive the formatting and style of your overall theme, from a visual standpoint (fonts, colors, images, and so on).

Every good PHP function has to come to an end. The `if` statement ends in the next line of code:

```
<?php endif; ?>
```

The Sidebar template

The filename of the Sidebar template is `sidebar.php`. Typically, the sidebar is displayed on the right or left side of your WordPress template. In the default Twenty Ten theme, the sidebar is displayed on the right side of the template, by default (refer to Figure 12-3).

Similarly to the Header template, the Sidebar template is called into the Main Index template with this function:

```
<?php get_sidebar(): ?>
```

This code calls the Sidebar template and all the information it contains into your blog page. Chapter 14 addresses some additional ways you can call in the Sidebar template, including having multiple Sidebar templates and using an include statement to pull them into the Main Index template.

In the "Using Tags with Parameters for Sidebars," section later in this chapter, you find information on template tags to use in the sidebar to display the usual sidebar elements, such as a list of the most recent posts or a list of categories.

The Footer template

The filename of the Footer template is footer.php. Usually, the footer sits at the bottom of the page (refer to Figure 12-3) and contains brief information about the site, such as copyright statements, credits to the theme designer or hosting company, or even a list of links to other pages within the site.

The default Twenty Ten theme shows the site title and a statement that says "Proudly powered by WordPress." You can use the footer to include all sorts of information about your site, however; you don't have to restrict it to small bits of information. In this chapter, I cover the typical footer that you see in the default Twenty Ten theme.

Similarly to the Header and Sidebar templates, the Footer template gets called into the Main Index template through this bit of code:

```
<?php get_footer(); ?>
```

This code calls the Footer and all the information it contains into your blog page.

Other templates

Other templates are in the default Twenty Ten theme, and I don't cover them in depth in this chapter, but having at least a basic understanding of them is a good idea. The ones I list in this section give you that good, solid kick in the pants you need to get started with understanding WordPress templates. When you have that task licked, you can move on to learning the rest.

These other (optional) templates include

- **Comments template (comments.php):** Table 12-9, later in this chapter, lists some useful template tags for WordPress. The Comments template is required if you plan to host comments on your blog; it provides all the template tags you need to display those comments. The template tag used to call the comments into the template is `<?php comments_template(); ?>`.

- ✔ **Single Post template (`single.php`):** When your visitors click the title or permalink of a post you've published to your blog, they're taken to that post's individual page. There, they can read the entire post, and if you have comments enabled, they see the comments form and can leave comments.

- ✔ **Page template (`page.php`):** You can use a Page template for static pages in your WordPress site.

- ✔ **Search Results (`search.php`):** You can use this template to create a custom display of search results on your blog. When someone uses the search feature to search your site for specific keywords, this template formats the return of those results.

- ✔ **404 template (`404.php`):** Use this template to create a custom 404 page, which is the page visitors get when the browser can't find the page requested and returns that ugly 404 Page Cannot Be Found error.

The templates in the preceding list are optional. If these templates don't exist in your WordPress `themes` folder, nothing breaks. The Main Index template handles the display of these items (the single post page, the search results page, and so on). The only exception is the Comments template. If you want to display comments on your site, you must have that template included in your theme.

Customizing Your Blog Posts with Template Tags

This section covers the template tags that you use to display the body of each blog post you publish. The body of a blog post includes information such as the post date and time, title, author name, category, and content. Table 12-3 lists the common template tags you can use for posts, available for you to use in any WordPress theme template. The tags in Table 12-3 work only if you place them within The Loop (covered earlier in this chapter and found in the `loop.php` template file).

Table 12-3	Template Tags for Blog Posts
Tag	**Function**
`get_the_date();`	Displays the date of the post.
`get_the_time();`	Displays the time of the post.
`the_title();`	Displays the title of the post.

Tag	Function
`the_permalink();`	Displays the permalink (URL) of the post.
`get_the_author();`	Displays the post author's name.
`the_author_link();`	Displays the URL of the post author's site.
`the_content('Read More...');`	Displays the content of the post. (If you use an excerpt [below], the words *Read More* appear and are linked to the individual post page.)
`the_excerpt();`	Displays an excerpt (snippet) of the post.
`the_category();`	Displays the category (or categories) assigned to the post. If the post is assigned to multiple categories, they'll be separated by commas.
`comments_popup_link('No Comments', 'Comment (1)', 'Comments(%)');`	Displays a link to the comments, along with the comment count for the post in parentheses. (If no comments exist, it displays a *No Comments* message.)
`next_posts_link('&laquo; Previous Entries')`	Displays the words *Previous Entries* linked to the previous page of blog entries.*
`previous_posts_link('Next Entries &raquo;')`	Displays the words *Next Entries* linked to the next page of blog entries.*

* These two tags aren't like the others. You don't place these tags in The Loop; instead, you insert them after The Loop but before the if *statement ends. Here's an example:*

```
<?php endwhile; ?>
<?php next_posts_link('&laquo; Previous Entries') ?>
<?php previous_posts_link('Next Entries &raquo;') ?>
<?php endif; ?>
```

Putting a Theme Together

In this section, you put together the guts of a basic Main Index template by using the information on templates and tags I've provided so far in this chapter. There seem to be endless lines of code when you view the `loop.php` template file in the Twenty Ten theme, so I've simplified it for you with the following steps. These steps should give you a basic understanding of the WordPress Loop and common template tags and functions that you can use to create your own.

You create a new WordPress theme, using some of the basic templates included in the default Twenty Ten theme. The first steps in pulling everything together are as follows:

1. **Connect to your Web server via FTP, click the** wp-content **folder, and then click the** themes **folder.**

   This folder contains the themes that are currently installed in your WordPress blog. (See Chapter 6 if you need more information on FTP.)

2. **Create a new folder, and call it** mytheme.

   In most FTP programs, you can right-click and choose New Folder. (If you aren't sure how to create a folder, refer to your FTP program's help files.)

3. **Upload the following files from the default Twenty Ten theme:**

   - sidebar.php

   - footer.php

   - header.php

   - style.css

   - comments.php

   - The images folder

   You find the default Twenty Ten theme files in the original WordPress files that you downloaded from the WordPress Web site (or installed directly from your Web server). Do not upload the index.php file, as you are about to create your own index.php file in the next section.

Using the tags provided in Table 12-4, along with the information on The Loop and the calls to the Header, Sidebar, and Footer templates provided in earlier sections, you can follow the next steps for a bare-bones example of what the Main Index template looks like when you put the tags together.

When typing templates, be sure to use a text editor such as Notepad or TextEdit. Using a word processing program such as Microsoft Word opens a whole slew of problems in your code. Word processing programs insert hidden characters and format quotation marks in a way that WordPress can't read.

To create a Main Index template to work with the other templates in your WordPress theme, open a new window in a text editor program and then follow these steps. (Type the text in each of these steps on its own line. Press the Enter key after typing each line so that each tag starts on a new line.)

1. **Type** <?php get_header(); ?>.

   This template tag pulls the information in the Header template of your WordPress theme.

2. **Type** <?php if (have_posts()) : ?>.

   This template tag is an if statement that asks, "Does this blog have posts?" If the answer is yes, it grabs the post content information from your MySQL database and displays the posts in your blog.

3. **Type** `<?php while (have_posts()) : the_post(); ?>`.

   This template tag starts The Loop.

4. **Type** `<a href="<?php the_permalink(); ?>"><?php the_title(); ?></a>`.

   This tag tells your blog to display the title of a post that's clickable (linked) to the URL of the post.

5. **Type** `Posted on <?php the_date(); ?> at <?php the_time(); ?>`.

   This template tag displays the date and time when the post was made. With these template tags, the date and time format are determined by the format you set in the Dashboard.

6. **Type** `Posted in <?php the_category(','); ?>`.

   This template tag displays a comma-separated list of the categories to which you've assigned the post — *Posted in: category 1, category 2,* for example.

7. **Type** `<?php the_content('Read More..'); ?>`.

   This template tag displays the actual content of the blog post. The `'Read More..'` portion of this tag tells WordPress to display the words *Read More,* which are clickable (hyperlinked) to the post's permalink, where the reader can read the rest of the post in its entirety. This tag applies when you're displaying a post excerpt, as determined by the actual post configuration in the Dashboard.

8. **Type** `Posted by: <?php the_author(); ?>`.

   This template tag displays the author of the post in this manner: *Posted by: Lisa Sabin-Wilson.*

9. **Type** `<?php comments_popup_link('No Comments', '1 Comment', '% Comments'); ?>`.

   This template tag displays the link to the comments for this post, along with the number of comments.

10. **Type** `<?php comments_template(); ?>`.

    This template tag calls in the Comments template (`comments.php`). All code and information in the Comments template is pulled into the Main Index template at this point. The Comments template is displayed only on the single post page, however, not on the front page of your blog site.

11. **Type** `<?php endwhile; ?>`.

    This template tag ends The Loop and tells WordPress to stop displaying blog posts here. WordPress knows exactly how many times The Loop needs to work, based on the setting in the WordPress Dashboard. That's exactly how many times WordPress will execute The Loop.

12. **Type** `<?php next_posts_link('&laquo; Previous Entries'); ?>`.

    This template tag displays a clickable link to the previous page of blog entries, if any.

13. **Type** `<?php previous posts link('&raquo; Next Entries'); ?>`.

    This template tag displays a clickable link to the next page of blog entries, if any.

14. **Type** `<?php else : ?>`.

    This template tag refers to the `if` question asked in Step 2. If the answer to that question is no, this step provides the `else` statement — IF this blog has posts, THEN list them here (Step 2 and Step 3), or ELSE display the following message.

15. **Type** `Not Found. Sorry, but you are looking for something that isn't here.`

    This is the message followed by the template tag that is displayed after the `else` statement from Step 14. You can reword this statement to have it say whatever you want.

16. **Type** `<?php endif; ?>`.

    This template tag ends the `if` statement from Step 2.

17. **Type** `<?php get_sidebar(); ?>`.

    This template tag calls in the Sidebar template and pulls that information into the Main Index template. (See the "Using Tags with Parameters for Sidebars" section later in this chapter, for further descriptions of tags for this template.)

18. **Type** `<?php get_footer(); ?>`.

    This template tag calls in the Footer template and pulls that information into the Main Index template. ***Note:*** The code in the `footer.php` template ends the `<body>` and the `<html>` tags that were started in the Header template (`header.php`).

    When you're done, the display of the Main Index template code looks like this:

```
<?php get_header(); ?>
<?php if (have_posts()) : ?>

  <?php while (have_posts()) : the_post(); ?>
<div <?php post_class() ?> id="post-<?php the_ID(); ?>">
  <a href="<?php the_permalink(); ?>"><?php the_title(); ?></a>
  Posted on: <?php the_date(); ?> at <?php the_time(); ?>
  Posted in: <?php the_category(','); ?>

  <?php the_content('Read More..'); ?>
```

```
Posted by: <?php the_author(); ?> | <?php comments_popup_link('No
          Comments', '1 Comment', '% Comments'); ?>
</div>
<?php comments_template(); ?>
 <?php endwhile; ?>
<?php next_posts_link('&laquo; Previous Entries') ?>
<?php previous_posts_link('Next Entries &raquo;') ?>

<?php else : ?>
 Not Found
 Sorry, but you are looking for something that isn't here.

<?php endif; ?>

<?php get_sidebar(); ?>
<?php get_footer(); ?>
```

19. Save this file as `index.php`, **and upload it to the** `mythemes` **folder.**

In Notepad, you can save it by choosing File⇨Save As. Type the name of the file in the File Name text box, and click Save.

20. Activate the theme in the WordPress Dashboard, and view your blog to see your handiwork in action!

 My Main Index template code has one template tag that is explained in Chapter 13: `<div <?php post_class() ?> id="post-<?php the_ ID(); ?>">`. This tag helps you create some interesting styles in your template using CSS, so check out Chapter 13 to find out all about it!

This very simple and basic Main Index template that you just built does not have the standard HTML mark up in it, so you will find that the visual display of your blog differs somewhat from the default Twenty Ten theme. This example was used to give you the bare bones basics of the Main Index template and the Loop in action. Chapter 13 goes into details about the use of HTML and CSS to create nice styling and formatting for your posts and pages.

Using Tags with Parameters for Sidebars

If you've been following along in this chapter as I've covered the Header and Main Index templates and tags, you have a functional WordPress blog with blog posts and various metadata displayed in each post.

In this section, I give you the template tags for the items commonly placed in the sidebar of a blog. I say "commonly placed" because it's possible to get creative with these template tags and place them in other locations (the Footer template, for example). To keep this introduction to sidebar template tags simple, I stick with the most common use, leaving the creative and uncommon uses to you to try when you're comfortable with building the basics.

This section also introduces *tag parameters,* which are additional options you can include in the tag to control some of its display properties. Not all template tags have parameters. You place tag parameters inside the parentheses of the tag. Many of the parameters discussed in this section were obtained from the WordPress software documentation in the WordPress Codex at `http://codex.wordpress.org`.

Table 12-4 helps you understand the three variations of parameters used by WordPress.

Table 12-4	Three Variations of Template Parameters	
Variation	*Description*	*Example*
Tags without parameters	These tags have no additional options available. Tags without parameters have nothing within the parentheses.	`the_tag();`
Tags with PHP function-style parameters	These tags have a comma-separated list of values placed within the tag parentheses.	`the_tag('1,2,3');`
Tags with query-string parameters	These types of tags generally have several available parameters. This tag style enables you to change the value for each parameter without being required to provide values for all available parameters for the tag.	`the_tag ('parameter=true);`

Identifying some blog-post metadata

Metadata is simply data about data. In WordPress, *metadata* refers to the data about each blog post, including:

✔ The author name

✔ The category or categories to which the post is assigned

✔ The date and time of the post

✔ The comments link and number of comments

You need to know these three types of parameters:

- ✔ **String:** A line of text that can be anything from a single letter to a long list of words. A string is placed between single quotation marks and sets an option for the parameter or is displayed as text.

- ✔ **Integer:** A positive or negative number. Integers are placed within the parentheses and either inside or outside single quotation marks. Either way, they'll be processed correctly.

- ✔ **Boolean:** Sets the parameter options to `true` or `false`. This parameter can be numeric (`0=false` and `1=true`) or textual. Boolean parameters aren't placed within quotation marks.

The WordPress Codex, located at `http://codex.wordpress.org`, has every conceivable template tag and possible parameter known to the WordPress software. The tags and parameters that I share with you in this chapter are the ones used most often.

The Calendar

The `calendar` tag displays a calendar that highlights each day of the week on which you've posted a blog. Those days are also hyperlinked to the original blog post. Here's the tag to use to display the calendar:

```php
<?php get_calendar(); ?>
```

The `calendar` tag has only one parameter, and it's Boolean. Set this parameter to `true`, and it displays the day of the week with one letter (Friday = F, for example.) Set this parameter to `false`, and it displays the day of the week as a three-letter abbreviation (Friday = Fri., for example). Here are examples of the template tag used to display the calendar on your WordPress blog:

```php
<?php get_calendar(true); ?>
<?php get_calendar(false); ?>
```

List pages

The `<?php wp_list_pages(); ?>` tag displays a list of the static pages you can create on your WordPress site (such as About Me or Contact pages). Displaying a link to the static pages makes them available so that readers can click the links and read the content you've provided.

WordPress has a very handy navigation menu building tool that I cover in Chapter 13. It allows you to build different custom navigation menus. If you like the navigation tool, you may never need to use the `wp_list_pages();` template tag. Still, I'm including it here because you may want to use it if you want to have complete control over how the list of pages appears on your Web site.

The `<list>` tag parameters use the string style. (Table 12-5 lists the most common parameters used for the `wp_list_pages` template tag.)

Table 12-5		Most Common Parameters (Query-String) for wp_list_pages();
Parameter	**Type**	**Description and Values**
`child_of`	integer	Displays only the subpages of the page; uses the numeric ID for a page as the value. Defaults to 0 (display all pages).
`sort_column`	string	Sorts pages with one of the following options: `'post_title'` — Sorts alphabetically by page title (default). `'menu_order'` — Sorts by page order (the order in which they appear in the Manage tab and Pages subtab of the Dashboard). `'post_date'` — Sorts by the date on which pages were created. `'post_modified'` — Sorts by the time when the page was last modified. `'post_author'` — Sorts by author, according to the author ID #. `'post_name'` — Sorts alphabetically by the post slug.
`Exclude`	string	Lists the numeric page ID numbers, separated by commas, that you want to exclude from the page list display (for example, `'exclude=10, 20, 30'`). There is no default value.
`Depth`	integer	Uses a numeric value for how many levels of pages are displayed in the list of pages. Possible options: 0 — Displays all pages, including main and subpages (default). -1 — Shows subpages but doesn't indent them in the list display. 1 — Shows only main pages (no subpages).

Parameter	Type	Description and Values
show_date	string	Displays the date when the page was created or last modified. Possible options: `' '` — Displays no date (default). `'modified'` — Displays the date when the page was last modified. `'created'` — Displays the date when the page was created.
date_format	string	Sets the format of the date to be displayed. Defaults to the date format configured in the Options tab and General subtab of the Dashboard.
title_li	string	Types text for the heading of the page list. Defaults to display the text: `"Pages"`. If value is empty (''), no heading is displayed; for example, `'title_li=My Pages"` displays the heading My Pages above the page list.

Page lists are displayed in an *unordered list* (you may know it by the term *bulleted list*). Whichever term you use, it's a list with a bullet point in front of every page link.

The following tag and query string displays a list of pages without the text heading `"Pages"`. In other words, it displays no title at the top of the page's link list:

```
<?php wp_list_pages('title_li='); ?>
```

The next tag and query string displays the list of pages sorted by the date when they were created; the date is also displayed along with the page name:

```
<?php wp_list_pages('sort_column=post_date&show_date='created'); ?>
```

Take a look at the way query-string parameters are written:

```
'parameter1=value&parameter2=value&parameter3=value'
```

The entire string is surrounded by single quotation marks, and there is no white space within the query string. Each parameter is joined to its value by the = character. When you use multiple parameters/values, you separate them with the & character. You can think of the string like this: parameter1=value**AND**parameter2=value**AND**parameter3=value. Keep this convention in mind for the remaining template tags and parameters in this chapter.

Bookmarks (blogroll)

In the WordPress Dashboard, you can manage your links from the Blogroll tab. Before I forge ahead and dig in to the template tag for the display of the blogroll, I want to clear up a little terminology.

A *blogroll* is a list of links that you add to the Blogroll area in the Dashboard. The specific template tag used to call those links into your template, however, refers to *bookmarks*. So this begs the question "Are they links, or are they bookmarks?" The answer is "Both." For simplicity, and to ensure that you and I are on the same wavelength, I refer to them the same way that half the planet does — as links.

Here is the tag used to display your blogroll:

```php
<?php wp_list_bookmarks(); ?>
```

In Chapter 8, I show you how to add links to your blogroll and also discuss the options you can set for each link. The parameters for this tag give you control of how the links are displayed and put some of the options to work. Table 12-6 shows the most common parameters used for the `wp_list_bookmarks` template tag.

In the Possible Values column of Table 12-6, values that appear in bold are the default values set by WordPress. Keep this convention in mind for all the parameter values in the rest of this chapter.

Table 12-6	Most Common Parameters (Query-String) for wp_list_bookmarks();	
Parameter and Type	*Possible Values*	*Example*
`categorize` (Boolean) Displays links within the assigned category.	1 (True) 0 (False)	`<?php wp_list_bookmarks ('categorize=0'); ?>` Returns the list of links not grouped into the categories.
`category` (string) Displays only the link categories specified; if none is specified, all link categories are shown.	Category ID numbers separated by commas	`<?php wp_list_ bookmarks('category=10, 20, 30'); ?>` Displays the list of links from the categories with ID numbers 10, 20, and 30.

Parameter and Type	Possible Values	Example
category_ orderby (string) Sorts the order in which links are displayed on your site.	Name id	`<?php wp_list_ bookmarks('category_ orderby=name'); ?>` Displays the link categories alphabetically by name.

title_li (string) Text title appears above the link list.	bookmarks If left blank, no title is displayed.	`<?php wp_list_ bookmarks('title_ li=Links'); ?>`
		
		Displays the Links header.
		`<?php wp_list_ bookmarks('title_li='); ?>`
		
		Displays no heading.

title_before (string) Formatting to appear before the category title — only if the 'categorize' parameter is set to 1 (true).	<h2>	`<?php wp_list_ bookmarks('title_ before='<strong>'); ?>` Inserts the `<strong>` HTML tag in front of the link category title.
title_after (string) Formatting to appear after the category title — only if the 'categorize' parameter is set to 1 (true).	</h2>	`<?php wp_list_ bookmarks('title_ after='</strong>'); ?>` Inserts the `</strong>` HTML tag after the link category title.
Include (string) Lists link ID numbers, separated by commas, to include in the display.	If no ID numbers are listed, displays all links.	`<?php wp_list_ bookmarks ('include="1,2,3'); ?>` Displays only links with the IDs of 1, 2, and 3.

(continued)

Table 12-6 *(continued)*

Parameter and Type	Possible Values	Example
Exclude (string) List of link ID numbers, separated by commas, to exclude from the display.	If no ID numbers are listed, all links are displayed.	`<?php wp_list_bookmarks ('exclude='4,5,6'); ?>` Displays all links except for the links with IDs of 4, 5, and 6.
After (string) Formatting to appear after each link in the list.	`</li>`	`<?php wp_list_ bookmarks('after= </strong'); ?>` Inserts the `</strong>` HTML tag after each link in the list.

Here are a couple of examples of tags used to set a link list.

The following tag displays a list of links in the category ID of 2 and orders that list by the length of the link name (shortest to longest):

```
<?php wp_list_bookmarks('categorize=1&category=2&orderby=length'); ?>
```

This next tag displays only the list of links in a category (the Espresso category, in this example):

```
<?php wp_list_bookmarks('category_name=Espresso'); ?>
```

Post archives

The `<?php wp_get_archives(); ?>` template tag displays the blog post archives in a number of ways, using the parameters and values shown in Table 12-7. Again, values that appear in bold are the default values set by WordPress. Here are just a few examples of what you can produce with this template tag:

✔ Display the titles of the last 15 posts you've made to your blog

✔ Display the titles of the posts you've made in the past ten days

✔ Display a monthly list of archives

Table 12-7	Most Common Parameters (Query-String) for wp_get_archives();	
Parameter and Type	**Possible Values**	**Example**
Type (string) Determines the type of archive to display	monthly daily weekly postbypost	`<?php wp_get_rchives ('type=postbypost'); ?>` Displays the titles of the most recent blog posts.
format (string) Formats the display of the links in the archive list	html — Surrounds the links with `<li>` `</li>` tags. option — Places archive list in drop-down menu format. link — Surrounds the links with `<link>` `</link>` tags. custom — Use your own HTML tags, using the before and after parameters.	`<?php wp_get_archives ('format=html'); ?>` Displays the list of archive links where each link is surrounded by the `<li>` `</li>` HTML tags.
limit (integer) Limits the number of archives to display.	If no value, all are displayed.	`<?php wp_get_archives ('limit=10'); ?>` Displays the last 10 archives in a list.
before (string) Places text or formatting before the link in the archive list when using the custom parameter.	No default	`<?php wp_get_archives ('before=<strong>'); ?>` Inserts the `<strong>` HTML tag before each link in the archive link list.

(continued)

Table 12-7 *(continued)*

Parameter and Type	Possible Values	Example
`after` (string) Inserts text or formatting after the link in the archive list when using the custom parameter.	No default	`<?php wp_get_archives ('after=</strong>'); ?>` Inserts the `</strong>` HTML tag after each link in the archive link list.
`show_post_ count` (Boolean) This value displays the number of posts in the archive. You would use this if you use the `'type'` of monthly.	`true` or 1 `false` or 0	`<? wp_get_archives ('show_post_count=1'); ?>` Displays the number of posts in each archive after each archive link.

Here are a couple of examples of tags used to display blog post archives.

This tag displays a linked list of monthly archives (for example, January 2011, February 2011, and so on).

```
<?php wp_get_archives('type=monthly'); ?>
```

This next tag displays a linked list of the 15 most recent blog posts:

```
<?php wp_get_archives('type=postbypost&limit=15'); ?>
```

Categories

WordPress lets you create categories and assign posts to a specific category (or multiple categories). Categories provide an organized navigation system that helps you and your readers find posts you've made on certain topics.

The `<?php wp_list_categories(); ?>` template tag lets you display a list of your categories by using the available parameters and values. (Table 12-8 shows some of the most popular parameters.) Each category is linked to the appropriate category page that lists all the posts you've assigned to it. The values that appear in bold are the default values set by WordPress.

Table 12-8	Most Common Parameters (Query-String) for wp_list_categories();	
Parameter and Type	**Possible Values**	**Example**
`orderby` (string) Determines how the category list will be ordered.	ID name	`<?php wp_list_categories ('orderby=name'); ?>` Displays the list of categories by name, alphabetically, as they appear in the Dashboard.
`style` (string) Determines the format of the category list display.	List none	`<?php wp_list_categories ('style=list'); ?>` Displays the list of category links where each link is surrounded by the `<li> </li>` HTML tags. `<?php wp_list_categories ('style=none'); ?>` Displays the list of category links with a simple line break after each link.
`show_count` (Boolean) Determines whether to display the post count for each listed category.	true or 1 false or 0	`<?php wp_list_categories ('show_count=1'); ?>` Displays the post count, in parentheses, after each category list. `Espresso (10)`, for example, means that there are ten posts in the Espresso category.
`hide_empty` (Boolean) Determines whether empty categories should be displayed in the list (meaning a category with zero posts assigned to it).	true or 1 false or 0	`<?php wp_list_categories ('hide_empty=0'); ?>` Displays only those categories that currently have posts assigned to them.

(continued)

Table 12-8 *(continued)*

Parameter and Type	Possible Values	Example
Feed (string) Determines whether the RSS feed should be displayed for each category in the list.	rss Default is no feeds displayed.	`<?php wp_list_categories ('feed=rss'); ?>` Displays category titles with an RSS link next to each one.
feed_image (string) Provides the path/filename for an image for the feed.	No default	`<?php wp_list_categories ('feed_image=/wp-content/ images/feed.gif'); ?>` Displays the feed.gif image for each category title. This image is linked to the RSS feed for that category.
hierarchical (Boolean) Determines whether the child categories should be displayed after each parent category in the category link list.	true or 1 false or 0	`<?php wp_list_categories ('hierarchical=0'); ?>` Doesn't display the child categories after each parent category in the category list.

Here are a couple of examples of tags used to display a list of your categories.

This example, with its parameters, displays a list of categories sorted by name without showing the number of posts made in each category and displays the RSS feed for each category title:

```
<?php wp_list_categories('orderby=name&show_count=0&feed=RSS'); ?>
```

This example, with its parameters, displays a list of categories sorted by name with the post count showing and shows the subcategories of every parent category:

```
<?php wp_list_categories('orderby=name&show_count=1&hierarchical=1'); '>
```

Getting widgetized

About 99.99 percent of the WordPress themes available today are coded with what is commonly referred to as *widgetized sidebars*. This coding means that you can use the widgets within WordPress to populate your sidebar area with content, navigation menus and lists. In Chapter 5, I go into detail about what widgets are and how you can use them to dress up your sidebar — so check out that chapter if you feel like you need more information about widgets.

With widgets in place, generally there is no reason to mess around with the code in the sidebar.php template file, because most of the content you want to add into your sidebar can be accomplished through the use of widgets.

In a WordPress theme, there are two places that create the functionality and the possibility for widgets to exist within your theme. You're not limited to where you place and use widgets, by and large. I am using the Sidebar template (sidebar.php) in this example.

First, you have to define the widgets in your theme. This means that you need to alert WordPress to the fact that this theme can handle widgets. This is also referred to as *registering* a widget with the WordPress software. To register a widget, the register_sidebar function needs to be added to the Theme Functions template (functions.php). In the functions.php file in the Twenty Ten theme, the code for registering a widget looks like this:

```
register_sidebar( array (
'name' => __( 'Primary Widget Area', 'twentyten' ),
'id' => 'primary-widget-area',
'description' => __( 'The primary widget area',
          'twentyten' ),
'before_widget' => '<li id="%1$s" class="widget-container
          %2$s">',
'after_widget' => "</li>",
'before_title' => '<h3 class="widget-title">',
'after_title' => '</h3>',
) );
```

Within that code, you see seven different *arrays*. An array is a set of values that tells WordPress how you would like your widgets handled and displayed:

- ✔ **name:** This name is unique to the widget and is displayed on the Widgets page in the Dashboard. It is helpful if you register several different widgetized areas on your site.

- ✔ **id:** This is the unique ID given to the Widget

- ✔ **description:** This is a text description of the Widget. The text that gets placed here will display on the Widgets page in the Dashboard.

- ✔ **before_widget:** This is the HTML markup that gets inserted directly before the widget. It is helpful for CSS styling purposes.

- ✔ **after_widget:** This is the HTML markup that gets inserted directly after the widget.

- ✔ **before_title:** This is the HTML markup that gets inserted directly before the widget title.

✔ `after_title:` This is the HTML markup that gets inserted directly after the widget title.

With that code in your `functions.php` file, WordPress now recognizes that you've registered a widget called Primary Widget Area for your theme and makes the widget area available for you to drag and drop widgets into on the Widgets page in the Dashboard. All that's left to do now is to call that widget into your `sidebar.php` file. By doing so, you allow the widgets to display on your site. Follow these steps to call widgets to your site (these steps assume the widget code isn't already in the Sidebar template):

1. **Click the Editor link below the Appearances menu.**

   The Edit Themes page opens.

2. **Click the Sidebar (sidebar.php) template.**

   The Sidebar template opens in the text box on the left side of the page.

3. **Type the following code in the Sidebar (sidebar.php) template:**

```php
<?php if ( ! dynamic_sidebar( 'Primary Widget Area' )
        ) : ?>
<?php endif; ?>
```

   The parameter within the `dynamic_sidebar` template tag corresponds to the name that you provided in the widget array called *'name'* earlier in this section. It must be the same, otherwise it will not display on your Web site.

4. **Click the Update File button.**

   The changes you've made to the Sidebar (`sidebar.php`) template file are now saved.

 You can register an unlimited number of widgets for your theme. This flexibility allows you to create several different widgetized areas and widget features in different areas of your site. Chapter 14 goes into more detail about using different sidebar templates to create different widgetized areas and features on your site.

Checking Out Miscellaneous but Useful Template Tags

In this chapter, I've picked the most common template tags to get you started. You can find all the rest of the template tags in the WordPress Codex at this URL:

```
http://codex.wordpress.org/Template_Tags
```

A few miscellaneous tags aren't included in the preceding sections, but I want to mention here briefly because they're helpful and sometimes fun. Table 12-9 lists some of these tags, their locations in the templates where they're commonly used, and their purposes.

Table 12-9	Some Useful Template Tags for WordPress

Tags Used in the Comments Template (`comments.php`)

Tag	Function
`<?php comment_author(); ?>`	Displays the comment author's name.
`<?php comment_author_link(); ?>`	Displays the comment author's name, linked to the author's Web site if a URL was provided in the comment form.
`<?php comment_text(); ?>`	Displays the text of a comment.
`<?php comment_date() ?>`	Displays the date when a comment was published.
`<?php comment_time(); ?>`	Displays the time when a comment was published.
`<?php echo get_avatar(); ?>`	Displays the Gravatar of the comment author (see Chapter 7).
`<?php previous_comments_link() ?>`	Displays navigation links to the previous page of comments, if you're using paged comments (see Chapter 7).
`<?php next_comments_link() ?>`	Displays navigation links to the next page of comments, if you're using paged comments (see Chapter 7).

Tags Used to Display RSS Feeds

Tag	Function
`<?php bloginfo('rss2_url'); ?>`	Displays the URL of the RSS feed for your blog. Usually surrounded by the `a href` HTML tag to provide a hyperlink to the RSS feed: `<a href=" <?php bloginfo('rss2_url'); ?>">RSS Feed</a>`
`<?php bloginfo('comments_rss2_url'); ?>`	Displays the URL of the RSS feed for your comments. Usually surrounded by the `a href` HTML tag to provide a hyperlink to the comments RSS feed: `<a href=" ="<?php bloginfo('comments_rss2_url'); ?>">Comments RSS</a>`

(continued)

Table 12-9 *(continued)*

Tags Used to Display Author Information

Tag	Function
`<?php the_author_ description(); ?>`	Pulls the information from the author bio located in the About Yourself section of your profile in the Dashboard, and displays that information in the blog.
`<?php the_author_ email(); ?>`	Pulls the author's e-mail address from the author profile in the Dashboard.

You can find additional hints, tips, and tricks on creative uses of WordPress templates and template tags in Chapters 13 and 14.

Chapter 13

Tweaking WordPress Themes

. . . .

In This Chapter

▶ Exploring basic CSS and defining CSS properties and values

▶ Setting a new background color, creating a header, and customizing navigation menus

▶ Changing fonts

. . . .

Chapter 11 shows how you can use free WordPress themes in your blog. Many people are quite happy to use these themes without making any adjustments to them at all. I can't tell you, however, how many times people have asked me how they can customize a theme that they've found. The answer to their questions is always, "Of course you can make changes on your own."

The practice of changing a few elements of an existing WordPress theme is *tweaking*. Thousands of WordPress blog owners tweak their existing themes on a regular basis. This chapter provides information on some of the most common tweaks you can make to your theme, such as changing the header image, changing the color of the background or the text links, and changing font styles — and these changes are pretty easy to make, too! You'll be tweaking your own theme in no time flat.

Before you go too wild with tweaking templates, make a backup of your theme so that you have the original files, from which you can easily restore if you need to. You can back up your theme files by connecting to your Web server via FTP (see Chapter 6) and downloading your theme folder to your computer. When you have the original theme files safe and secure on your hard drive, feel free to tweak away, comfortable in the knowledge that you have a backup.

Styling with CSS: The Basics

A Cascading Style Sheet (CSS) is a style sheet that controls the appearance of content on a Web site. Every single WordPress theme you use in your blog uses CSS. The CSS provides style and design flair to the template tags in your templates. (See Chapter 12 for information about WordPress template tags.)

The CSS for your WordPress theme is pulled in through the Header template (`header.php`) and is named `style.css`.

In your Dashboard, click the Editor link on the Appearances menu, and look at the Header template for the Twenty Ten WordPress theme by clicking the Header link on the Edit Themes page. You find the following line of code, which pulls the CSS (`style.css`) into the page to provide the formatting of the elements of your blog:

```
<link rel="stylesheet" type="text/css" media="all" href="<?php bloginfo(
                'stylesheet_url' ); ?>" />
```

Don't tweak the line of code that pulls in the `style.css` file; otherwise, the CSS won't work for your blog.

Chapter 12 covers the commonly used parameters for the `bloginfo()`; template tag used in WordPress themes.

CSS selectors

With CSS, you can provide style (such as size, color, and placement) to the display of elements on your blog (such as text links, header images, font size and colors, paragraph margins, and line spacing). *CSS selectors* contain names, properties, and values to define which HTML elements in the templates you will style with CSS. Table 13-1 provides some examples of CSS selectors and their use.

Table 13-1			Basic CSS Selectors
CSS Selector	**Description**	**HTML**	**CSS**
body	Sets the style for the overall body of the site, such as background color and default fonts	`<body>`	`body {background-color: white}` The background color on all pages is white.
p	Defines how paragraphs are formatted	`<p>This is a para-graph</p>`	`p {color:black}` The color of the fonts used in all paragraphs is black.

CSS Selector	Description	HTML	CSS
h1, h3, h3, h4	Provide bold headers for different sections of your site	`<h1>This is a site title</h1>`	`h1 {font-weight: bold;}` The fonts surrounded by the `<h1>..</h1>` HTML tags will be bold.
a	Defines how text links display in your site	`<a href= "http:// wiley.com"> Wiley Publishing </a>`	`a {color: red}` All text links appear in red.

Classes and IDs

You can find the stylesheet (`style.css`) for the default Twenty Ten theme on the Edit Themes page in your Dashboard (see Figure 13-1). Everything in it may look foreign to you right now, but I want to bring your attention to two items you see when you scroll down through that template:

- **#container:** One type of CSS selector. The hash mark (#) indicates that it's a CSS *ID*.

- **.onecolumn:** Another type of CSS selector. The period (.) indicates that it's a CSS *class*.

IDs and classes define styling properties for different sections of your WordPress theme. Table 13-2 shows examples of IDs and classes from the `header.php` template in the Twenty Ten WordPress theme. Armed with this information, you'll know where to look in the stylesheet when you want to change the styling for a particular area of your theme.

Figure 13-1:
The
WordPress
default
theme
stylesheet
(style.
css).

Table 13-2	**Connecting HTML with CSS Selectors**	
HTML	**CSS Selector**	**Description**
`<div id= "wrapper">` In this case, the CSS selector name is `page`.	`#wrapper`	Styles the elements for the `wrapper` ID in your template(s).
`<div id= "header">`	`#header`	Styles the elements for the `header` ID in your template(s).
`<div id= "masthead">`	`#masthead`	Styles the elements for the `masthead` ID in your template(s).
`<h1 id="site- title">`	`#site-title`	Styles the elements for your `site-title` ID in your template(s), but also follows rules for the `h1` values set in the CSS.

HTML	CSS Selector	Description
`<div id="site-description">`	`#site-description`	Styles the elements for your `site-description` ID in your template(s).
`<div class="skip-link screen-reader-text">`	`.skip-link` and `.screen-reader`	Styles the elements for your `skip-link` and `screen-reader` classes in your template(s).

If you find an element in the template code that says id (such as div id= or p id=), look for the hash symbol in the stylesheet. If you find an element in the template code that says class (such as div class= or p class=), look for the period in the stylesheet followed by the selector name.

CSS properties and values

CSS properties are assigned to the CSS selector name. You also need to provide values for the CSS properties to define the style elements for the particular CSS selector you're working with.

In the default Twenty Ten WordPress theme, for example, the first piece of markup in the Header template (header.php) is <div id="wrapper">. This ID, with the name wrapper, provides styling for the site page.

In the default Twenty Ten WordPress theme stylesheet, the CSS defined for the wrapper ID is as follows:

```
#wrapper {
margin: 0 auto;
width: 940px;
background: #fff;
padding: 0 20px;
}
```

Every CSS property needs to be followed by a colon (:), and each CSS value needs to be followed by a semicolon (;).

The CSS selector is #page, which has three properties:

- The first CSS property is margin, which has the value of 0 auto;.
- The second CSS property is width, which has the value 940px (absolute, fixed pixel width).

- ✔ The third CSS property is `background`, which has the value `#fff` (which is the correct hex code for the color white.

- ✔ The fourth, and final, CSS property is `padding`, which has the value: `0 20px` (no padding on the top and bottom, 20 pixels of padding on the right and left sides).

Table 13-3 provides some examples of commonly used CSS properties and values.

Table 13-3	Common CSS Properties and Values	
CSS Property	*CSS Value*	*Examples*
`background-color`	Defines the color of the background (such as red, black, or white)	**Markup:** `<div id="wrapper">` **CSS:** `#wrapper {background-color: white}`
`background`	Defines a background image	**Markup:** `<div id="header">` **CSS:** `#header {background: url(images/header.jpg) no-repeat;}`
`font-family*`	Defines the fonts used for the selector	**Markup:** `<body>` **CSS:** `body { font-family: 'Lucida Grande', Verdana, Arial, Sans-Serif;}`
`color`	Defines the color of the text	**Markup:** `<h1>Website Title</h1>` **CSS:** `h1 {color: blue}`
`afont-size**`	Defines the size of the text	**Markup:** `<h1>Website Title</h1>` **CSS:** `h1 {font-size: 18px;}`
`text-align`	Defines the alignment of the text (left, center, right, or justified)	**Markup:** `<div id="wrapper">` **CSS:** `#wrapper {text-align: left;}`

* *W3Schools has a good resource on the font-family property here:*
http://w3schools.com/CSS/pr_font_font-family.asp

** *W3Schools has a good resource on the font-size property here:*
http://w3schools.com/CSS/pr_font_font-size.asp

Changing the Background Color

In Chapter 12, I discuss the Header template (`header.php`) in detail. In this section, I show you how to tweak the background color in the default Twenty Ten theme. If you're not using the default Twenty Ten theme, you can also use the `<body>` tag in a Header template to change the background color of your Web site.

Creating a custom background

The Twenty Ten WordPress theme is packaged with an option that allows you to change the background to a different color or use an image for your background. To use the nifty, built-in custom background feature to change the Twenty Ten background for your blog, follow these steps:

1. **Click the Background link under the Appearances menu.**

   The Custom Background page loads in the Dashboard.

2. **To change the background color, type the hexadecimal color code in the Color text box.**

   If you don't know what hex code you want to use, click the Select a Color link and click on a color within the provided color wheel (see Figure 13-2).

   A hexadecimal (or *hex*) code represents a certain color. Hex codes always start with a hash symbol (#) and have six letters and/or numbers to represent a particular color; in this case, `#d5d6d7`. I talk more about hexadecimal values in the section "Changing the background using CSS," later in this chapter.

3. **To use an image file for the background, upload an image from your computer.**

   Click the Browse button under the Upload New Background Image and select a file from your computer. Then click the Upload button.

4. **Change the display options for your new background image.**

   - **Position:** Select Left, Center, or Right to set the screen position of the background image on your Web site.

   - **Repeat:** Select No Repeat, Tile, Tile Horizontally, or Tile Vertically in the drop-down menu to set the image repeat behavior of the background image on your Web site.

   - **Attachment:** Select Scroll to set the background image to scroll down the page or select Fixed to set the background image in a static position (so it doesn't scroll down the page).

Figure 13-2:
The color
wheel
selector on
the Custom
Background
page.

5. Save your changes.

Be sure to click the Save Changes button before navigating away from
the Custom Background page. Otherwise, your new settings won't be
saved.

You can add the Custom Background option to any theme with just a few
lines of code. Just follow these steps:

**1. Browse to the Edit Themes page and click the Theme Functions
(functions.php) template.**

The Theme Functions template opens in the text editor on the left side
of the page.

2. Add the following line of code to the Theme Functions template:

```
add_custom_background();
```

This line of code tells WordPress that your theme has added the Custom
Background feature.

3. **Click the Save File button.**

   The Theme Functions template is saved, along with your changes. The Background link now displays below the Appearances menu.

4. **View your Web site page to see your changes.**

Changing the background using CSS

The `<body>` tag is simple HTML markup. Every theme has this tag, which defines the overall default content for each page of your Web site — the site's *body*.

In the stylesheet (`style.css`), the background for the body is defined like this:

```
body {
  background: #f1f1f1;
}
```

The background for the `<body>` tag uses a hexadecimal color code of `#f1f1f1` that gives the background a light gray color. You can use a color or an image (or both) to style the background of your Web site:

- **Color:** The W3Schools Web site has a great resource on hex codes at `http://w3schools.com/HTML/html_colornames.asp`.

- **Image:** You can easily use an image as a background for your site by uploading the image to the `images` folder in your theme directory. That value looks like `background: url(images/yourimage.jpg)`. (***Note:*** The `url` portion of this code automatically pulls in the URL of your blog, so you don't have to change the `url` part to your URL.)

You can also use a combination of colors and images in your backgrounds.

In the case of some basic colors, you don't have to use the hex code. For colors such as white, black, red, blue, and silver, you can just use their names — `background-color: white`, for example.

If you want to change the background color of your theme, follow these steps:

1. **In the WordPress Dashboard, click the Editor link on the Appearance menu.**

   The Edit Themes page opens.

2. **From the Select Theme to Edit drop-down menu, choose the theme you want to change.**

3. **Click the Stylesheet template link.**

   The `style.css` template opens in the text editor on the left side of the Theme Editor page (refer to Figure 13-1).

4. **Scroll down in the text editor until you find the CSS selector body.**

   If you're tweaking the default theme, this section is what you're looking for:

   ```
   body {
     background: #f1f1f1;
   }
   ```

   If you're tweaking a different template, the CSS selector body will look similar.

5. **Edit the `background` property's values.**

   For example, in the default template, if you want to change the background color to black, you can enter either

   ```
   background: #000000;
   ```

   or

   ```
   background: black;
   ```

6. **Click the Update File button in the bottom-left corner of the page.**

   Your changes are saved and applied to your theme.

7. **Visit your site in your Web browser.**

   The background color of your theme has changed.

Using Your Own Header Image

Most themes have a header image that displays at the top of the page. This image is generated by a graphic defined either in the CSS value for the property that represents the header area, or through the use of a feature in WordPress called a custom header. In the WordPress default Twenty Ten theme, all the hard work's been done for you. Including a custom header image on a blog that uses the Twenty Ten theme is pretty darn easy.

To use existing header images, follow these steps:

1. **Click the Header link in the Appearances menu in your Dashboard.**

   The Your Header Image page appears.

2. **Choose from one of seven header images.**

   Scroll down to the bottom of the page and select one of the cool header images that WordPress provides for you by clicking the circle to the left of your chosen image.

3. **Click the Save Changes button.**

   The header image you've chosen is now saved. When you view your Web site, you should see it displayed at the top.

To upload a new header image, follow these steps:

1. **Click the Browse button under the Upload New Header Image title. Select the image from your computer then click Open.**

2. **Click Upload.**

   Your image uploads to your Web server. The Crop Header page appears, where you can crop the image and adjust which portion of the header image you would like displayed (see Figure 13-3).

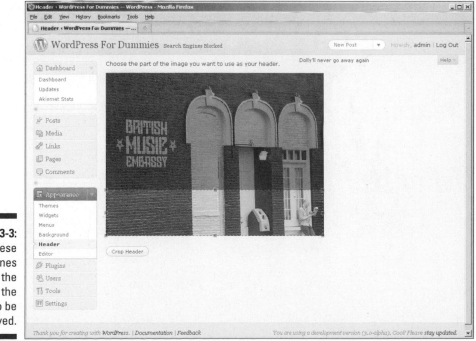

Figure 13-3: These dotted lines indicate the area of the header to be displayed.

3. **Click the Crop Header button.**

   The Header Image page appears, and your new header image is now displayed.

4. **View your Web site.**

   Your new header image is now displayed at the top of your Web site.

In themes that do not have the custom header image feature, you can easily define a background image for the header image using CSS.

For purposes of this example, the HTML mark up for the header in the template is:

```
<div id="header"></div>
```

In the CSS (style.css) file, you can use a background image by defining it in the CSS properties for #header. Use this code:

```
#header {
background: url(/images/header-image.jpg) no-repeat;
width: 980px;
height: 100px;
}
```

The background value indicates an image called: header-image.jpg. In order for it to display on your site, you need to create the image and upload it to your Web server under /images/ directory.

Creating Custom Navigation Menus

A *navigation menu* is a listing of links displayed on your site. These links can be links to pages, posts, or categories within your site, or they can be links to other sites. Either way, you can define navigation menus on your site through the use of the built-in feature in WordPress called Custom Menus.

It's to your advantage to provide at least one navigation menu on your site so that readers can see everything your site has to offer. Providing visitors with a link — or several — to click is in keeping with the point-and-click spirit of the Web.

Adding the Custom Menu feature to your theme

The Custom Menu feature is already built in to the default Twenty Ten WordPress theme, so you don't have to worry about preparing your theme for it. However, if you're using a different theme, adding this functionality is easy:

1. **Click the Editor link under the Appearances menu. Then click the Theme Functions (**functions.php**) template.**

   The Theme Functions template opens in the text editor on the left side of the Edit Themes page.

2. **Type the following function on a new line in the Theme Functions template file:**

   ```
   add_theme_support( 'nav-menus' );
   ```

3. **Click the Update File button to save the changes to the template.**

   This template tag tells WordPress that your theme can use the Custom Menu feature, and a Menus link now displays under the Appearances menu in the Dashboard.

4. **Open the Header template (**header.php**)**

   Click on the Header link on the Edit Themes page to open the Header template in the text editor on the left side of the Edit Themes page.

5. **Add the following template tag by typing it on a new line in the Header template (**header.php**):**

   ```
   <?php wp_nav_menu(); ?>
   ```

   This template tag is needed so the menu you build using the Custom Menu feature will display at the top of your Web site. Table 13-4 gives the details on the different parameters you are able to use with the wp_nav_menu(); template tag in order to further customize the display to suit your needs.

6. **Save the changes you've made to the Header template.**

   Click the Update File button at the bottom of the page.

Table 13-4   Common Tag Parameters for wp_nav_menu();

Parameter	Information	Default	Tag
`id`	The unique ID of the menu (because you can create several menus, each has a unique ID number)	Blank	`wp_nav_menu ( array( 'id' => '1' ) );`
`slug`	The menu name in slug form (for example, `nav-menu`)	Blank	`wp_nav_menu ( array( 'slug' => 'nav-menu' ) );`
`menu`	The menu name	Blank	`wp_nav_menu ( array( 'menu' => 'Nav Menu' ) );`
`menu_class`	The CSS class used to style the menu list	Menu	`wp_nav_menu ( array( 'menu_class' => 'mymenu' ) );`
`format`	The HTML markup used to style the list (either an unordered list (`ul/li`) or `div` class)	div	`wp_nav_menu ( array( 'format' => 'ul' ) );`
`fallback_cb`	The parameter that creates a fall back if a custom menu doesn't exist	`wp_page_menu` (the default list of page links)	`wp_nav_menu ( array( ' fallback_cb' => 'wp_page_menu') );`
`before`	The text that displays before the link text	None	`wp_nav_menu( array( 'before' => 'Click Here' ) );`
`after`	The text that displays after the link text	None	`wp_nav_menu( array( 'after' => '&raquo;' ) );`

Building custom navigation menus

After you add the menu feature to your theme (or if you're already using a theme that has it added), building menus is super easy — just follow these steps:

1. **Click the Menus link in the Appearances menu on your Dashboard.**

   The Menus page opens on your WordPress Dashboard.

2. **Type a name in the Menu Name box and click the Create Menu button.**

   The Menus page is reloaded with a message that tells you your new menu has been created.

3. **Add new links to your newly created menu.**

   There are three ways that WordPress allows you to add new links to the new menu you just created:

   - **Custom Links:** In the URL field, type the URL of the Web site that you want to add (`http://www.google.com`). Then type the name of the link that you want displayed in your menu in the Text field (Google). Then click the Add to Menu button.

   - **Pages:** Click the View All link to display a list of all the page(s) you have currently published on your site. Place a checkmark in the box next to the page names you would like to add to your menu. Then click the Add to Menu button.

   - **Categories:** Click the View All link to display a list of all the categories you've created on your site. Place a checkmark in the box next to the category names you would like to add to the menu. Then click the Add to Menu button.

4. **Review your menu choices on the right side of the page.**

   When you add new menu items, the column on the right side of the Menus page populates with your menu choices. In Figure 13-4, I've populated my menu with one custom link, one page link, and one category link (Home, About and Books, respectively).

5. **Edit your menu choices, if needed.**

   Click the Edit link to the right of the menu link name () to edit the information of each individual link in your new menu.

6. **Save your menu before leaving the Menus page.**

   Be sure to click the Save Menu button under Menu Settings on the right side, at the top of the Menus page. A message confirming that the new menu has been saved appears.

Figure 13-4:
The Build
Custom
Menus
options on
the Menus
page on the
Dashboard.

You can create as many menus as you need to for your Web site. Just follow the parameters for the menu template tag to make sure you're pulling in the correct menu in the correct spot on your theme. Pay attention to either the menu ID or menu name in the template tag.

Changing Font Styles, Colors, and Sizes

Fonts come in all shapes and sizes, and you can use CSS to define the font styles that display in your blog. Changing the font can change the look and feel of your blog dramatically, as well as improve your readers' experience by making the text easy on the eyes. Table 13-5 displays some of the most commonly used CSS properties and values for applying font styling to your stylesheet.

Table 13-5	Common Font Styles in CSS
Font Properties	*Sample Value*
`font-family`	Times New Roman
`color`	black or #000000
`font-size`	12px

The Web is actually kind of picky about how it displays fonts, as well as what kind of fonts you can use in the `font-family` property. Not all fonts display correctly on the Web. To be safe, here are some commonly used font families that display correctly in most browsers:

✔ **Serif fonts:** Times New Roman, Georgia, Garamond, Bookman Old Style
✔ **Sans-serif fonts:** Verdana, Arial, Tahoma, Trebuchet MS

Serif fonts have little tails, or curlicues, at the edges of letters. (This text is in a serif font.) Sans-serif fonts have straight edges and are devoid of any fancy styling. (The heading in Table 13-5 uses a sans-serif font.)

When you want to change a font family in your CSS, open the stylesheet (`style.css`), search for `property: font-family`, change the values for that property, and save your changes.

In the default template CSS, the font is defined in the `<body>` tag like this:

```
font-family: 'Lucida Grande', Verdana, Arial, Sans-Serif
```

You can easily change the color of your font by changing the `color` property of the CSS selector you want to tweak. You can use hex codes to define the colors.

In the default template CSS, the font color is defined in the `<body>` tag like this:

```
color: #333;
```

To tweak the size of your font, change the `font-size` property of the CSS selector you want to change. Font sizes generally are determined by units of measurement, as in these examples:

✔ **px:** pixel measurement. Increasing or decreasing the number of pixels increases or decreases the font size (12px is larger than 10px).

✔ **pt:** point measurement. As with pixels, increasing or decreasing the number of points affects the font size accordingly (12pt is larger than 10pt).

✔ **%:** percentage measurement. Increasing or decreasing the percentage number affects the font size accordingly (50% is the equivalent to 7 pixels; 100% is the equivalent to 17 pixels).

In the default template CSS, the font size is defined in the body tag as a percentage, like this:

```
font-size: 62.5%;
```

Putting all three elements (font-family, color, and font-size) together in the `<body>` tag, they style the font for the overall body of your site. Here's how they work together in the `<body>` tag of the default template CSS:

```
body {
font-size: 62.5%; /* Resets 1em to 10px */
font-family: 'Lucida Grande', Verdana, Arial, Sans-Serif;
color: #333;
}
```

Chapter 14

Beyond Blogging: WordPress as a Content Management System

In This Chapter

▶ Defining a Content Management System

▶ Setting the home page

▶ Creating a template for each static page, post category, and sidebar

▶ Custom styles for sticky posts, categories, and tags

▶ Using custom post types

▶ Optimizing for search engine success

*I*f you've avoided using WordPress as a solution for building your own Web site because you think it's only a blogging platform, and you don't want to have a blog (not every Web site owner does, after all), it's time to rethink your position. The self-hosted version of WordPress, WordPress.org, is a powerful Content Management System (CMS) that is flexible and extensible enough to run an entire Web site — with no blog at all, if you prefer.

A *Content Management System* (CMS) is a system used to create and maintain your entire site. It includes tools for publishing and editing, as well as for searching and retrieving information and content. A CMS lets you maintain your Web site with little or no knowledge of HTML. You can create, modify, retrieve, and update your content without ever having to touch the code required to perform those tasks.

This chapter shows you a few ways that you can use the self-hosted WordPress.org software to power your entire Web site, with or without a blog. It covers different template configurations that you can use to create separate sections of your site. You also discover how to use the front page of your site as a *landing page* (a static page) or *portal* (a page that contains snippets from other sections of your site, with links to those sections), which can include a link to an internal blog page, if you want a blog.

Creating the Front Page of Your Web Site

For the most part, when you visit a blog powered by WordPress, the blog is on the main page. My personal blog at `http://justagirlintheworld.com`, powered by WordPress (of course), shows my latest blog posts on the front page, along with links to the post archives (by month or by category). This setup is typical of a site run by WordPress (see Figure 14-1).

But the front page of my business site at `http://ewebscapes.com`, also powered by WordPress, contains no blog (see Figure 14-2). It doesn't display any blog posts; rather, it displays the contents of a static page I created in the WordPress Dashboard. This static page serves as a portal to my design blog, my portfolio, and other sections of my site. The site includes a blog but also serves as a full-blown business Web site, with all the sections I need to provide my clients the information they want.

Both of my sites are powered by the self-hosted version of WordPress.org, so how can they differ so much in what they display on the front page? The answer lies in the templates in the WordPress Dashboard.

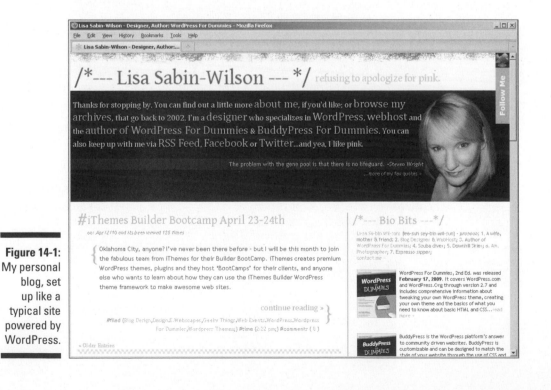

Figure 14-1: My personal blog, set up like a typical site powered by WordPress.

Figure 14-2: My business site, set up as a business Web site, rather than a blog.

You use static pages in WordPress to create content that you don't want to display as part of your blog but do want to display as part of your overall site (such as a bio page, a page of services, and so on).

Creating a front page is a three-step process: Create a static page, designate that static page as the front page of your site, and tweak the page to look like a Web site rather than a blog.

Using this method, you can create unlimited numbers of static pages to build an entire Web site. You don't even need to have a blog on this site unless you want to include one.

Creating the static page

To have a static page display on the front page of your site, you need to create that page. Follow these steps:

1. **Click the Add New link on the Pages menu.**

The Add New Page page opens where you can write a new page to your WordPress blog, as shown in Figure 14-3. (Check out Chapter 7 for the difference between a page and a post in WordPress.)

2. **In the Title text box, type a title for the page.**

3. **Type the content of your page in the text box.**

4. **Set the options for this page.**

   I explain all these options in Chapter 7.

5. **Click the Publish button.**

   The page is saved to your database and published to your WordPress site with its own, individual URL (or *permalink*). The URL for the static page consists of your blog URL and the title of the page. For example, if you titled your page "About Me," then the URL of the page is `http://yourdomain.com/about-me`. (See Chapter 8 for more information about permalinks.)

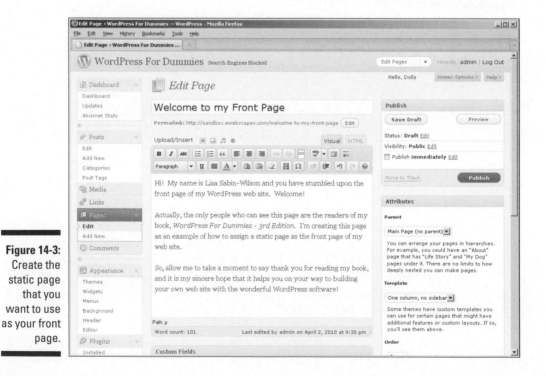

Figure 14-3:
Create the static page that you want to use as your front page.

Note that the Page Template option is set to Default Template. This setting tells WordPress that you want to use the default page template (page.php in your theme template files) to format the page you're creating. The default template is the default setting for all pages you create; assigning a page to a different template is something I discuss in the "Defining Specific Templates for Static Pages" section in this chapter.

Assigning a static page as the front page

Next, you need to tell WordPress that you want the static page to serve as the front page of your site. Follow these steps:

1. **Click the Reading link on the Settings menu to display the Reading Settings page.**

2. **In the Front Page Displays section, select the A Static Page radio button.**

3. **From the Front Page drop-down menu, choose the static page that you want to serve as your front page.**

   In Figure 14-4, I'm choosing to display a static page, and Welcome to My Front Page is the page I want to display.

Figure 14-4:
Choosing which page to display as the front page.

Reading Settings

Front page displays

○ Your latest posts

⦿ A static page (select below)

Front page: — Select —

Posts page: — Select —
About
Welcome to my Front Page

4. **Click the Save Changes button at the bottom of the Reading Settings page.**

   WordPress displays the page you selected in Step 4 as the front page of your site. Figure 14-5 shows my site displaying the page I created as my front page.

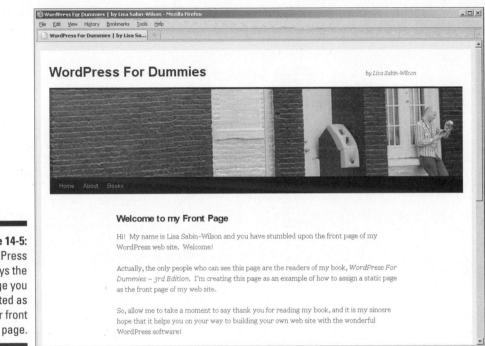

Figure 14-5:
WordPress
displays the
page you
selected as
your front
page.

Adding a Blog to Your Web Site

If you want a blog on your site but don't want to display the blog on the front page, you can add one with the WordPress Dashboard. To create the blog for your site, follow these steps:

1. **Click the Add New link on the Pages menu.**

   The page where you can write a new post to your WordPress blog opens.

2. **Type** Blog **in the Title text box.**

   This automatically sets the page slug to /blog. (Read more about slugs in Chapter 8.)

3. **Leave the Page Content box blank.**

4. **Click the Publish button.**

   The page is saved to your database and published to your WordPress site.

Now you have a blank page that redirects to http://yourdomain.com/blog. Next, you need to assign the page you just created as your blog page. To do so, follow these steps:

1. **Click the Reading link on the Settings menu to display the Reading Settings page.**

   The Reading Settings page opens.

2. **From the Posts Page drop-down menu, choose the page you just created.**

   The page is set as your blog page.

3. **In the Blog Pages Show at Most section, type the number of posts you want to display in the Posts text box.**

   This setting specifies the number of posts you want to display on that page at any time. If you enter **5**, the blog page shows the last five posts you've made to your blog.

4. **Click the Save Changes button.**

   The options you just set are saved, and your blog is now at `http://yourdomain.com/blog` (where *yourdomain.com* is the actual domain name).

Now when you navigate to `http://yourdomain.com/blog`, your blog displays. Figure 14-6 shows my blog page with my latest post.

Figure 14-6:
My blog at
`/blog` with
one post
displayed.

This method of using the `/blog` page slug works only if you're using custom permalinks with your WordPress installation. (See Chapter 8 if you want more information about permalinks.) If you're using the default permalinks, the URL for your blog page is different; it looks something like `http://yourdomain.com/?p=4` (where 4 is the ID of the page you created for your blog).

Easily add a link to your blog in the navigation menu (as shown on my site in Figure 14-6) by adding it to your custom menu. To find out how to build your own custom menu, check out Chapter 13.

Defining Specific Templates for Static Pages

As I explain in "Creating the Front Page of Your Web Site," earlier in this chapter, a *static page* contains content that is not displayed on the blog page, but as a separate page within your site. You can have numerous static pages on your site, and each page can have a different design, which is governed by the template you create. (See Chapter 12 to find out all about choosing and using templates.) You can create several static-page templates and assign them to specific pages within your site by adding code to the top of the static-page templates.

Following is the code that appears at the top of the static-page template I use for my About Us and Our Blog Designers page at `http://ewebscapes.com/about`:

```php
<?php
/*
Template Name: About Page
*/
?>
```

Using a template on a static page is a two-step process: Upload the template, and tell WordPress to use the template by tweaking the page's code.

In Chapter 13, I cover information about Custom Menus, including how to create different navigation menus for your Web site. You can create a menu of links that includes all the pages you've created in your WordPress Dashboard. You can display that menu on your Web site using the Custom Menus feature.

Uploading the template

To use a page template, you have to create one. You can create this file in a text-editor program, such as Notepad. (To see how to create a template, flip to Chapter 12.) To create an About page, for example, you can name your template `about.php`.

When you have your template created, follow these steps to make it part of WordPress:

1. **Upload the template file to your WordPress theme folder.**

   You can find that folder on your Web server in `/wp-content/themes/`. (See Chapter 6 for more information about FTP.)

2. **Log in to your WordPress Dashboard, click the Editor link on the Appearance menu.**

   The Edit Themes page opens.

3. **Click the about.php template link located on the right side of the page.**

4. **Type the Template Name tag directly above the header template tag.**

   The header tag looks like this: `<?php get_header(); ?>`.

   If you're creating an About Page, the code to create the Template Name looks like this:

   ```
   <?php
   /*
   Template Name: About Page
   /*
   ?>
   ```

5. **Click the Update File button.**

   The file is saved, and the page refreshes. If you created an About Page template, the `about.php` template is now called About Page in the template list on the right side of the page.

Figure 14-7 shows the Page template and displays the code needed to define a specific name for the template.

Assigning the template to a static page

When you have the template created and named the way you want it, you assign that template to a page by following these steps:

1. **Click the Add New link on the Pages menu.**

   The Add New Page page opens, where you can write a new post to your WordPress blog.

2. **Type the title in the Title text box and the page content in the text box.**

3. **Choose the page template from the Page Template drop-down menu.**

   The Page Template drop-down menu in the Attributes module by default is shown on the right side of the page. You can reposition the modules on this page; see Chapter 7 for more information.

4. **Click the Publish button to save and publish the page to your site.**

Figure 14-8 shows the layout of my home page on my business site at `http://ewebscapes.com` and the information it contains, whereas Figure 14-9 shows the layout and information provided on the Services page at `http://ewebscapes.com/services`. Both pages are on the same site, in the same WordPress installation, with different static-page templates to provide different looks, layouts, and sets of information.

Figure 14-8:
My home
page at
E.Web-
scapes.

Figure 14-9:
The
Services
page at
E.Web-
scapes.

Creating a Template for Each Post Category

You don't have to limit yourself to creating a static-page template for your site. No, you can completely gorge yourself at the table of WordPress templates and create unique sections for your site, as I did (with an espresso chaser, of course).

Figure 14-10 shows my design portfolio. Design Portfolio is the name of a category that I created in the WordPress Dashboard. Instead of using a static page for the display of my portfolio, I used a category template to handle the display of all posts made to the Design Portfolio category.

You can create category templates for all categories in your blog simply by creating template files with filenames that correspond to the category ID numbers and then uploading those templates to your WordPress `themes` directory (see Chapter 12). The logic to this is as follows:

Figure 14-10: My Design Portfolio page, using a category template file.

✔ A template with the filename `category.php` is a catch-all for the display of categories.

✔ Add a dash and the category ID number to the end of the filename (as shown in Table 14-1) to specify a template for an individual category.

✔ If you don't have a `category.php` or `category-#.php` file, the category display pulls from the Main Index template (`index.php`).

Table 14-1 shows three examples of the category template naming requirements.

Table 14-1   WordPress Category Template Naming Conventions

If the Category ID Is . . .	The Category Template Filename Is . . .
1	`category-1.php`
2	`category-2.php`
3	`category-3.php`

Pulling In Content from a Single Category

WordPress makes it possible to pull in very specific types of content on your Web site through the `<query_posts>` template tag. You place this template tag before The Loop (see Chapter 12), and it lets you specify which category you want to pull information from. If you have a category called WordPress, and you want to display the last three posts from that category on your front page, in your blog sidebar, or somewhere else on your site, you can use this template tag.

The `<query_posts>` template tag has several parameters that let you display different types of content, such as posts in specific categories and content from specific pages/posts or dates in your blog archives. The `<query_posts>` tag lets you pass so many variables and parameters that it's impossible for me to list all the possibilities. Instead, you can visit this page in the WordPress Codex and read about the options available with this tag: `http://codex.wordpress.org/Template_Tags/query_posts`.

First, you have to find the ID number for the category you want to use; then you have to tell WordPress how to display the content with the `<query_posts>` tag.

Finding the category ID number

The unique ID number for a category is not easy to find unless you know where to look. Follow these steps:

1. **Click the Categories link on the Posts menu.**

   The Categories page opens.

2. **Hover your mouse over the name of the category that you need the ID number for.**

3. **Look in the status bar of your browser to view the category ID number.**

   Figure 14-11 shows the category ID in the status bar of Mozilla Firefox. (Internet Explorer and Safari have similar status bars.) The last part of the URL displayed in the status bar is `cat_ID=1`, which means that 1 is the category ID for my Uncategorized category.

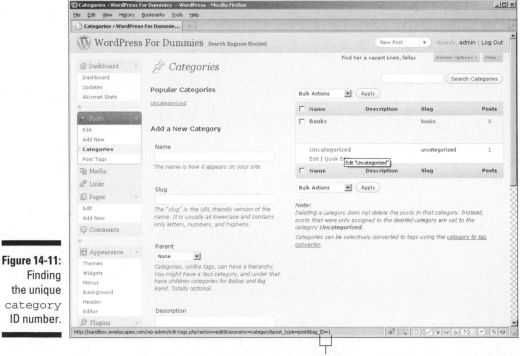

Figure 14-11: Finding the unique `category` ID number.

Category ID

Adding the <query_post> tag

When you have the category ID number in hand, you're ready to add the <query_post> tag to your template.

Here is an example of two parameters you can use with the <query_posts> tag:

- ✔ **showposts=X:** This parameter tells WordPress how many posts you want to display. If you want to display only three posts, enter **showposts=3**.

- ✔ **cat=X:** This parameter tells WordPress that you want to pull posts from the category with this specific ID number. If the ID category is 40, enter **cat=40**.

Follow these steps to add the <query_post> tag to your template:

1. **Click the Editor link on the Appearance menu.**

   The Edit Themes page opens.

2. **Click the template in which you want to display the content.**

   If you want to display content in a sidebar, for example, choose the Sidebar template: sidebar.php.

3. **Locate the ending </ul> tag at the bottom of the template for the theme you're using.**

   If you're using the Twenty Ten theme, the ending </ul> tag is the second-to-the-last line.

4. **Type the following code directly above the ending </ul> tag:**

```php
<?php query_posts('showposts=3&cat=40'); ?>
<h2>Type Your Desired Title Here</h2>
<?php if (have_posts()) : while (have_posts()) : the_
       post(); ?>
<strong><a href="<?php the_permalink() ?>"
       rel="bookmark" title="Permanent Link to <?php
       the_title_attribute(); ?>"><?php the_title();
       ?></a></strong>
<?php the_excerpt();endwhile;endif; ?>
```

In the first line, I indicated the following: showposts=3&cat=40. You can change these numbers to suit your specific needs. Just change 3 to whatever number of posts you'd like to display (there is no limit!), and change 40 to the specific category ID number that you want to use.

5. **Click the Update File button.**

   The changes you just made are saved to the sidebar.php template.

Using Sidebar Templates

You can create separate sidebar templates for different pages of your site by using a simple `include` statement. When you write an `include` statement, you're simply telling WordPress that you want it to include a specific file on a specific page.

The code that pulls the usual Sidebar template (`sidebar.php`) into all the other templates, such as the Main Index template (`index.php`), looks like this:

```
<?php get_sidebar(); ?>
```

What if you create a page and want to use a sidebar that has different information from what you have in the Sidebar template (`sidebar.php`)? Follow these steps:

1. **Create a new sidebar template in a text editor such as Notepad.**

   See Chapter 12 for information on template tags and themes.

2. **Save the file as `sidebar2.php`.**

   In Notepad, choose File➪Save. When you're asked to name the file, type **sidebar2.php** and then click Save.

3. **Upload `sidebar2.php` to your `themes` folder on your Web server.**

   See Chapter 6 for FTP information, and review Chapter 12 for information on how to locate the `themes` folder.

   The template is now listed in your theme files on the Edit Themes page (log in to your WordPress Dashboard, click the Editor link on the Appearance menu).

4. **To include the `sidebar2.php` template in one of your page templates, find this code:**

   ```
   <?php get_sidebar(); />
   ```

5. **Replace it with this `include` code:**

   ```
   <?php include (TEMPLATEPATH . '/sidebar2.php'); ?>
   ```

Using that `include (TEMPLATEPATH` statement, you can include virtually any file in any of your WordPress templates. You can use this method to create footer templates for pages on your site, for example. To do this, first create a new template with the filename `footer2.php`. Then locate the following code in your template:

```
<?php get_footer(); ?>
```

and replace it with this code:

```
<?php include (TEMPLATEPATH . '/footer2.php'); ?>
```

You can do multiple things with WordPress to extend it beyond the blog. This chapter gives you a few practical examples using the default Twenty Ten theme. The point is to show you how to use WordPress to create a fully functional Web site with a CMS platform — anything from the smallest personal site to a large business site.

Custom Styles for Sticky, Category, and Tag Posts

In Chapter 12, I discussed the method of putting a very basic WordPress theme together, which included a Main Index template using the WordPress Loop. You can use a custom tag to display custom styles for sticky posts, categories, and tags on your blog. That special tag looks like this:

```
<div <?php post_class() ?> id="post-<?php the_ID(); ?>">
```

The part of that template tag that is so cool is the post_class() section. This template tag tells WordPress to insert specific HTML markup in your template that allow you to use CSS to make custom styles for sticky posts, categories, and tags.

In Chapter 8, I tell you all about how to publish new posts to your blog, including the different options you can set for your blog posts, such as categories, tags, and publishing settings. One of the settings is the Stick This Post to the Front Page setting. In this chapter, I show you how to custom style those sticky posts — it's not as messy as it sounds!

For example, I have published a post with the following options set for that post:

- ✔ Stick this post to the front page
- ✔ Filed in a category called WordPress
- ✔ Tagged with News

By having the post_class() tag in my template, WordPress inserts HTML markup that allows me to use CSS to style sticky posts, or posts assigned to specific tags or categories, differently. WordPress inserted the following HTML markup for my post:

```
<div class="post sticky category-wordpress tag-news">
```

In Chapter 13, I talk about CSS selectors and HTML markup and how they work together to create style and format for your WordPress theme. I can now go to my CSS file and define styles for the following CSS selectors:

- ✔ **.post:** Use this as the generic style for all posts on your blog. Te CSS for this tag is

```
.post {background: #ffffff; border: 1px solid silver;
       padding: 10px;}
```

   A style is created for all posts that have a white background with a thin silver border and 10 pixels of padding space between the post text and the border of the post.

- ✔ **.sticky:** The concept of sticking a post to your front page is to call attention to that post, so you may want to use different CSS styling to make it stand out from the rest of the posts on your blog:

```
.sticky {background: #ffffff; border: 4px solid red;
        padding: 10px;}
```

   This creates a style for all sticky posts that display with a white background, a thicker red border, and 10 pixels of padding space between the post text and border of the post.

- ✔ **.category—wordpress:** Because I blog a lot about WordPress, my readers may appreciate it if I gave them a visual cue as to which posts on my blog are about that topic. I can do that through CSS by telling WordPress to display a small WordPress icon on the top-right corner of all my posts in the WordPress category:

```
.category-wordpress {background: url(wordpress-icon.
        jpg) top right no-repeat; height: 100px;
        width: 100px;}
```

   This code inserts a graphic — wordpress-icon.jpg — that is 100 pixels in height and 100 pixels in width at the top-right corner of every post I've assigned to the WordPress category on my blog.

- ✔ **.tag—news:** I can style all posts tagged with News the same way I've styled the categories:

```
.tag-news {background: #f2f2f2; border: 1px solid
        black; padding: 10px;}
```

   This CSS styles all posts tagged with News with a light grey background and a thin black border with 10 pixels of padding between the post text and border of the post.

Using the post-class() tag, combined with CSS, to create dynamic styles for the posts on your blog is fun and easy!

Working with Custom Post Types

Brand new to the latest version of WordPress (version 3.0) is a feature called Custom Post Types. This feature allows you, the site owner, to create different content types for your WordPress site that give you more creative control over how different types of content are entered, published, and displayed on your WordPress Web site.

By default, WordPress already has different post types built in to the software, ready for you to use. These default post types include:

✔ Blog posts
✔ Pages
✔ Navigation menus (see Chapter 13)
✔ Attachments
✔ Revisions

Custom post types give you the ability to create new and useful types of content on your Web site, including a smart and easier way to publish those content types to your site.

The possibilities for the use of Custom Post Types are really endless, but here are a few ideas that will kick start your imagination, as well as being some of the more popular and useful ideas that others have implemented on sites:

✔ Photo Gallery
✔ Podcast or Video
✔ Book Reviews
✔ Coupons and Special Offers
✔ Events Calendar

In order to create and use Custom Post Types on your site, you need to be sure that your WordPress theme contains the correct code and functions. In the following steps, I am creating a very basic and generic Custom Post Type called "Generic Content" — follow these steps to create the same basic Custom Post Type and later in this section, you find detailed information on the different parameters you can use with Custom Post Types to create different types to suit your needs:

1. **Open the Theme Functions template file (`functions.php`).**

   Click the Editor link under the Appearances menu to open the Theme Editor page. Then click the Theme Functions template link to open the `functions.php` file in the text editor on the left side of the page.

2. **Add the Custom Post Types code to the bottom of the Theme Functions template file.**

   Scroll down to the bottom of the `functions.php` file and include the following code to add a 'Generic Content' Custom Post Type to your site:

   ```
   add_action( 'init', 'create_my_post_types' );

   function create_my_post_types() {
   register_post_type( 'generic_content',
   array(
   'label' => __( 'Generic Content' ),
   'singular_label' => __( 'Generic Content' ),
   'description' => __( 'This is a description of
   the Generic Content type' ),
   'public' => true,
   );
   }
   ```

3. **Save your changes.**

   Click the Update File button to save the changes made to the `functions.php` file.

The function: `register_post_type` can accept several different arguments and parameters, which are detailed in Table 14-2. You can use a variety and combination of different arguments and parameters to create a specific post type. You can find more information on Custom Post Types and using the `register_post_types` function in the official WordPress Codex here: `http://codex.wordpress.org/Function_Reference/register_post_type`.

Now that you have completed the steps to add the Generic Content post type to your site, you see that there is a new post type added to the left navigation menu in the Dashboard labeled Generic.

You add and publish new content using the new Custom Post Type just as you would when you write and publish blog posts (see Chapter 8). The published content is not added to the chronological listing of blog posts, but are, rather, treated as separate content, just like static pages.

View the permalink for it, and you see that it adopts the post type name, Generic Content, and uses it as part of the permalink structure, creating a permalink that looks like: `http://yourdomain.com/generic-content/new-article`.

Table 14-2 Arguments and Parameters for: register_post_types();

Parameter	Information	Parameters	Example
label	The name of the post type	None	`'label' => __( 'Generic Content' ),`
singular_label	Same as label	None	`'singular_label' => __( 'Generic Content' ),`
description	The description of the post type; displayed in the Dashboard to represent the post type	None	`'description' => __( 'This is a descrip-tion of the Generic Content type' ),`
public show_ui publicly_queryable exclude_from_search	Sets whether the post type is public, or not. There are three other arguments. show_ui: show admin screens, or not. publicly_queryable: query for this post type from the front end, or not. exclude_from_search: show post type in search results, or not	true or false. Default is false	`'public' => true,` `'show_ui' => true,` `'publicly_queryable' => true,` `'exclude_from_search' => false,`

(continued)

Table 14-2 *(continued)*

Parameter	Information	Parameters	Example
menu_position	Sets the position of the post type menu item in the Dashboard navigation menu	Default: 20 By default, custom post types appear after the Comments menu in the Dashboard Set integer in intervals of 5 (ie: 5, 10, 15, 20, etc)	'menu_position' => 25,
menu_icon	Define a custom icon (graphic) to the post type menu item in the Dashboard navigation menu Create and upload the image into the images directory of your theme folder	None	'menu_icon' => get_stylesheet_directory_uri() . '/images/generic-content.png',
hierarchical	Tells WordPress whether to display the post type content list in a hierarchical manner, or not	true or false Default is true	'hierarchical' => true,
query_var	Allows you to control whether or not this post type can be used with a query variable such as query_posts (see previous section) or WP_Query	true or false Default is false	'query_var' => true,

Parameter	Information	Parameters	Example
`capability_type`	Defines permissions for users to edit, create, or read the custom post type (see Chapter 7)	`post` (default) Gives the same capabilities for those who can edit, create and read blog posts	`'query_var' => post,`
`supports`	Defines what meta boxes, or modules, are available for this post type in the Dashboard	`title` `editor` `comments` `track-backs` `revisions` `author` `excerpt` `thumbnail` `custom-fields` `page-attributes`	`'supports' => array ( 'title', 'editor', 'excerpt', 'custom-fields', 'thumbnail' ),`
`rewrite`	Rewrite the permalink structure for the post type	true or false Two other arguments are available: `slug:` permalink slug to prepend your custom post types `with_front:` if you've set your permalink structure with a specific prefix such as / `blog`	`'rewrite' => array( 'slug' => 'my-content', 'with_front' => false ),`

(continued)

Table 14-2 *(continued)*

Parameter	Information	Parameters	Example
taxonomies	Allows you to use existing WordPress taxonomies (category and tag)	Category post_tag	'taxonomies' => array ('post_tag', 'category'),

Optimizing Your WordPress Blog

Search engine optimization (SEO) is the practice of preparing your site to make it as easy as possible for the major search engines to crawl your site and cache your data in their systems so that your site appears as high as possible in the search returns.

If you visit Google's search engine page at http://google.com and do a search using the keywords *WordPress blog design,* my own site at E.Webscapes is in the top ten search results for those keywords (at least, it is as I'm writing this chapter). Those results can change from day to day, so by the time you read this book, someone else may very well have taken over that coveted position. The reality of chasing those high-ranking search engine positions is that they're here today, gone tomorrow.The goal of search engine optimization is to make sure that *your* site ranks as high as possible for the keywords that you think people will use to find your site. After you attain those high-ranking positions, the next goal is to keep them. Check out *Search Engine Optimization For Dummies,* by Peter Kent (Wiley Publishing), for some valuable information on keeping those high rankings through ongoing optimization of your site.

WordPress is equipped to create an environment that is friendly to search engines, giving them easy navigation through your archives, categories, and pages. This environment is provided by a clean code base, content that is easily updated through the WordPress interface, and a solid navigation structure.

To extend search engine optimization even further, you can tweak five elements of your WordPress posts, pages, and templates:

✔ **Custom permalinks:** Use custom permalinks, rather than the default WordPress permalinks, to fill your post and page URLs with valuable keywords. Check out Chapter 8 for information on WordPress permalinks.

✔ **Posts and page titles:** Create descriptive titles for your blog posts and pages to provide rich keywords in your site.

✔ **Text:** Fill your blog posts and pages with keywords for search engines to find and index. Keeping your site updated with descriptive text and phrases helps the search engines find keywords to associate with your site.

✔ **Category names:** Use descriptive names for the categories you create in WordPress to place great keywords right in the URL for those category pages, if you use custom permalinks.

✔ **Images and** ALT **tags:** Place <ALT> tags in your images to further define and describe the images on your site. You can accomplish this task easily by using the description field in the WordPress image uploader.

Planting keywords in your Web site

If you're interested in a higher ranking for your site, I strongly recommend using custom permalinks. By using custom permalinks, you're automatically inserting keywords into the URLs of your posts and pages, letting search engines include those posts and pages in their databases of information on those topics. If your site is hosted by a provider that has the Apache mod_ rewrite module enabled, you can use the custom permalink structure for your WordPress-powered site.

Keywords are the first step on your journey toward great search engine results. Search engines depend on keywords, and people use keywords to look for content.

The default permalink structure in WordPress is pretty ugly. When you're looking at the default permalink for any post, you see a URL something like this:

```
http://yourdomain.com/p?=105
```

This URL contains no keywords of worth. If you change to a custom permalink structure, your post URLs automatically include the titles of your posts to provide keywords, which search engines absolutely love. A custom permalink may appear in this format:

```
http://yourdomain.com/2007/02/01/your-post-title
```

I explain setting up and using custom permalinks in full detail in Chapter 8.

Optimizing your post titles for search engine success

Search engine optimization doesn't completely depend on how you set your site up. It also depends on you, the site owner, and how you present your content.

One way to present your content in a way that lets search engines catalog your site easily is to give your blog posts and pages titles that make sense and coordinate with the actual content being presented. If you're doing a post on a certain topic, make sure that the title of the post contains at least one or two keywords about that particular topic. This practice gives the search engines even more ammunition to list your site in searches relevant to the topic of your post.

As your site's presence in the search engines grows, more people will find your site, and your readership will increase as a result.

A blog post with the title A Book I'm Reading isn't going to tell anyone what book it is, making it difficult for people searching for information on that particular book to find the post.

If you give the post the title WordPress For Dummies: My Review, you provide keywords in the title, and (if you're using custom permalinks) WordPress automatically inserts those keywords into the URL, giving the search engines a triple keyword play:

- ✔ Keywords exist in your blog post title.
- ✔ Keywords exist in your blog post URL.
- ✔ Keywords exist in the content of your post.

Writing content with readers in mind

When you write your posts and pages, and want to make sure that your content appears in the first page of search results so that people will find your site, you need to keep those people in mind when you're composing the content.

When search engines visit your site to crawl through your content, they aren't seeing how nicely designed your site is. What they're looking for are words — which they're grabbing to include in their databases. You, the site owner, want to make sure that your posts and pages use the words and phrases that you want to include in search engines.

If your post is about a recipe for fried green tomatoes, for example, you need to add a keyword or phrase that you think people will use when they search for the topic. If you think people would use the phrase *recipe for fried green tomatoes* as a search term, you may want to include that phrase in the content and title of your post.

A title such as A Recipe I Like isn't as effective as a title such as A Recipe for Fried Green Tomatoes, right? Including it in your post or page content gives the search engines a double keyword whammy.

Here's another example: I once wrote a post about a rash that I developed on my finger, under my ring. I wrote that post well over a year ago, not really meaning to attract a bunch of people to that particular post. However, it seems that many women around the world suffer from the same rash, because a year later, that post still gets at least one comment a week. When people do a Google search using the keywords *rash under my wedding ring,* out of a possible 743,000 results returned, my blog post appears in the top five slots.

This is how great blogs are! I was actually able to solve my problem with the rash under my finger because one woman from Australia found my blog through Google, visited my blog post, and left a comment with a solution that worked. Who says blogs aren't useful?

Creating categories that attract search engines

One little-known SEO tip for WordPress users: The names you give the categories you've created for your blog provide rich keywords that attract search engines like bees to honey. A few services — Technorati.com being one of the biggest — treat categories in WordPress like tags. These services use those categories to classify recent blog posts on any given topic. The names you give your categories in WordPress can serve as topic tags for Technorati and similar services.

Search engines also see your categories as keywords that are relevant to the content on your site. In this regard, it's important to make sure that you're giving your categories names that are relevant to the content you're providing on your site.

If you sometimes blog about your favorite recipes, you can make it easier for search engines to find your recipes if you create categories specific to the recipes you're blogging about. Instead of having one Favorite Recipes category, you can create multiple category names that correspond to the types of recipes you blog about — Casserole Recipes, Dessert Recipes, Beef Recipes, and Chicken Recipes, for example.

Creating specific category titles not only helps search engines, but also helps your readers.

You can also consider having one category called Favorite Recipes and creating subcategories (also known as *child categories*) that give a few more details on the types of recipes you've written about. (See Chapter 8 for information on creating categories and child categories.)

Categories use the custom permalink structure as well. So links to your WordPress categories also become keyword tools within your site to help the search engines — and ultimately, search engine users — find the content. Using custom permalinks gives you category page URLs that look something like this:

```
http://yourdomain.com/category/Category_Name
```

The `Category_Name` portion of that URL puts the keywords right into the hands of search engines.

Using the <ALT> tag for images

When you use the WordPress image uploader to include an image in your post or page, you're given a Description text box in which you can enter a description of the image. (I cover using the WordPress image uploader in detail in Chapter 9.) This text automatically becomes what is referred to as the <ALT> tag.

The <ALT> tag's real purpose is to provide a description of the image for people who, for some reason or another, can't actually see the image. In a text-based browser that doesn't display images, for example, visitors see the description, or <ALT> text, telling them what image would be there if they could see it. Also, the tag helps people with impaired vision who rely on screen-reading technology, because the screen reader reads the <ALT> text from the image. You can read more about Web site accessibility for people with disabilities at www.w3.org/WAI/References/Browsing.

An extra benefit of <ALT> tags is that search engines gather data from them to further classify the content of your site. The following is the code for inserting an image, with the <ALT> tag of the code in bold to demonstrate what I'm talking about:

```
<img src="http://yourdomain.com/image.jpg" alt="This is an
          ALT tag within an image" />
```

Search engines harvest those <ALT> tags as keywords. The WordPress image uploader gives you an easy way to include those <ALT> tags without having to worry about inserting them into the image code yourself. Just fill out the Description text box before you upload and add the image to your post. Chapter 9 covers in-depth information on adding images to your site content, including how to add descriptive text for the ALT tag and keywords.

Chapter 15

Hosting Multiple Sites with WordPress

In This Chapter

▶ Understanding if multiple sites are for you

▶ Exploring Web hosting considerations

▶ Enabling the WordPress network capabilities

▶ Choosing subdirectories or sub-domain

▶ Understanding the Super Admin role

▶ Exploring network settings and options

▶ Using plugins within the network

▶ Finding WordPress network news and resources

*I*n this chapter, I introduce you to the network feature that is built in to the WordPress software. The network feature allows you, the site owner, to add and maintain multiple blogs within one installation of WordPress. This feature was introduced into WordPress as of the 3.0 version — prior to that, if you wanted to run multiple WordPress blogs with one installation of the software, you needed to use different software called WordPress MU (Multi User).In this chapter, you discover how to set up the WordPress network feature, explore settings and configurations, gain an understanding of the Super Admin role, determine which configuration is right for you (do you want sub-directories or subdomains?), and find some great resources to help you on your way.

With the network features enabled, users of your network can run their own sites within your installation of WordPress. They also have access to their own Dashboard with the same options and features as you've read about in the past 14 chapters. Heck, it would probably be a great idea to buy a copy of this book for every member within your network so everyone can become familiar with the WordPress Dashboard and features, too. At least have a copy on hand so people can borrow yours!

Considering Web Hosting Services

This chapter assumes that you already have the WordPress software installed and running correctly on your Web server, and that your Web server meets the minimum requirements to run WordPress (see Chapter 6).

Before you enable the WordPress network feature, you need to determine how you are going to use the feature. You have a couple of options:

- ✔ Manage just a few of your own WordPress blogs or Web sites.
- ✔ Run a full-blown blogging network with several hundred different blogs and multiple users.

If you are planning to run just a few of your own sites with the WordPress network feature, then your current hosting situation is probably well suited (see Chapter 6 for information on Web hosting services). However, if your plans are to host a large network with hundreds of blogs and multiple users, you should consider contacting your host and increasing your bandwidth, as well as the disk space limitations on your account.

The best example of a large blog network with hundreds of blogs and users (actually, more like millions) would be the hosted service at WordPress. com (see Part I of this book, which covers WordPress.com in great detail). At WordPress.com, people are invited to sign up for an account and start a blog using the network feature within the WordPress platform on the WordPress server. When you enable this feature on your own domain and enable the user registration feature (covered later in this chapter), you are inviting users to:

- ✔ Create an account.
- ✔ Create a blog on your WordPress installation (on your domain).
- ✔ Create content by publishing blog posts.
- ✔ Upload media files such as photos, audio, and video.
- ✔ Invite their friends to view their blog, or sign up for their own account.

In addition to the necessary security measures, time, and administrative tasks that go into running a community of blogs, you've got a few things to worry about. Creating a community will increase the resource use, bandwidth, and disk space on your Web server. In many cases, if you go over your allotted limits given to you by your Web host, you will incur great cost as a result. Make sure you anticipate your bandwidth and disk space needs before running a large network on your Web site! (Don't say I didn't warn you.)

Many WordPress Network communities start with grand dreams of being a large and active community — be realistic on how your community will operate in order to make the right hosting choice for yourself, and your community.

Small blogging communities can be easily handled using a shared-server solution, whereas larger, more active communities should really consider a dedicated server solution for operation. The difference between the two lies in their names:

- **Shared-server solution:** You have one account on one server that has several other accounts on it. Think of this as apartment living. One apartment building has several apartments for multiple people to live, all under one roof.

- **Dedicated server:** You have one account. You have one server. That server is dedicated to your account, and your account is dedicated to the server. Think of this as owning a home where you don't share your living space with anyone else.

A dedicated server solution is a more expensive investment for your blog community, while a shared-server solution is the most economical. Your decision on which solution to go with for your WordPress Network blogging community will be based on your realistic estimates on how big and how active your community will be. You can move from a shared-server solution to a dedicated server solution if your community gets larger than you expected; however it is easier to start with the right solution for your community from day one.

Enabling the WordPress Network Feature

WordPress makes it pretty easy to enable the network feature, but it does require opening a file on your Web server called `wp-config.php`, and making a small alteration. Follow these steps to get the process started:

1. **Download the file called `wp-config.php` from the WordPress installation on your Web server.**

   It's easiest to use an FTP program to download a copy of this file from your Web server to your computer. Chapter 6 covers the information you need about using FTP.

2. **Using your preferred text editor, open the `wp-config.php` file.**

   PC users can use Notepad to edit the file; Mac users can use TextMate.

3. **Find the line that says:** `define('DB_COLLATE', '');`

   Click at the end of that line. Press Enter and a new, blank line is created.

4. **Type**

   ```
   define ('WP_ALLOW_MULTISITE', true ) ;
   ```

   Save the file to your computer as `wp-config.php`. Your `wp-config.php` file should look like mine, shown in Figure 15-1. Save the `wp-config.php` file to your computer.

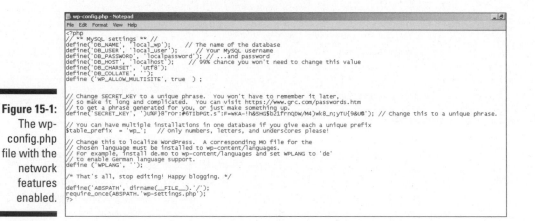

Figure 15-1:
The wp-config.php file with the network features enabled.

5. **Upload the new** `wp-config.php` **to your Web server in your WordPress installation directory.**

6. **Go to your WordPress Dashboard in your browser.**

   You now see a new item, labeled Network, under the Tools menu.

7. **Click the Network link in the Tools menu.**

   A page called Create a Network of WordPress Sites loads in your browser window, shown in Figure 15-2.

Preparing Your Web Server

Before proceeding with the final steps in enabling the WordPress network feature, you need to get a few items in order on your Web server. You also need to make a decision about how the multiple blogs within your network will be handled. These configurations need to be in place in order to run the WordPress Network successfully. If you can perform the configurations in this section yourself (and if you have access to the Apache configuration files), this section is for you. If you don't know how, are uncomfortable with adjusting these settings, or don't have access to change the configurations in your Web server software, you'll need to ask your hosting provider for help or hire a consultant to perform the configurations for you.

DNS (domain name server)

The WordPress network feature gives you two different ways to run a network of blogs on your domain. You can use the subdomain option or the subdirectory option. The most popular option (and recommended structure) sets up subdomains for the blogs created by your WordPress Network. With the subdomain option, the username of the blog appears first, followed by your domain name. With the subdirectory option, your domain name appears first, followed by the username of the blog. Which one should you choose? The choice is yours. You can see the difference in the URLs of these two options by comparing the following examples:

- A **subdomain** looks like this: `http://username.yourdomain.com`.
- A **subdirectory** looks like this: `http://yourdomain.com/username`.

Figure 15-2: Create a Network of WordPress Sites page on your WordPress Dashboard.

If you want to use a subdomain for each blog in your WordPress Network, you must add a wildcard record to your DNS records. You need to add a hostname record pointing at your Web server in the DNS configuration tool available in your Web server administration software (like WebHost Manager (WHM), a popular Web host administration tool). The hostname record looks like this: `*.yourdomain.com` (where `yourdomain.com` is replaced with your actual domain name).

Apache mod_rewrite

Apache (`http://httpd.apache.org`) is Web server software that's loaded and running on your Web server. Not everyone has access to Apache files, however. Usually, the only person who has access to those files is the Web server administrator. (This is usually your Web host.) Depending on your own Web server account and configuration, you may or may not have access to the Apache software files.

The Apache module that's necessary in order for the WordPress Network to create nice permalink URLs (see Chapter 8 for information on *pretty perma-links*) is called `mod_rewrite`. This must be configured so that it's active and installed on your server.

You or your Web host can make sure that the Apache `mod_rewrite` is activated on your server; open the `httpd.conf` file and verify that the following line is included within:

```
LoadModule rewrite_module /libexec/mod_rewrite.so
```

If it isn't, type that line on its own line and save the file. You will probably need to restart Apache before the change takes effect.

Virtual Host

In the same `httpd.conf` file that I discuss two paragraphs ago, you need to make some adjustments to the `<VirtualHost>` section of that file. Follow these steps:

1. **Find the** `<VirtualHost>` **section in the** `httpd.conf` **file.**

   This line of the `httpd.conf` file provides directives, or configurations, that apply to your Web site.

2. **Find a line in the** `<VirtualHost>` **section of the** `httpd.conf` **that looks like this:**
   ```
   AllowOverride None
   ```

3. **Replace that line with this line:**
   ```
   AllowOverride FileInfo Options
   ```

4. **On a new line, type** `ServerAlias *.yourdomain.com`.

   Replace `yourdomain.com` with whatever your domain is. This line defines the host name for your Network site and is essential for the virtual host to work correctly.

5. **Save the** `httpd.conf` **file and close it.**

PHP (PHP Hypertext Processor)

In this section, you edit the PHP configuration on your Web server. PHP needs to have the following configurations in place in the `php.ini` file on your Web server in order to run WordPress MU on your server:

- Set your PHP to *not* display any error messages in the visitor's browser window. (This is usually already turned off by default; just double-check that to be sure.)

- Find out if your PHP is compiled with memory limit checks. You can find this out by looking for the text `memory_limit` in the `php.ini` file. Usually, the default limit is 8MB. Increase the memory limit to at least 32MB, or even 64MB, to avoid PHP memory errors when running WordPress MU.

- Global variables should be set to Off. Usually, the default setting does have global variables turned off; double-check to be sure. An easy way to configure this is to open the `.htaccess` file (found on your Web server in the same directory you installed the WordPress MU files) and add the following two lines to the very top of the `.htaccess` file:

```
php_flag register_globals 0
php_flag display_errors 0
```

Setting Up the WordPress Network

Now that I've covered the initial steps to enable the Network feature, and you have made your decision on whether to go with the subdomain or subdirectory set up, it's time to set it up and make it work! The rest of the steps in setting up the network feature are easy:

1. **Click the Network link under the Tools menu in the Dashboard.**

   A page called Create a Network of WordPress Sites appears.

2. **Select subdomains or subdirectories as the addresses of the sites in your network.**

> Make sure you've made your final decision on this issue, because you can't change this selection later.

3. **Type the title of your network in the box labeled Network Title.**

4. **Type the e-mail address of the site administrator in the box labeled Admin E-mail Address.**

   Typically, the site administrator is you. This is the e-mail address to which all site-related items will be sent. For example, all messages about new sign ups, newly created blogs, and other administrative communications will be sent to this address.

5. **Click the Install button.**

   A page called Enabling the Network, shown in Figure 15-3, appears. You need to follow several instructions to enable the network.

6. **Create a directory on your Web server called:** `blogs.dir`.

   In your WordPress installation directory there is a folder labeled `/wp-content/`. It's in that folder that you create a new directory called `blogs.dir`. The entire path should look something like this: `/public_html/wp-content/blogs.dir`. This is the directory that stores all uploaded media (photos, videos, audio, and other media) within the network blogs on your domain.

Figure 15-3:
The Enabling the Network page in the WordPress Dashboard.

Most FTP programs allow you to create a new directory (or a new folder) by right-clicking in the Web server window and selecting Make New Directory. I discuss FTP in Chapter 6.

7. **Add the Network related configuration lines to the** `wp-config.php`.

On the Enabling the Network page, in Step 2, WordPress gives you up to 15 lines of configuration rules that need to be added to the `wp-config.php` file.

Earlier in this chapter, in the section called "Enabling the WordPress Network Feature," you added a line of code to enable the network feature. Follow those instructions to add these lines to that same file, in the same manner. Copy the lines from the Enabling the Network page, and paste them into the `wp-config.php` file, then save and upload them to your Web server again. The code I was giving during this process can be seen in Figure 15-3.

The lines of code that are given to you on the Enabling the Network page are unique to *your* installation of WordPress. Don't copy the lines of code you see in Figure 15-3. Make sure you copy the lines of code that are given to you on the Enabling the Network page.

8. **Add the Rewrite Rules to the** `.htaccess` **file on your Web server.**

As in Step 7, WordPress gives you up to 13 lines of code that you need to add to a file called `.htaccess` on your Web server. You will find that file in the WordPress installation directory.

9. **Copy the lines of code from the Enabling a Network page in Step**

8. **Then open the** `.htaccess` **file and paste the lines of code there.** Completely replace the rules that already exist in that file.

10. **Save the** `.htaccess` **file and upload again it to your Web server.**

11. **Return to the Dashboard. Click the Dashboard link at the top of the menu navigation in the WordPress Dashboard.**

You may be asked to log in to WordPress again, because by following these steps you have changed some of the browser cookie handling rules in the `wp-config.php` and `.htaccess` files.

Exploring the Super Admin Dashboard Menu

It's a bird . . . it's a plane . . . it's really predictable that I start in with the "Super" jokes right about now, isn't it? With the WordPress Network now fully enabled and configured, you see a new item at the top of the left navigation menu in your WordPress Dashboard: Super Admin. In this section, I show you how to don your cap and tights and discover everything you need to know about being a Super Admin in your new WordPress Network.

Within the Super Admin menu, you find six different items that you will use to configure manage and maintain your new Network:

- **Admin:** Create new sites and new users in your network.

- **Sites:** View a list of the sites in your network, along with details about them.

- **Users:** See detailed info about current users in your network.

- **Themes:** View all the Currently available themes to enable or disable them for use in your network.

- **Options:** Change settings and configure your network.

- **Update:** Upgrade all sites in your network with one click.

All of the items in the Super Admin menu are important, and you will use them all frequently throughout the life of your network.I suggest that you make the Options link your first stop. Clicking that link takes you to the Network Options page and allows you to set up some important preliminary configurations for your Network. In the next section, I cover the network options first, followed by the rest of the items you find in the Super Admin menu.

Configuring network options

Click the Options link in the Super Admin menu to see the Network Options page. Not surprisingly, you will be greeted with a variety of options for configuring sites in your network. For one thing, you can change operational settings such as the site name, administrator e-mail address, the text of the welcome e-mail that gets sent to new users, and other stuff (see Figure 15-4). The options are many, and the following steps take you through each setting:

1. **Type the name of your Network in the Network Name text box.**

2. **Type your e-mail address in the Network Admin Email text box.**

   You use this e-mail address to send site registration notices, password reminders, and support e-mails to the users within your WordPress Network. Just a suggestion — make it an easy, generic one like support@*yourdomain*.com. You want to keep in mind that this e-mail address is used to send out notices to your users, so some of those users may e-mail you back at that e-mail address seeking support or assistance.

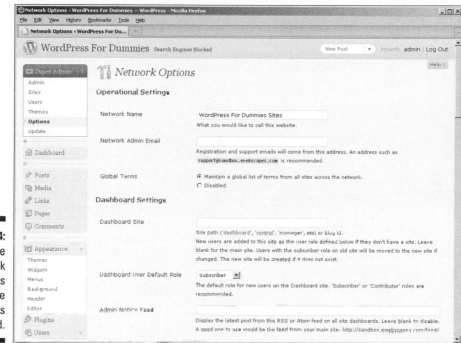

Figure 15-4:
The
Network
Options
page in the
WordPress
Dashboard.

3. **Select Global Terms.**

   The global list of terms allows site administrators (that's you) to maintain a fixed list of post tags and categories that are used on all blogs within a network. This is a helpful option for navigation purposes, because it allows visitors to navigate through your network of blog using tags or categories. You can activate or disable this option by clicking the button to the left of the options.

4. **Type the main site name in the Dashboard Site text box.**

   The Dashboard Site is the main blog for your Web site. If this field is left blank, the main site for your Network will default to your main domain (*yourdomain.com*) when people visit your site. New users are added as subscribers to the dashboard blog if they don't have a blog within your community.

5. **Set the Dashboard User Default Role for new users on the dashboard blog.**

   Your drop-down menu choices are:

   - *Subscriber:* Users can access their profile only and cannot access any of the back-end features or settings of your main blog.

- *Contributor:* Users can upload files and write, edit, and manage posts on your main blog. However, when a contributor writes a post, the post is saved as a draft to await administrator approval. Contributors cannot post to the blog without approval, which is a nice way to moderate content written by new authors.

- *Author:* In addition to having the same access and permissions as a contributor, an author can publish posts without administrator approval. Authors can also edit and delete their own posts.

- *Editor:* In addition to having the same access and permissions as an author, an editor can moderate comments, manage categories, manage links, edit pages, and edit other author's posts. Editors can also read and edit private posts.

- *Administrator:* This user has access to all menus and settings within the WordPress Dashboard and has the authority to change any of those options and settings, as well.

I highly recommend leaving the default role set to Subscriber because you don't want community users to have access to any of the back-end settings and options for your main blog (unless that's your intention; then by all means, change it!).

6. **Set the Admin Notice Feed.**

If you want to display the latest post from your main blog within the Dashboard of each of your users, type the RSS feed of the blog into this text box. By default, the text box is blank.

7. **Select an Allow New Registrations option:**

- *Registration is Disabled:* Disallows new user registration completely. When selected, this option prevents people who visit your site from registering for a user account.

- *User accounts may be registered:* Gives people the ability to create only a user account; users will not be able to create a blog within your network.

- *Logged in users may register new sites:* Allows only existing users — that is, those who are already logged in — to create a new blog within your network. This also disables new user registration completely. This is an option you would use if you don't want just anyone registering for an account. Instead you, as the site administrator, can add new users at your own discretion.

- *Both sites and user accounts can be registered:* Gives users the ability to register an account and a site on your network during the registration process.

8. **Select registration notification preferences.**

   Choose Yes or No to whether you want to be notified via e-mail each time a new user registers in your network.

9. **Select whether to allow blog administers to add new users to their blog(s).**

   Choose Yes or No to whether you want to allow your community blog owners to add new users to their own community blog via the Users page within their individual dashboards.

10. **Type disallowed usernames in the Banned Names text box.**

    By default, WordPress bans several usernames from being registered within your community, including *www, web, root, admin, main, invite, administrator,* and so on. For good reason, you don't want a random user to register a username, such as *admin,* because you don't want that person misrepresenting himself as an administrator on your site. You can enter an unlimited amount of usernames that you do not want to allow on your site in the Banned Names text box.

11. **Limit registration to certain e-mail addresses.**

    This option allows you to enter an unlimited amount of e-mail addresses to limit new user registration to only certain e-mail addresses. For example, if I wanted to create a community of people from my publishing company, Wiley Publishing — I can put *wiley.com* in this field to restrict registration to only people with access to that email domain. People who try to register with an e-mail that is not on the list cannot register. To keep registration open to everyone, regardless of their address, leave this field blank.

12. **In the Welcome Email text box, type the text of the e-mail you want new site owners to receive when they register a new site within your Network.**

    Alternatively, you can leave this area alone and use the default text provided for you by WordPress. The body of this e-mail is sent to new site owners.

    A few variables you can use in this e-mail aren't explained entirely on the Site Options page, including:

    - SITE_NAME: Inserts the name of your WordPress site.
    - BLOG_URL: Inserts the URL of the new member's blog.
    - USERNAME: Inserts the new member's username.
    - PASSWORD: Inserts the new member's password.

- `BLOG_URLwp-login.php`: Inserts the hyperlinked login URL for the new member's blog.

- `SITE_URL`: Inserts the hyperlinked URL for your WordPress site.

13. **In the Welcome User Email text box, type the text of the e-mail you want new users to receive when they register with your Network.**

    Alternatively, you can leave this area alone and use the default text provided for you by WordPress. The body of this e-mail is sent to new users owners. You are also able to use the different variables I explained in Step 11.

14. **In the First Post text box, type the text that you want to appear in the first post on every site that's created in your community.**

    You can use this area to provide useful information about your site and services. This also serves as a nice guide for new users, as they can view that post in their dashboard, on the Edit Post page, and see how it was entered and formatted and use that as a guide for creating their own blog posts. You can also use the variables mentioned in Step 11 to have WordPress automatically add some information for you.

15. **In the First Page text box, type the text that you want to appear in the first page on every site that's created in your community.**

    Similar to Step 13, only this is the text for a page, rather than a post. The variables from Step 11 can also be utilized here.

16. **In the First Comment text box, type the text that you want to appear in the first comment on every site that's created in your community.**

    Similar to Step 13, only this is the text for a sample comment, rather than a post. The variables from Step 11 can also be used here.

17. **In the First Comment Author text box, type the name of author of the first comment from Step 15.**

    This is a nice way to personalize your Network. When someone sets up a brand new site, WordPress has a sample comment in the first blog post of that site (from Step 13). Type in your name in the First Comment Author box to personalize the message a bit more.

18. **In the First Comment URL text box, type in the URL (Web address) of the first comment for the new site.**

    Typically, this will be your main site URL.

19. **Select Media Upload buttons.**

    The choices are Images, Videos, and Music. Select the media that you'll allow community users to upload to their own site.

20. **Type the number for the maximum storage space allowed for blog uploads.**

   The amount is in megabytes (MB), and the default storage space is 10MB. This amount of hard drive space is what you give users to store the files they upload to their blog.

21. **Select upload file types.**

   Users cannot upload any file types that do not appear in this text box. By default, WordPress includes the following file types: .jpg, .jpeg, .png, .gif, .mp3, .mov, .avi, .wmv, .midi, .mid, and .pdf. You can remove any default file types, and add new ones.

22. **Set the maximum uploaded file size.**

   This amount is in kilobytes (K), and the default file size is 1500K. This means that a user cannot upload a file that is larger than 1500K. Adjust this number as you see fit.

23. **In the Menus section, select the Plugins check box.**

   The Plugins page will be visible to users on their own blog dashboard. If you leave this option unselected, users will not have access to the plugins list. For more information about using plugins with WordPress, see Chapter 10.

24. **Click the Save Changes button.**

   When you finish the Network Options settings, don't forget to click the Save Changes button to save your settings. This reloads the Site Options page with your saved settings.

Exploring the Network Admin Page

The first item on the Super Admin menu is Admin. Click Admin, and the Network Admin page appears where you can search for users and sites within your community. Obviously, you won't perform this search if you don't have any users or sites yet. However, this function is extremely useful when you have a community of users and sites within your network.

The Search Users feature allows you to search usernames and user e-mail addresses. If you search for the user *Lisa,* for instance, your results will include any user whose username or e-mail address contains *Lisa* — so you can receive multiple returns when using just one search word or phrase. The Search Sites feature returns any blog content within your community that contains your search term, too.

The Network Admin page has two links near the top of the page that are very useful:

- ✔ **Create a New Sites:** Click this link to create a new site within your Network. Once clicked, the Sites page appears where you can add a new site. I cover how to do this in the upcoming "Discovering the Sites Page" section.

- ✔ **Create a New User:** Click this link to create a new user account within your community. Once clicked, the Users page appears where you can add a new user to your community. I cover how to do this in the upcoming "Using the Users Page" section.

Additionally, the WordPress Network Admin page gives you a real-time count of how many sites and users you have in your network, which is nice-to-know information for any Super Admin.

Discovering the Sites Page

The second item on the Super Admin menu is Sites. The Sites page is where you find several options for managing your network sites (Figure 15-5).

At the top of the Sites page is a search box that allows you to search through your network sites by name, ID, or IP address. This is especially helpful if you have a large network and a user contacts you with a question about his site. You can visit the Sites page and pull up that particular site pretty quickly with the search feature.

The Sites page also lists all the sites within your network. The listing shows the following statistics about each community site:

- ✔ **ID:** The blog's ID number assigned when it was created.
- ✔ **Site Path:** The domain URL (Web address) of the site.
- ✔ **Last Updated:** The date the site was last updated (or published to).
- ✔ **Registered:** The date the site was registered in your network.
- ✔ **Users:** The username and e-mail address associated with the user(s) of that site.

Figure 15-5:
The Sites
page in the
WordPress
Dashboard.

Underneath the listing of existing site in your community, you see a handy area under the heading "Add a Site" where you are able to add a new site easily by following these few steps:

- **Type in the address in the Site Address text box.**

  The Site Address is also the URL (Web address) of the site you are creating. For example, if you typed in the word *site1*, then the URL of the site will be `http://site1.yourdomain.com` if you're using subdomains. If you're using subdirectories in your network, the URL will be `http://yourdomain.com/site1`.

- **Type in the title in the site Title text box.**

  This is the title of the new site you are creating. An example of a title would be something like "My New Site" — this title can be changed at any time in the future within the WordPress Dashboard settings, unlike the Site Address, which cannot be changed.

- **Type in the e-mail of the site owner in the Admin Email text box.**

  This is the e-mail address of the person who is the owner of this site. If the user is not already a member of your network, WordPress will create a new user and send that person an e-mail with his or her username and password for the new site.

✔ **Click the Add Blog button.**

This action creates the blog in your network, and the Blogs page refreshes; you now see the newly created blog in the listing of blogs within your community.

Using the Users Page

The third item on the Super Admin menu is Users, shown in Figure 15-6. The Users page lists all your users and provides the following information about each one:

✔ **Username:** This is the login name the member uses when she logs in to her account in your community.

✔ **Name:** This is the user's real name, taken from her profile. If the user has not provided her name in her profile, this column will be blank.

✔ **E-mail:** This is the e-mail address the user entered when she registered on your site.

✔ **Registered:** This is the date when the user registered.

✔ **Sites:** If you enable sites within your WordPress Network, this lists any sites the user is a member of.

When you hover on a username with your mouse, an Edit link appears that you can click to edit that user's profile if you need to.

Also on the Users page, you can add new users with the interface near the bottom of the page, as seen in Figure 15-6.

Perhaps you have a reluctant friend who's been dragging her feet about joining your network. You've been begging and pleading with her to join, and she keeps promising she will, yet days go by, and her user registration doesn't come through your e-mail. (Mom, are you paying attention?) Well, fix her up with an account within your network right this very minute! Here's how to add a new user to your network:

1. **Type the desired username in the Username text box.**

2. **Type the user's e-mail address in the Email text box.**

3. **Click the Add User button.**

   The page reloads with an Options Saved message at the top. You now see the new user in the list of users on the Users page.

Figure 15-6:
The Users
page in the
WordPress
Dashboard.

The new user you created receives a confirmation e-mail. You've graciously
helped your friend along, but she still has to confirm the registration.
Nevertheless, you're one step closer to having your friend on board in your
network!

Enabling network themes

Chapter 11 goes into great detail on how to find, install, and activate new
themes with your WordPress installation. However, when it comes to
enabling themes on a WordPress site that has the network feature-enabled,
you have an extra hoop you need to jump through as the Super Admin (good
thing Super Admins can leap tall buildings in a single bound!).

On a WordPress Network site, to use a theme, it needs to be enabled in the
Super Admin menu under Themes. Taking this step allows your network
users to use the themes that you have enabled. Themes that aren't enabled
are, in fact, hidden from network users and are only available to the Super
Admin. You can enable Network Themes for your users in these few steps:

1. **Browse to the Network Themes page.**

   Click the Themes link in the Super Admin menu, and you see the Network Themes page, as seen in Figure 15-7.

2. **Locate the theme you want to enable on the Network Themes page.**

3. **Make the theme active.**

   Select Yes to the left of the theme name to make the theme active on your site.

4. **Update your options.**

   Click the Update Themes button to save your settings; the Network Themes page reloads and displays a message informing you that the site themes have been saved.

With the theme(s) enabled, you can now browse to the Manage Themes page to activate the theme of you choice on your main site. Also, users who have a site within your network are now able to view the enabled theme in their Dashboard and can browse and select the themes, as well.

Figure 15-7:
The Network Themes page in the WordPress Dashboard.

Updating Your Network

The final item on the Super Admin menu is Update. You use the Update Network page (shown in Figure 15-8) to update your network whenever you upgrade the WordPress software to a new version. This update ensures that all sites across your network get the latest and greatest features and functions with the latest version, and it also makes sure that the database associated with your WordPress installation is fully up to date with the latest version, across all network sites.

When WordPress releases a new version, a message is shown at the top of your WordPress Dashboard alerting you that you need to upgrade. Upgrading is an easy process that I describe in Chapter 7.

You're not upgrading for one anymore! You have to make sure each site within your community is upgraded, also. To accomplish this upgrade, simply click the Update Network button on the Update Network page. After you do that, WordPress runs a script that updates each site within your network. Simple as that. One caveat, though: Depending on the size of your network — particularly if there are several sites — this can take a very long time.

Using Plugins within Your Network

By and large, all WordPress plugins will work on your network. There are, however, some special plugins and some special considerations for using plugins with a network.

First, if you need a refresher on how to find, install, and activate plugins in WordPress, page back through and find Chapter 10.

Browse to the Manage Plugins page in your WordPress Dashboard by clicking the Installed link under the Plugins menu. You find that the Manage Plugins page is just as I described it in Chapter 10, but there is one very small, subtle difference that you could easily miss if you don't know where to look. Check out Figure 15-8 and have a look below the name of the plugin. Do you see the Network Activate link? Guess what! That link is only there if you are administrating a network.

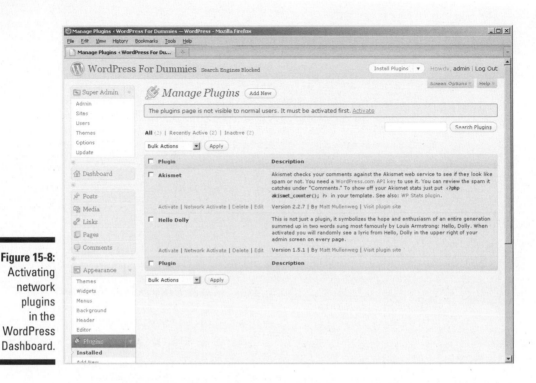

Figure 15-8:
Activating
network
plugins
in the
WordPress
Dashboard.

The difference is pretty easy to understand:

- **Activate:** Clicking this link activates the plugin only on the site you are currently logged in to. For example, if you log in to your main site and visit the Manage Plugins page and click Activate under the Akismet plugin, you can activate that plugin only on your one main site.

- **Network Activate:** Clicking this link activates the plugin on all sites within your network, no matter what the network users' preference might be. This is very helpful with plugins that add universal features such as spam protection. As the site administrator, you probably want your whole network — across the board — to be protected from spam comments. The Network Activate feature lets you manage that problem.

When a plugin is Network Activated, the users don't see the plugin displayed in their listing of available plugins. The plugin is automatically activated, and they have access to the settings and options for that plugin.

It's important to note that users who have sites within your network can't view the Manage Plugins page unless you, the Super Admin, have given them the ability to do so. Refer back to Step 23 in the "Configuring network options" section earlier in this chapter; it is there than you can enable or disable the Plugins menu. If you want your users to be able to activate and deactivate plugins on their own sites within your network, be sure to enable the plugin administration menus under Network Options.

Part VI
The Part of Tens

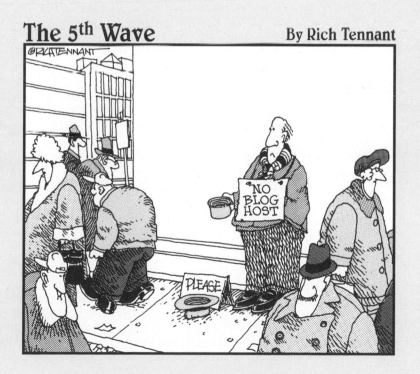

The 5th Wave   By Rich Tennant

PLEASE

NO BLOG HOST

In this part . . .

Welcome to The Part of Tens! In this part, I tell you about ten fabulous WordPress themes and ten great plugins that you can use to enhance your WordPress blogging. I also present ten WordPress–powered sites that effectively use WordPress as a CMS (content management system).

Chapter 16

Ten Great Sites That Use WordPress as a CMS

In This Chapter

▶ Seeing examples of how WordPress powers Web sites

▶ Discovering sites that use WordPress for more than just blogging

A tremendous number of well-designed WordPress sites are floating around the Web. Picking only ten of them would be a near-impossible task for me. Sometimes, you can look at a Web site and not even know that it's a blog or a site built with blogging software. Because users can extend the WordPress software to function as so much more than just a blog, people refer to WordPress as a CMS (content management system), rather than merely a blogging platform. You can do much more with it than just blog; you can also build fully functional Web sites with it. In this chapter, I reveal ten sites that go beyond the blog.

Many Web sites using WordPress as a CMS have a blog as part of their content. However, just as many don't include a blog. These sites are using WordPress to power their small business, magazine, news, or e-commerce Web site with dynamic features such as:

✔ Shopping cart

✔ Event calendar

✔ Links directories

✔ Discussion forums

✔ Multimedia galleries

✔ Podcasts and/or Internet radio shows

✔ User-submitted content

Harvard Gazette

http://news.harvard.edu/gazette

The Harvard Gazette, on first glance, looks like an online magazine of articles, resources, and information. Dig a little deeper, and you find that it's a Web site that is rich in multimedia offerings, such as videos and photography. All these additions provide a beautiful accent to the written content.

Included in the Harvard Gazette Web site is an extensive calendar of events that is updated routinely and offers the visitor a glimpse into the types of events — giving visitors the capability to add the event to their own calendars with applications from Facebook, Google, Yahoo!, Apple iCal, and more.

 If you take away one idea from this site, it's the use of category archiving coupled with fully customizing the different category templates. This touch creates an interesting and clean browsing experience.

Icon Dock

http://icondock.com

Icon Dock is a Web site created by the folks from N.Design Studio and is a perfect example of using WordPress as an online shop. Icon Dock has a fully functional and easy-to-navigate e-commerce shop where visitors can purchase high-quality designed icons and graphics.

 If you use one good idea from Icon Dock, it's the site's smart use of a great WordPress plugin to power its online shop. The plugin is called WP E-Commerce, which you can find here: www.instinct.co.nz/e-commerce. You can install the plugin on any WordPress–powered Web site, and you immediately have a state-of-the-art e-commerce platform that allows you to host a full-featured shopping cart. Very professional! The possibilities of this plugin are literally endless.

Mosaic Consulting, Inc.

http://mosaic-consulting.com

Mosaic Consulting is a small legal IT consulting company whose work spans the globe. Mosaic chose WordPress as a CMS because of the software's flexibility and extensibility.

The company doesn't run a blog on its site. Instead, it offers an unlimited number of static pages on the site — pages that someone created without ever having to touch a piece of the underlying code in the theme (that's the WordPress way). The site also uses WordPress categories and subcategories in a nice dynamic navigation menu that takes visitors through the various sections of the site. The different layouts for individual pages and categories are accomplished through extensive use of custom page and category templates within the WordPress theme.

CSS Collection

http://csscollection.com

CSS Collection is a showcase site powered by WordPress. The purpose of the site is to showcase what people can do with Cascading Style Sheets when building Web sites and blogs.

Here are some of the site's features:

- **Thumbnails:** The front page includes thumbnail images of highlighted sites. Click a thumbnail to visit the Web site. The thumbnailing is accomplished through the image handler in WordPress, along with some custom coding done with the Custom Fields tool.
- **Interactive ratings:** Click any Web site's title, and you go to a single page where you can comment on the entry. Through the use of a plugin called Rate My Stuff (http://deadcantrant.com/projects/rate/), the folks at CSS Collection let readers rate each site with a star-rating system.

CSS Collection also makes good use of the typical blog layout and functions that you are used to seeing with WordPress. But the blog is not the primary part of the site. Rather, the site keeps a news section active with announcements and updates, using the old-fashioned blog layout that you've come to expect with WordPress. It uses RSS and Categories extensively to accomplish these goals.

Queensryche

http://queensryche.com

I never really envisioned myself writing about the rock band Queensryche, especially since what I have to say has nothing to do with dissecting the psychology behind its *Operation:Mindcrime* albums.

Nope, this is all about the Web design. Using a relatively simple layout that is rich in photographs and imagery, and powered by WordPress, Queensryche has provided a fun place on the Web for members of its fan club to get news, information, tour dates, recordings, videos, photos, and a growing Members Only discussion forum.

Visitors to the Web site are first met with the latest update and news from the band, along with photographs and graphic imagery.

Streamy Awards

www.streamys.org

If you've ever found yourself wondering. . . . *"Hmm, do they have an awards program for online Web television programming?"* — yes, they do! The Streamy Awards is a Web site and organization dedicated to honoring excellence in the field of original Web television programming. This organization is no joke, either. Past winners include industry greats such as Felicia Day, Joss Whedon, William Shatner, Rosario Dawson, Alex Albrecht, Zadi Diaz, Jane Espenson, Neil Patrick Harris, Paul Rudd, and Ronald D. Moore.

The Streamy Awards Web site, powered by WordPress, of course, mixes up traditional written content with multimedia offerings such as videos and a live-streaming of its annual Streamy Awards show, available on demand. Visitors to the Streamy Awards Web site can participate in some of the following activities:

✔ Vote for the Audience Choice award for your favorite online television programming.

✔ Watch videos from last year's event, including acceptance speeches, photo montages, and more.

✔ View or download Streamy media to various mobile devices (iPhone, Blackberry, Android).

✔ Connect with Streamy through Facebook and Twitter.

MommyCast

http://mommycast.com

MommyCast lives in the genre of *mommy blogs* — blogs owned and maintained by mothers. But MommyCast takes that concept quite a bit further through its radio program. MommyCast.com is a unique online audio company by and for women who are immersed in the fullness of motherhood and life; the site's motto is "Holding the world together, one child at a time." MommyCast offers interviews with people on topics that encompass all things having to do with motherhood.

I had the chance to speak with Joelle Reeder of Moxie Design Studios (`http://moxiedesignstudios.com`), the design brain behind the MommyCast brand. Joelle had this to say about the decision to use WordPress as the CMS for the project: "The MommyCast show has sponsors who use WordPress, so it was a natural choice for them to go in the same direction. The people behind the project also have used WordPress in the past and were very familiar with the platform."

Joelle also implemented a really neat way to bring some visual vitality to each post through image thumbnailing, combined with Custom Fields, that lets them insert small images into each post that calls attention not only to the post but to the post topic. These Custom Fields are called *Call Outs,* and they draw the eye in and make you pay attention.

Mendocino Beauty

`www.mendocinobeauty.com`

This Web site is a professional business Web site for the beauty and skin-care studio, Mendocino Beauty. Powered by WordPress, the site contains a blog — however, the blog isn't front and center like you see with a lot of WordPress installations. Instead, you're met with a beautifully designed front page that invites you into its site by providing you with navigation links to the different areas and offerings.

If you take away anything from this site, it's the use of its Look Book — a full photo gallery powered by a nifty WordPress plugin called NextGEN Gallery by plugin author Alex Rabe. The plugin was developed for the WordPress platform, and it allows you to create an unlimited number of photo albums and galleries for your Web site. You can check out, and download, the NextGEN Gallery in the official WordPress Plugin Directory here: `http://wordpress.org/extend/plugins/nextgen-gallery`.

John James Jacoby

`http://johnjamesjacoby.com`

John James Jacoby is one of two core developers on the BuddyPress team. He is a specialist in new media development and design. I am including his Web site here because he runs a very simple but elegant online portfolio with

WordPress. This Web site doesn't contain a blog. What you will find is a gallery of work and projects that he has been directly involved with.

Additionally, you will find a few static pages that John uses to publish a short bio, information about his rates, and an explanation of the services he offers. Using a plugin called Easy Contact, John also provides an easy-to-use e-mail form that allows visitors to contact him via e-mail using a form on his Contact Page. The Easy Contact plugin (`http://wordpress.org/extend/plugins/easy-contact`) was developed by Scott Allan Wallick and has features that include an options menu so that you can customize form content, built-in spam reduction measures, customizable CSS, and trackable information such as referrals and user agents.

E.Webscapes Design Studio

`http://ewebscapes.com`

I have to issue a disclaimer for this listing: I've owned and operated this site since 1998. I include it in this chapter not so much to self-promote (although that is a bonus!) but as a way to illustrate some great things that you can do with just one installation of the WordPress software. I often refer people to my site when I explain how WordPress not only powers a great blog, but also is the foundation of a fully functional business Web site.

E.Webscapes has several sections:

- ✔ **The front page:** This page contains an introductory message to visitors, some examples of my work, links, case studies, and news.

- ✔ **The Design Blog:** I update this blog regularly with information about the design projects that my designers and I have completed for our clients.

- ✔ **FAQ/Services/Resources:** These are examples of several different pages I have created within the E.Webscapes Web site — each use a slightly different custom page template to display the information in the way I wanted to arrange it.

- ✔ **Our Work:** This section is the design portfolio that spotlights all the projects that my designers and I have done in the past.

Chapter 17

Ten Popular WordPress Plugins

In This Chapter

▶ Finding popular WordPress plugins
▶ Using plugins to enhance your blog

*I*n this chapter, I list ten of the most popular plugins available for your WordPress blog. This list isn't exhaustive by any means; hundreds of excellent WordPress plugins can, and do, provide multiple ways to extend the functionality of your blog. And if these ten plugins aren't enough for you, you can find many more at the official WordPress Plugin Directory (`http://wordpress.org/extend/plugins`).

The greatest plugin of all is Akismet, which I describe in Chapter 10. Akismet is the answer to comment and trackback spam; it kills spam dead. It's installed with WordPress. Chapter 10 contains information on how to locate, download, unpack, install, activate, and manage plugins in your WordPress blog.

WP Print

Developer: Lester Chan

`http://wordpress.org/extend/plugins/wp-print`

WP Print is one of several WordPress plugins developed by Lester Chan. While visiting the official WordPress Plugin Directory, do a search for the term *gamerz,* and you will find all of the plugins created by Lester. They're all great plugins and worth a look.

WP Print is an easy-to-use plugin that provides a clean, printable version of your blog posts and/or pages. Unless your blog theme has a specialized stylesheet for printing, posts and pages print rather messily. WP Print strips most of the style from your theme design (images and formatting, for example) and outputs a clean print of your article with black text on a white background.

You can configure these options:

- ✔ **Print Text Link for Post:** This option configures a Print This Post link.
- ✔ **Print Text Link for Page:** This option configures a Print This Page link.
- ✔ **Print Icon:** Choose between two icons: `print.gif` and `printer_fam fam fam.gif`. The icon you choose appears on your site.
- ✔ **Print Text Style Link:** This drop-down menu presents settings for displaying the print link on your site.
- ✔ **Additional printing options:** You can specify whether comments, links, images, video, and disclaimer or copyright text will print.

WP Print doesn't automatically appear on your blog. You need to add a small snippet of code to your blog template in the area where you want the print link to appear:

```
<?php if(function_exists('wp_print')) { print_link(); } ?>
```

Place the code within The Loop. (See Chapter 12 for information about The Loop.)

Subscribe to Comments

Developer: Mark Jaquith

`http://wordpress.org/extend/plugins/subscribe-to-comments`

The Subscribe to Comments plugin adds a very nice feature to your blog by letting your visitors subscribe to individual posts you've made to your blog. When your readers subscribe to individual posts on your blog they receive notification via e-mail whenever someone leaves a new comment on the post. This feature goes a long way toward keeping your readers informed and making the discussions lively and active!

The plugin includes a full-featured subscription manager that your commenters can use to unsubscribe to certain posts, block all notifications, or even change their notification e-mail address.

ShareThis

Developer: Alex King

`http://wordpress.org/extend/plugins/share-this`

Every social bookmarking service has its own icon. People put these icons on their blogs as a way to let their visitors know that they can share their content with each social bookmarking service. This was a good concept when only a handful of services existed. Now there are dozens.

ShareThis is a plugin that combines an "e-mail this" plugin and social bookmarking service, allowing visitors to share content through e-mail and popular social bookmarking services such as Technorati, del.icio.us, and Digg.

When you've installed the plugin, go to the Options page for ShareThis, and set these options:

- ✔ **Enter the Widget Code:** Obtain the code from the ShareThis Web site; then copy the code into the text box.

- ✔ **Display the Link Only on Certain Pages of Your Blog:** By default, the ShareThis link is added at the very end of your blog post and page. You can turn off this default option. Choose No from the Automatically Add ShareThis to Your Posts and the Automatically Add ShareThis to Your Pages drop-down menus that appear on the ShareThis Options page. Then add the ShareThis template tag to your template wherever you want it to display in your blog:

```
<?php if (function_exists('sharethis_button')) { sharethis_button(); } ?>
```

This plugin requires the `wp-footer()` call in the footer (`footer.php`) of your template. If your theme doesn't include a `wp_footer()` call, you can add it easily by opening the `footer.php` template and adding this bit of code:

```
<?php wp_footer(); ?>
```

All in One SEO Pack

Developer: Michael Torbert

http://wordpress.org/extend/plugins/all-in-one-seo-pack/

Almost everyone is concerned about search engine optimization (SEO) in blogs. Good SEO practices help the major search engines (such as Google, Yahoo!, and Bing) easily find and cache your blog content in their search databases so that when people search for keywords, they can find your blog in the search results. All in One SEO Pack helps you fine-tune your blog to make that happen. It automatically creates optimized titles and generates HTML keywords for your individual posts. If you're a beginner, this plugin works for you out of the box with no advanced configuration necessary. Woo hoo! If you're an advanced user, you can fine-tune all of the All In One SEO settings to your liking.

WPtouch iPhone Theme

Developer: Brave New Code

`http://wordpress.org/extend/plugins/wptouch`

The WPtouch iPhone Theme plugin transforms your WordPress powered Web site into an iPhone-compatible browsing experience. It's designed specifically for visitors using an Apple iPhone. As an extra added bonus, it also creates a nice interface for visitors browsing in on an Android phone or Blackberry, as well.

This plugin doesn't affect how your WordPress Web site appears on a desktop or laptop. It only affects the view for people browsing your site on different mobile devices. The switch happens automatically without you having to touch one bit of code, which is always great news!

WP-DB-Backup

Developers: Austin Matzko

`http://wordpress.org/extend/plugins/wp-db-backup/`

Throughout this book, I often remind you to back up your files. In my work outside this book, I'm always encouraging my friends and clients to back up.

WP-DB-Backup is a plugin that provides a very easy method of creating a backup of your MySQL database. Remember, the database stores all the important data for your blog: your posts, pages, links, categories, comments, trackbacks, and settings.

If something happens to your database, and you don't have a backup, you'll be starting over from page one. Do yourself a huge favor: Make regular backups of your database by using this plugin. You can choose to have the backup file sent to an e-mail address of your choosing, downloaded to your computer, or stored on your Web sever in a backup folder inside your `wp-content` folder.

WP Super Cache

Developer: Donncha O'Caoimh

`http://wordpress.org/extend/plugins/wp-super-cache`

WP Super Cache creates static HTML files from your dynamic WordPress content. Why is this useful? On a high-traffic site, having cached versions of your posts and pages can speed up the load time of your Web site considerably. A *cached* version simply means that the content is converted to static HTML pages (as opposed to dynamically created content pulled from your database through a series of PHP commands) that are then stored on the server. This process eases the efforts the Web server must take to display the content in your visitors' browsers.

You can also read a very helpful article written by the plugin developer, Donncha O'Caoimh on his Web site here: `http://ocaoimh.ie/wp-super-cache/`.

In Chapter 2, I explain the relationship between PHP and MySQL. Twitter Tools

Developer: Alex King

`http://wordpress.org/extend/plugins/twitter-tools`

Social media networking is insanely popular on the Web right now. One of the more popular services is Twitter (`www.twitter.com`). Almost everyone who has a blog also has a Twitter account (you can even follow me on Twitter at `http://www.twitter.com/LisaSabinWilson`).

One of the nicer things that came about shortly after Twitter hit the scene was Alex King's plugin for WordPress called Twitter Tools. This plugin lets you tweet an announcement every time you publish a new post on your blog. The announcement appears on your Twitter stream and is read by all of your Twitter followers. People can then click the link and read your article. It's just one more nice way to use social media to promote your blog and content! There's more to this plugin, however; it also has some pretty nifty tools that enable you to

- ✔ Publish a post on your blog with your Twitter updates from the day.

- ✔ Publish a tweet directly from your blog, so you don't have to use another browser window or application.

- ✔ Tag your blog posts with Twitter hash tags — which are like keywords for Twitter that help other people search for and find your content within the Twitter universe.

Google XML Sitemaps

Developer: Arne Brachhold

`http://wordpress.org/extend/plugins/google-sitemap-generator`

This plugin lets you create a Google-compliant site map of your entire blog. Every single time you create a new post or page, the site map is updated and submitted to several major search engines, including Google, Yahoo!, and Bing. This plugin helps the search engines find and catalog new content from your site, so your new content appears in the search engines faster than it would if you didn't have a site map.

WordPress.com Stats

Developer: Andy Skelton and Michael D. Adams

`http://wordpress.org/extend/plugins/stats`

With the rise in popularity of the hosted WordPress.com service came a huge demand for the statistics that WordPress.com provides in its Dashboard pages. Users of the self-hosted WordPress.org software drooled when they saw the stats available to WordPress.com users, and the cry for a similar stats plugin for WordPress.org went out across the blogosphere.

Andy Skelton answered that call with the release of the WordPress.com Stats plugin for WordPress.org users. This plugin collects all the important statistics, including the number of hits on the site per hour, day, or month; the most popular posts; the sources of the traffic on the blog; and the links people click to leave the site.

The stats are provided for you on one easy-to-view page. This plugin doesn't count your own visits to your blog, so you can be assured that the counts are accurate.

You need a WordPress.com API key for the stats plugin to work. (See Chapter 10 for information on how to obtain a WordPress.com API key.) To enter the key, click the Plugins link in the Dashboard, click the WordPress.com Stats subtab, and type the API key there.

After you've activated the plugin and inserted your WordPress.com API key, click the Dashboard link in the Dashboard. Click the Blog Stats subtab to view your stats.

Chapter 18

Ten Free WordPress Themes

In This Chapter

▶ Finding good WordPress themes

▶ Using popular WordPress themes to style your blog

The list I present here isn't exhaustive by any means. Chapters 11, 12, and 13 give you a few more resources to find a theme that suits your needs.

All the themes in this chapter meet the following criteria:

✔ They're user-friendly, which means you don't have to tinker with anything to get things to look the way you want them to.

✔ They're compatible with widgets. In a word, widgets are wonderful. I cover widgets completely in Chapter 5.

✔ They're free. There are some very nice premium themes out there, but why pay if you don't have to?

✔ They use valid code. Although you may not notice it, valid code that meets W3C (www.w3c.org) standards won't cause errors in browsers.

Hybrid

Theme designers: Justin Tadlock

http://themehybrid.com

Hybrid is more of a theme *framework*, or parent theme that can be modified endlessly to create the perfect child theme, than it is a theme to use straight out of the box, but don't let that intimidate you! It's crazy easy to use, and Hybrid is very user-friendly.

By default, the Hybrid theme is very plain and simple, but it encompasses any and all of the WordPress features and functions that you would want:

- ✓ **It's SEO ready:** Hybrid comes completely optimized for SEO (search engine optimization).

- ✓ **It's highly customizable:** Hybrid has 15 custom page templates for you to choose from. Each custom page is set up slightly differently, giving you an array of options.

- ✓ **It's widget ready:** Hybrid has multiple widgetized areas for you to easily drop content into, making your WordPress theme experience easy and efficient.

You can read about the Hybrid theme at the developer, Justin Tadlock's Web site at `http://www.themehybrid.com` — and you can also download and install the theme directly into WordPress Web site by using the automatic theme installer built in to your WordPress Dashboard.

Check out options for installing and tweaking WordPress themes in Chapters 11, 12, and 13. Those chapters give you information on CSS, HTML, and theme tweaking, as well as guide you through working with parent/child themes.

designPile

Theme designer: Smashing Magazine

`http://wordpress.site5.net/designpile/`

The highlights of this theme are the following:

- ✓ Three different color schemes: black and pink, black and green, and black and blue

- ✓ Widgets are configured for use in the sidebar and footer areas of this design

- ✓ Allows you to create post thumbnails with an easy-to-use plugin called Simple Post Thumbnails (which you can find and download here: `http://wordpress.org/extend/plugins/simple-post-thumbnails`)

- ✓ Provides space for monetization with ads

- ✓ Includes built-in social networking links and sharing

The designPile theme (shown in Figure 18-1) is a sharp design and an easy-to-use free WordPress theme for any new user.

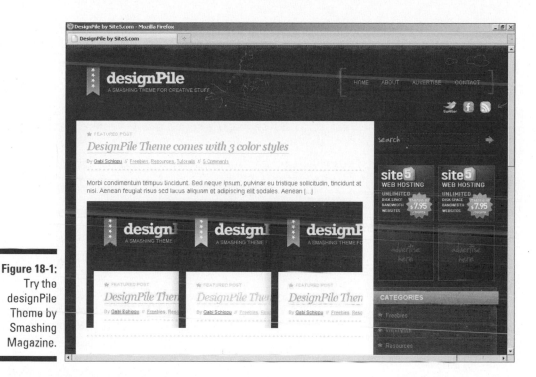

Figure 18-1:
Try the
designPile
Theme by
Smashing
Magazine.

Elegant Grunge

Theme designer: Michael Tyson

`http://wordpress.org/extend/themes/elegant-grunge`

Michael Tyson's Elegant Grunge theme is designed with some of the most popular design elements around the Web: grunge design, paper-like effects, and a monochromatic color scheme.

The Elegant Grunge theme also has very nicely designed frames for photos, photo blog handling, custom page templates, and a wide footer area that allows you to add widgets.

P2

Theme designer: Noel Jackson

`http://wordpress.org/extend/themes/p2`

You can easily see the Twitter-esque inspiration behind P2 by looking at the post text box displayed at the top of the theme. As with Twitter, users can post quick updates, and logged-in visitors can leave feedback on the updates. All this stuff happens from the convenience of the front page of your site — without having to click through to a different page on your site, locate the comment form, type, and submit the comment. The P2 theme also features:

- Live tag suggestions for your posts and updates
- Threaded comment display
- A show/hide feature for comments
- Real-time notification for posts, updates, and comments
- Keyboard shortcuts

Stargaze

Theme designer: Joni Ang

`http://taintedsong.com/2008/02/20/stargaze-wordpress-theme`

By the designer's own admission, this theme is a bit more "girly" than most. Most free WordPress themes do seem to have a distinct lack of femininity, so I thought I would present a female-oriented one here.

Stargaze is a beautiful two-column theme that is widget ready (meaning that you can use WordPress widgets with this theme without having to do any special adjustments to the theme). The color scheme is a nice combination of blue, yellow, and pink, with a variety of nicely placed icons and design elements drawing attention to specific areas of your content.

Carrington Blog

Theme designer: Alex King`http://wordpress.org/extend/themes/carrington-blog`

Carrington (see Figure 18-2) is a theme built upon a framework that organizes different WordPress features that can be styled distinctly by the users, based on their own, individual tastes. Inside the admin options of the Carrington theme, users find they have the ability to customize the color of links and header of the theme with an easy-to-use color picker, as well as a customizable header image that allows users to further customize Carrington to suit their tastes. Carrington is a clean, simple, and minimalistic theme and supports WordPress features — such as threaded comments, image galleries, and simplified CSS — to make it as easy as possible for users to customize the CSS styling. (See Chapter 13 for great information on tweaking WordPress themes using CSS.)

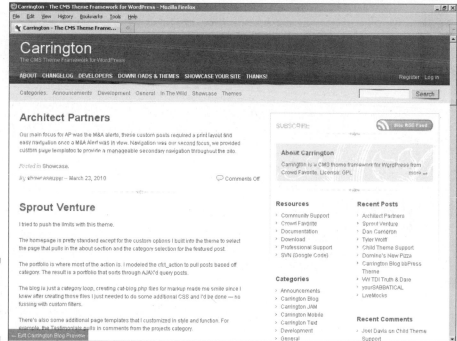

Figure 18-2:
Carrington
Blog by Alex
King.

iTheme

Theme designer: Nick La

```
http://www.ndesign-studio.com/demo/wordpress/
```

iTheme is a WordPress theme designed with Macintosh lovers in mind. The theme emulates the design elements and features of the Macintosh operating system, with beautiful blue gradients and Maclike menu headers and icons. This theme has a fully configurable sidebar that allows you to use WordPress widgets, and when they're in your blog, you can drag those widgets around in the sidebar.

Redoable

Theme designer: Dean J. Robinson

`http://deanjrobinson.com/wordpress/redoable`

Redoable is the only dark theme that made my list of top tens. The light-text-on-a-dark-background type of theme has gained popularity among designers and theme fans across the blogosphere, but it can make your blog difficult for some visitors to read. I include this theme because of the popularity of this type of look. Aside from readability issues, Redoable is a beautiful theme with a lot of detailed treatment, built on the popular K2 theme.

Redoable has a two-column layout, and its sidebar is widget ready. It supports multiple popular WordPress plugins. (See the theme's Web page for details.) This theme also gives detailed treatment to many design classes, letting you create a unique blog site.

Corporate

Theme designer: Ori Pearl

`http://wordpress.org/extend/themes/corporate`

The Corporate theme by Ori Pearl is a very clean, professional-looking free theme for WordPress that you can begin using immediately after you install and activate it through your WordPress.

The color scheme is a cool light blue and white with a gray gradient background. The design has trendy rounded corners and a tidy text box on the front page to welcome visitors to your site. If you want to tweak this theme to make it more individual to you, the header is highly customizable (see Chapter 13 for information on tweaking WordPress themes).

Gridline Lite

Theme designer: Thad Allender

`http://gridline.thadallender.com`

Gridline Lite is a minimalist WordPress theme. The theme has clean, simple, light elements, which lets your design focus mainly on content rather than appearance. The theme uses black, white, and gray tones and a two-column layout, with content on the left and sidebar on the right.

Appendix

Migrating Your Existing Blog to WordPress

In This Appendix

▶ Preparing your current blog for migration

▶ Converting your template for use in WordPress

▶ Importing from different blog platforms

▶ Discovering other import resources

So you have a blog on a different blogging system and want to move your blog to WordPress? This appendix helps you accomplish just that. WordPress makes it relatively easy to pack up your data and archives from one blog platform and move to a new WordPress blog.

WordPress lets you move your blog from platforms such as Blogspot, TypePad, and Movable Type. It also gives you a nifty way to migrate from any blogging platform via RSS feeds, as long as the platform you're importing from has an RSS feed available. Some platforms, such as MySpace, have some limitations on RSS feed availability, so be sure to check with your platform provider. In this appendix, you discover how to prepare your blog for migration and how to move from the specific platforms for which WordPress provides importer plugins.

For each blogging platform, the WordPress.org platform provides you with a quick and easy to install plugin that allows you to import and use your content right away. The importers are packaged in a plugin format because most people use an importer just once, and some people don't use the importer tools at all. The plugins are there for you to use if you need them. WordPress. com, on the other hand, has the importers built right into the software. Note the differences for the version you are using.

Movin' On Up

Bloggers have a variety of reasons to migrate away from one system to WordPress:

- ✓ **Simple curiosity:** There is a *lot* of buzz around the use of WordPress and the whole community of WordPress users. People are naturally curious to check out something that all the cool kids are doing.

- ✓ **More control of your blog:** This reason applies particularly to those who have a blog on Blogspot, TypePad, or any other hosted service. Hosted programs limit what you can do, create, and mess with. When it comes to plugins, add-ons, and theme creation, hosting a WordPress blog on your own Web server wins hands down. In addition, you have complete control of your data, archives, and backup capability when you host your blog on your own server.

- ✓ **Ease of use:** Many people find the WordPress interface easier to use, more understandable, and a great deal more user-friendly than many of the other blogging platforms available today.

Both the hosted version of WordPress.com and the self-hosted version of WordPress.org allow you to migrate your blog to their platforms; however, WordPress.com accepts a few less than WordPress.org does. Table A-1 lists blogging platforms that have built in importers, or import plugins, for migration to WordPress.

Table A-1	Compatible Blogging Platforms for Migration	
Blogging Platform	*WordPress.com*	*WordPress.org*
Blogger (Blogspot)	Yes	Yes
Blogli	Yes	No
LiveJournal	Yes	Yes
Movable Type	Yes	Yes
Posterous	Yes	No
RSS import	No	Yes
TypePad	Yes	Yes
Vox	No	Yes
WordPress	Yes	Yes

In the WordPress.org software (self-hosted), the importers are added to the installation as plugins. The importer plugins included in Table A-1 are the plugins that are packaged within the WordPress.org software by default; there are several other platforms you can import content from by installing other plugins available from the official WordPress plugins directory, which you can find here: `http://wordpress.org/extend/plugins/search.php?q=importer`.

Preparing for the Big Move

Depending on the size of your blog (that is, how many posts and comments you have), the migration process can take anywhere from 5 to 30 minutes. As with any major change or update you make, no matter where your blog is hosted, the very first thing you need to do is create a backup of your blog. You should back up the following:

- **Archives:** Posts, comments, and trackbacks
- **Template:** Template files and image files
- **Links:** Any links, banners, badges, and elements you have in your current blog
- **Images:** Any images you use in your blog

Table A-2 gives you a few tips on creating the export data for your blog in a few major blogging platforms. *Note:* This table assumes that you are logged in to your blog software.

Table A-2	Backing Up Your Blog Data on Major Platforms
Blogging Platform	*Backup Information*
Movable Type	Click the Import/Export button in the menu of your Movable Type Dashboard; then click the Export Entries From link. When the page stops loading, save it on your computer as a .txt file.
TypePad	Click the name of the blog you want to export; then click the Import/Export link in the Overview menu. Click the Export link at the bottom of the Import/Export page. When the page stops loading, save it on your computer as a .txt file.

Table A-2 *(continued)*

Blogging Platform	Backup Information
Blogspot	Back up your template by copying the text of your template to a text editor such as Notepad. Then save it on your computer as a .txt file.
LiveJournal	Browse to http://livejournal.com/export.bml and enter your information; choose XML as the format. Save this file on your computer.
WordPress	Click the Export link on the Tools menu in the Dashboard; the Export page opens. Choose your options on the Export page and then click the Download Export File button, and save this file on your computer. (Chapter 17 lists ten great WordPress plugins, including one that lets you back up your entire database.)
RSS feed	Point your browser to the URL of the RSS feed you want to import. Wait until it loads fully (you may need to set your feed to display all posts). View the source code of the page, copy and paste that source code into a .txt file, and save the file on your computer.

This import script allows for a maximum file size of 128MB. If you get an "out of memory" error, try dividing the import file into pieces and uploading them separately. The import script is smart enough to ignore duplicate entries, so if you need to run the script a few times to get it to take everything, you can do so without worrying about duplicating your content.

Converting Templates

Every blogging program has a unique way of delivering content and data to your blog. Template tags vary from program to program; no two are the same, and each template file requires conversion if you want to use *your* template with your new WordPress blog. In such a case, two options are available to you:

✔ **Convert the template yourself.** To accomplish this task, you need to know WordPress template tags and HTML. If you have a template that you're using on another blogging platform and want to convert it for use with WordPress, you need to swap the original platform tags for WordPress tags. Chapters 12 and 13 give you the rundown on basic WordPress template tags; you may find that information useful if you plan to attempt a template conversion yourself.

✔ **Hire an experienced WordPress consultant to do the conversion for you.** See Chapter 15 for a list of WordPress consultants.

To use your own template, make sure that you have saved *all* the template files, the images, and the stylesheet from your previous blog setup. You need them to convert the template(s) for use in WordPress.

Hundreds of free templates are available for use with WordPress, so it may be a lot easier to abandon the template you're currently working with and find a free WordPress template that you like. If you've paid to have a custom design done for your blog, contact the designer of your theme, and hire him to perform the template conversion for you. Also, you can hire several WordPress consultants to perform the conversion for you — including yours truly.

Moving Your Blog

You've packed all your stuff, and you have your new place prepared. Moving day has arrived!

This section takes you through the steps for moving your blog from one blog platform to WordPress. This section assumes that you already have the WordPress software installed and configured on your own Web server (see Chapter 6 for information about installing WordPress.org). You can also apply these steps to moving your blog to a WordPress.com hosted blog (Part II is all about WordPress.com).

Find the import function that you need by following these steps:

1. **In the Dashboard, click the Import link on the Tools menu.**

   The Import page opens, listing blogging platforms from which you can import content (such as Blogger and Movable Type). Figure A-1 shows the Import page for WordPress.com, and Figure A-2 shows this page for WordPress.org.

2. **Click the link for the blogging platform you're working with.**

   Click the Install Now button to install the importer plugin to begin using it.

The following sections provide some import directions for a few of the most popular blogging platforms (other than WordPress, that is). Each platform has its own content export methods, so be sure to check the documentation for the blogging platform that you are using.

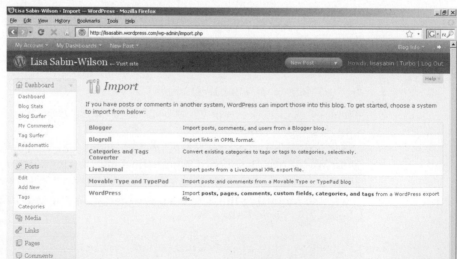

Figure A-1:
The Import
feature of
the (hosted)
WordPress.
com
Dashboard.

Figure A-2:
The Import
feature of
the (self-
hosted)
WordPress.
org
Dashboard.

Importing from Blogspot/Blogger

I call it Blogspot; you call it Blogger — a rose by any other name would smell as sweet. The blogging application owned by Google is referenced either way: Blogspot or Blogger. In the end, we're talking about the same application.

To begin the import process, first complete the steps in the "Moving Your Blog" section, earlier in this chapter. Then follow these steps:

1. **Click the Blogger link on the Import page.**

   The Import Blogger page loads and you see a message that says, Howdy! This importer allows you to import posts and comments from your Blogger account into your WordPress blog. The message goes on to explain that you need a Google account, and that you need to tell Google you're authorizing your WordPress blog to access your Blogger blog.

2. **Click the Authorize button to tell WordPress to access your account.**

   A page from Google opens with a message that says your WordPress blog is trying to access your Google account (see Figure A-3).

3. **Enter the e-mail address and password you use for Google; then click the Sign In button.**

   The Access Request page in your Google Account opens.

   When you have successfully logged in, you receive a message from Google stating that your blog at WordPress is requesting access to your Blogger account so that it can post entries on your behalf.

4. **Give your permission by clicking the Grant Access button on the Access Request page.**

   If you have many posts and comments in your Blogger blog, the import can take 30 minutes or more.

   After the import script has performed its magic, you're redirected to your WordPress Dashboard, where the name of your Blogger blog is listed.

5. **To finish importing the data from Blogger, click the Import button (below the Magic Button header).**

   The text on the button changes to *Importing . . .* while the import takes place. When the import is complete, the text on the button changes to *Set Authors* (no wonder it's called the Magic Button!).

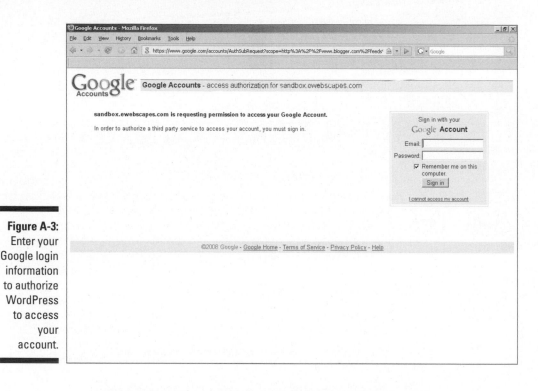

Figure A-3:
Enter your
Google login
information
to authorize
WordPress
to access
your
account.

6. **Click the Set Authors button to assign the authors to the posts.**

   The Blogger username appears on the left side of the page; a drop-down menu on the right side of the page displays the WordPress login name.

7. **Assign authors using the drop-down menu.**

   If you have just one author on each blog, the process is especially easy: Use the drop-down menu on the right to assign the WordPress login to your Blogger username. If you have multiple authors on both blogs, each Blogger username is listed on the left side with a drop-down menu to the right of each username. Select a WordPress login for each Blogger username to make the author assignments.

8. **Click Save Changes.**

   You're done!

Importing from LiveJournal

Both WordPress.com and WordPress.org offer an import script for LiveJournal users, and the process of importing from LiveJournal to WordPress is the same for each platform.

To export your blog content from LiveJournal, log in to your LiveJournal blog and then type this URL in your browser's address bar: `www.livejournal.com/export.bml`.

LiveJournal lets you export the XML files one month at a time, so if you have a blog with several months' worth of posts, be prepared to be at this process for a while. First, you have to export the entries one month at a time, and then you have to import them into WordPress — yep, you guessed it — one month at a time.

To speed the process a little, you can save all the exported XML LiveJournal files in one text document by copying and pasting each month's XML file into one plain-text file (created in a text editor such as Notepad), thereby creating one long XML file with all the posts from your LiveJournal blog. Then you can then save the file as an XML file to prepare it for import into your WordPress blog.

After you export the XML file from LiveJournal, return to the Import page in your WordPress Dashboard, and follow these steps.

1. **Click the LiveJournal link.**

   The Import LiveJournal page opens, from which you can extract the XML file into your WordPress blog.

2. **Click the Browse button.**

   A window opens, listing files on your computer.

3. **Double-click the name of the XML file you saved earlier.**

4. **Click the Upload and Import button.**

   When the import script finishes, it reloads the page with a confirmation message that the process is complete. Then WordPress runs the import script and brings over all your posts from your LiveJournal blog.

Importing from Movable Type and TypePad

Movable Type and TypePad were created by the same company, Six Apart. These two blogging platforms run on essentially the same code base, so the import/export procedure is basically the same for both. Refer to Table A-2, earlier in this chapter, for details on how to run the export process in both Movable Type and TypePad. This import script moves all your blog posts, comments, and trackbacks to your WordPress blog.

Go to the Import page in your WordPress Dashboard by following Steps 1 and 2 in the "Moving Your Blog" section, earlier in this chapter. Then follow these steps:

1. **Click the Movable Type and TypePad link.**

   You see instructions for importing the data you exported from your Movable Type or TypePad blog.

2. **Click the Browse button.**

   A window opens, listing your files.

3. **Double-click the name of the export file you saved from your Movable Type or TypePad blog.**

4. **Click the Upload File and Import button.**

   Sit back and let the import script do its magic. When it's done, it reloads the page with a confirmation message that the process is complete.

When the import script is done, you can assign users to the posts, matching the Movable Type or TypePad usernames with WordPress usernames. If you have just one author on each blog, this process is easy; you simply assign your WordPress login to the Movable Type or Typepad username using the drop-down menu. If you have multiple authors on both blogs, match the Movable Type or TypePad usernames with the correct WordPress login names and then click Save Changes. You're done!

Importing from WordPress

With this WordPress import script, you can import one WordPress blog into another, and this is true for both the hosted and self-hosted versions of WordPress. WordPress imports all your posts, comments, custom fields, and categories into your blog. Refer to Table A-2, earlier in this chapter, to find out how to use the export feature to obtain your blog data.

Only files 15MB or smaller can upload via the Import page of the WordPress. com Dashboard. If you have a file that is larger than 15MB in size, you can break it into smaller files and import them as separate files.

When you complete the exporting, follow these steps:

1. **Click the WordPress link on the Import page.**

   To get to the Import page, follow Steps 1 and 2 of the "Moving Your Blog" section, earlier in this chapter.

2. **Click the Browse button.**

   A window opens, listing the files on your computer.

3. **Double-click the export file you saved earlier from your WordPress blog.**

4. **Click the Upload File and Import button.**

   The import script gets to work, and when it's done, it reloads the page with a confirmation message that the process is complete.

Importing from an RSS feed

If all else fails, or if WordPress doesn't provide an import script that you need for your current blog platform, you can import your blog data via the RSS feed for the blog you want to import. With the RSS import method, you can import posts only; you can't use this method to import comments, trackbacks, categories, or users. WordPress.com currently does not allow you to import blog data via an RSS feed; this function works only with the self-hosted WordPress.org platform.

Refer to Table A-2, earlier in this chapter, for the steps required to create the file you need to import via RSS. Then follow these steps:

1. **On the Import page in the WordPress Dashboard, click the RSS link.**

   You find the instructions to import your RSS file, as shown in Figure A-4.

2. **Click the Browse button on the Import RSS page.**

   A window opens, listing the files on your computer.

3. **Double-click the export file you saved earlier from your RSS feed.**

4. **Click the Upload File and Import button.**

   The import script does its magic and then reloads the page with a confirmation message that the process is complete.

Finding Other Import Resources

The WordPress Codex has a long list of other available scripts, plugins, work-arounds, and outright hacks for importing from other blog platforms. You can find that information at `http://codex.wordpress.org/Importing_Content`.

Note, however, that the WordPress Codex is run by a group of volunteers. When you refer to the Codex, be aware that not everything listed in it is necessarily up to date or accurate, including import information (or any other information about running your WordPress blog).

Index

• A •

abandoned domain names, 98
accounts, 29–32, 50, 108, 130
Adams, Michael D. (developer), 362
add-ons. *See* plugins
addresses
  e-mail, 111, 130, 146–147, 152
  FTP, 103
  images, 163
  posts. *See* permalinks
  registration restrictions, 339
  RSS feeds, 163, 171–172
  URLs, 112, 130
Admin Color Scheme, 49, 146
administrative control, 22, 70, 131, 338
Adobe Flash, 57, 188
advertising, 18, 93, 364
Akismet (spam filter), 25, 37, 78, 183–184,
    210–212
alignment, 174–175, 190, 192–193, 287
All in One SEO Pack, 359
Allender, Thad (designer), 368
ALT tags, 323, 326
Android phone-compatible browsing, 360
Ang, Joni (designer), 366
Apache
  configuration, 330–331
  mod_rewrite, 169, 170–171, 332
API key, 210, 362
appearance, 87, 150–151, 232. *See also specific
    elements of appearance*
Apple iPhone-compatible browsing, 360
approving comments, 74, 76–77, 138–139, 150,
    181–182
archives, 19–21, 272–274, 371
arrays, 277–278
article settings, 136–137
ASCII transfer mode, 108
Atom publishing protocol, 134, 172
audio
  disk space for, 103
  embedding, 143
  inserting, 54, 59, 176, 199
  plugins for, 202
Audio Player, 202

authors
  adding, 152, 338
  comments from, 37, 119
  posts from, 69
  requirements for, 73
  role of, 131
Auto Renew (domain names), 99
autodetect transfer mode, 108
autodiscoverable RSS feeds, 23, 171
Auto-Embed feature, 197–198
auto-installation, plugins, 213, 215
Automattic (WordPress manufacturer), 25,
    78, 183–184, 210, 212
autosaving, 54, 175
avatars, 72, 76, 139–142
avi files, 54

• B •

b2 platform, 224
background, 151, 287–290
BackUp Buddy, 225
backups, 19, 281, 360, 371
bandwidth, 100, 102–103, 327
base code files, 15
Best Buy (Web site), 16
Billboard, 225
binary transfer mode, 108
biographical information, 147
BlackBerry-compatible browsing, 360
blacklists, 74–75, 139
blip.tv, 198
Blog of the Day, 46
bloginfo parameters, 249–250
Blogli, 370
Bloglines, 23
blogs. *See also* multiple site hosting
  about, 17–18
  blogrolls (link lists), 65–69, 158–165, 270–272
  categories, 153–158
  comments. *See* comments
  configuration, 330–331
  content management system. *See* content
    management system (CMS)
  domain names, 97–100
  File Transfer Protocol, 103–104
  front page, 80–82, 135, 179, 300–304

blogs *(continued)*
  installation, 104–114
  migration from. *See* migration
  names, 253–254
  networks, 16, 18
  OpenID, 83–84
  optimization, 322–326
  organization, 63–65
  page layout, 87
  permalinks, 165–171
  planning for, 25
  posts
    how to, 51–54
    media files, 54–59
    publishing, 61–62
    refinements, 59–61
  primary, 50
  publicity/privacy options, 62, 82–83, 134, 144, 164, 177, 179
  RSS feeds, 171–172
  spam, 78
  static pages, 78–80
  taglines, 253–254
  technologies, 18–25
  titles, 111, 129
  trackbacks, 181–184
  users, 69–71
  Web hosting, 100–103
  writing, 173–180
Blogs About Hosting, 101
Blogspot, 13, 369, 370, 372, 375–376
BlueHost, 101
body templates, 245, 260–261
bookmarks, 65–69, 158–165, 270–272
Boolean parameters, 267
Brachhold, Arne (developer), 362
Brave New Code, 360
browsers
  connection options, 49
  errors, 363
  links in, 66–67
  RSS feed alerts, 23
  screens, 53
  uploading, 57
BuddyPress team, 355
bug fixes, 224
bulk-editing, 183
bulleted lists (list pages), 267–269
Burmeister, Mary (author)
  HTML 4 For Dummies, 5th Edition, 242
business blogs, 18

• C •

Cagle, Daryl (editorial blogger), 18
calendar, 267
calling templates, 244, 254–256
capabilities, extensibility of, 10, 11–12
Cascading Style Sheets (CSS)
  about, 85, 246, 281–286
  background changes with, 289–290
  classes/IDs, 283–285
  CSS Collection, 353
  CSS selectors, 282–283, 284–286
  customization, 92–93
  photo galleries, 194
  templates, 246, 262
  in theme design, 242
categories
  archives, 19–21
  blogrolls, 65–69
  blogs, 153–158
  customization, 315–317
  ID numbers, 312
  links, 134, 149, 159–160
  naming conventions, 311
  number of, 36, 118
  posts, 61, 63–65, 134, 148, 177, 310–311
  for search engines, 323, 325–326
  tag parameters/conversions, 152, 158, 274–276
category children, 154
centering images, 287
Chan, Lester (developer), 357
character encoding/entities, 82, 252–253
chat programs, 146
child categories, 326
chronology, archives, 19–21
citizen journalism, 18
classes, 283–285
clockwise rotation, 191
closing (collapsing) categories/modules, 35, 117, 161, 164, 173
CMS (content management system). *See* content management system (CMS)
coding. *See also* MySQL; PHP Hypertext Preprocessor
  Apache `mod_rewrite`, 169, 170–171, 332
  backgrounds, 288, 289, 290
  base code files, 15
  blogrolls (link lists), 270–272
  calendar, 267
  Cascading Style Sheets (CSS), 282
  categories, 274–276
  character entities, 252–253

clean, 229
conditional statements, 257–258
CSS selectors, 282–286
errors, 247
executable, 90
fonts, 297, 298
header templates, 248–249
HTML. *See* HTML coding
images, 57, 292
list pages, 267–269
The Loop, 256
main index template, 262–265
malicious, 229–230, 236
navigation, 293–294
networks, 330
photo galleries, 195
PHP configuration, 333
posts
  archives, 272–274
  customization, 260–261, 315, 316, 318–322
  query tags, 313
removing, 223
RSS feeds, 171, 172
sidebars, 258–259
simplifying, 261–265
static pages, 307, 308, 309
tags, 278–280
templates, 241–242, 258–259, 266
UTF-8, 82, 135
collapsing (closing) categories/modules, 117, 161, 164, 173
color, 282–286, 296–298, 364, 366–367. *See also specific plugins; specific themes*
Comment Reply via E-mail, 75
comments
  allowing, 177
  approving, 74, 76–77, 138–139, 150, 181–182
  blacklists, 139
  blogging, 72–77, 181–184
  coding, 262
  data about, 119–120
  managing, 37
  menu, 76, 150, 181
  moderating, 37, 73–75, 120, 138–139, 150, 181–183
  number of, 36, 118–119
  from other blogs, 24, 60
  from readers, 21–22, 60
  recent, 37
  settings for, 137–138
  spam, 24–25, 137, 150
  subscriptions to, 75
  templates, 259–260
  from users, 73
  viewing, 37, 76, 120

compatibility, server/permalinks, 169–171
compression formats, 105
conditional statements, 257–258
configuration
  for cookies, 116
  of Dashboard
    about, 34–35
    general settings, 129–132
    media, 142–144
    Permalinks, 144–145
    privacy, 144
    profiles, 145–147
    reading, 134–142
    writing, 132–134
  discussion settings, 72
  image options, 57
  multiple site hosting, 330–331
  networks, 16, 335, 336–341
  PHP Hypertext Preprocessor, 333
  plugins, 219
  text widgets, 90
contact information, 45, 146–147
content
  delivery, 172
  duplicate, 372
  indexing, 112, 168
  organization, 87
  from other blogs, 91–92
  pulling in, 311–313
  for search engine optimization, 324–325
  sidebars, 89
  storage, 105
content management system (CMS)
  about, 299
  blogs, 304–306, 322–326
  front page, 300–304
  posts, 315–321
  pulling in content, 311–313
  templates, 306–309, 310–311, 314–315
  Web sites
    CSS Collection, 353
    E.Webscapes Design Studio, 356
    Harvard Gazette, 352
    Icon Dock, 352
    John James Jacoby, 355–356
    Mendocino Beauty, 355
    MommyCast, 354–355
    Mosaic Consulting, Inc, 352–353
    Queensryche, 353–354
    Streamy Awards, 354
contributors, 69, 131, 338
conventions in this book, 2–3
conversation, 21–22, 60
cookies as login credentials, 32, 116

Coordinated Universal Time (UTC), 43, 131
corrections, coding, 133
costs
  domain names, 92, 94, 98–99
  free price tag
    File Transfer Protocol, 103
    plugins, 11
    themes, 227–232, 246, 363–368
    WordPress, 9
  plugins, 11
  premium products, 225, 228, 236–238
  upgrades, 92–93
  Web hosting, 15–16, 100, 328–329
  WordPress, 9
counter-clockwise rotation, 190
cPanel, 105–106
cropping
  images, 57, 190, 291–292
  photos, 47
CSS. *See* Cascading Style Sheets (CSS)
CSS Collection, 353
CSS selectors, 282–283, 284–286
customer testimony, 237, 238
customization
  background, 287–289
  body templates, 260–261
  Cascading Style Sheets, 92–93
  Dashboard, 125–127
  fields, 177
  headers, 151, 366–367
  menus, 151, 292–296
  permalinks, 167–168, 306, 323
  themes, 16, 85, 228, 241, 364
  WordPress.com limitations, 15
Cyberduck (for Mac), 103

• D •

DailyMotion, 59, 198
Dashboard
  about, 10
  administrative control through, 22
  blogging format, 147–152
  configuration
    general settings, 129–132
    media, 142–144
    permalinks, 144–145
    privacy, 144
    profiles, 145–147
    reading, 134–142
    writing, 132–134
  content, 19
  installation from, 234–236
  logging in, 115–116

during migration, 374
  navigation, 116–125
  options, 128
  rearranging, 117, 125–127
  shortcut links to, 32, 34, 35
  WordPress.com, 34–40
Database Host, 110
database names, 110
dates
  filtering by, 201
  format, 131–132
  organization by, 143
  in permalinks, 166, 167–168
  publishing, 62
  settings, 42–43
daylight savings time (DST), 43
deactivating plugins, 206
dedicated server, 329
Default Article Settings, 72, 136–137
Del.icio.us, 204, 359
design, themes, 85–86
designer-credit links, 228
development news, 123–125
dialog, 21–22, 60
diaries, 17
Digg, 204, 359
directory of community blogs, 47
discussion, 21–22, 60
disk space, 59, 101, 327
DNS (domain name server), 331–332
doc files, 54, 59
DOCTYPE, 248
domain name server (DNS), 331–332
domain names, 92, 94, 97–100
downloading, 12, 15, 230–232. *See also*
    specific applications; specific plugins
drafts
  recent, 39, 123
  saving, 61–62, 148, 178, 179
dragging and dropping, 34–35, 104, 161, 162, 164
DreamHost, 101
drop-down menus. *See* menus
DST (daylight savings time), 43
duplicate content, 372

• E •

ease of use, 10
Easy Contact (plugins), 356
editorial bloggers, 18
editors, 69, 131, 338
e-mail
  addresses, 111, 130, 146–147, 152
  Easy Contact, 356

notification, 204
with photos, 48
posting from, 134
registration restrictions, 339
settings, 42, 82
with Web hosting, 100
E-Mail Me Whenever option, 73–74, 138
embedding files, 143
embellishments, 11
emoticons, 133
enhancements
  domain names, 94
  hosting upgrades, 92–93
  themes, 85–87
  widgets, 87–92
errors/error messages, 114, 223, 258, 260, 333, 363, 372
E. Webscapes Design Studio, 356
excerpts, 37, 60, 177
executable coding, 90
expanding modules, 117
expired domain names, 98
exporting to other blogs, 152
extensibility, capabilities, 10, 11–12

• **F** •

fact-checking news media, 18
family-friendly blogs, 140
feed generator, 171
feed readers, 23–24
FeedDemon, 23
Feldman, Loren (blogger), 197
fields, customized, 177
File Transfer Protocol (FTP), 100, 103–104, 333–335
files
  embedding, 143
  extensions, 98
  filtering, 201
  permissions, 108, 209
  size, 59, 142–143, 190, 378
FileZilla, 103
filtering spam, 75
500 error messages, 114
five-minute installation, 105, 110
Flash (Adobe), 57, 188
Flickr, 198
flipping images, 57
flipping vertically/horizontally, 191
fonts, 174–175, 296–298
footer templates, 246, 259, 262, 359

format
  date/time, 43, 131–132
  fonts, 174–175
  page breaks, 73
  posts, 52–53, 133–134, 174–175
  setting up, 147–152
formats, compression, 105
403/404/500 error messages, 114
404 template, 260
free price tag
  File Transfer Protocol, 103
  plugins, 11
  themes, 227–232, 246, 363–368
  WordPress, 9
front page, 80–82, 135, 179, 300–304
FTP (File Transfer Protocol), 100, 103, 333–335
FTP Explorer, 103
Fun Mode, 49

• **G** •

galleries, photo, 193–196
Gardner, Brian (designer), 238
global variables, 333
GoDaddy, 99
Google
  blog visibility to, 112
  Blogsearch, 38
  Blogspot, 13, 369, 370, 372, 375–376
  Reader, 23
  Video, 59
  Videom, 198
  XML Sitemaps, 362
graphs, statistical, 39
Gravatars, 46, 139
Greenwich Mean Time, 131
guestbooks, 21–22, 24–25

• **H** •

hackers, protection against, 49
hard drives, 56–57, 100
Harvard Gazette, 352
Hawt Post, 47
headers
  Cascading Style Sheets with, 282
  color, 366–367
  customization, 151
  images, 290–292, 366–367
  templates, 245, 248–254, 262
Hello Dolly, 213
hexadecimal (hex) code, 287
horizontal flipping, 191

horizontal tiling, 287
hosted versions, 1, 10, 13–15, 92–93. *See also*
    WordPress.com
hosting. *See* Web hosting
HTML, XML, and CSS Bible, 3rd Edition
    (Pfaffenberger et al.), 242
HTML 4 For Dummies, 5th Edition (Tittel &
    Burmeister), 242
HTML coding
  with CSS selectors, 284–285
  divergence from, 265
  in header templates, 248
  HTML tab, 52, 53, 175
  photo galleries, 194
  static, 360–361
  in theme design, 242
HTTPS connections, 49
Hulu, 198

• I •

ICANN (Internet Corporation for Assigned
    Names and Numbers), 99
Icon Dock, 352
icons
  audio, 199
  images, 188, 189
  in this book, 6
  RSS feeds, 23
  social networking, 359
  video, 198
IDs, 283–285, 312
If, then, else, 257–258
Image editor, 58
images. *See also* photos
  addresses, 67, 163
  alignment, 192–193
  as background, 287
  backups, 371
  for search engine optimization, 323, 326
  headers, 290–292
  inserting, 54–59, 176, 188–196
  posts represented as, 177
  uploading, 151, 262
importing, 15, 152
Imthiaz, 196
Incoming Links module, 38, 120
index templates, 170, 246, 254–258, 255
indexing content, 112, 168
install script, 109–114
installation
  plugins, 122, 151–152, 210, 213–218
  readme files, 218

  themes, 150, 234–236
  WordPress, 11, 15, 101, 104–114
instructions, 218
integer parameters, 267
interface, hosting, 105–106
Interface Language option, 49
Internet Corporation for Assigned Names and
    Numbers (ICANN), 99
Internet Explorer, 218
inviting friends, 70–71
iPhone-compatible browsing, 360
iThemes, 225, 238

• J •

Jackson, Noel (designer), 365
Jaquith, Mark (developer), 214, 215–217, 218,
    219, 358
JavaScript, 90, 108
jazz as naming inspiration, 213
John James Jacoby (developer), 355–356
journalism, 18

• K •

Kent, Peter (author)
    Search Engine Optimization For Dummies,
    322
keyboard shortcuts, 49, 146
keywords for searching, 39, 60–61, 201, 323, 324
King, Alex (developer), 358, 361, 366, 367

• L •

La, Nick (designer), 367
landing pages. *See* static pages
languages
  interface, 49
  of publication, 42
  scripting, 16, 18–19
Laughing Squid, 101
layout, 87, 125–127
library, media, 148
licensing restrictions, 237
Link Relationship (XFN) options, 162–163
links
  backups, 371
  blogrolls (link lists), 65–69, 158–165, 270–272
  categories, 134
  color, 366–367
  comment management, 37, 120
  to Dashboard, 32, 34, 35

to further information, 246
menus, 33–34, 149, 292
options, 149, 165
to posts, 38, 120–121
on Profile page, 45–46
relationships (XFN), 68
for site creation, 342
sorting, 165
spam as, 229–230
unlinking, 53
viruses as, 229–230
lists, ordered/unordered, 174, 267–269
LiveJournal, 370, 372, 376–377
localhost, 110
logging in, 32, 112–113, 115–116, 152
The Loop, 256–257

• *M* •

Macintosh elements, 367
mailing lists, 13
main (parent) categories, 154
main index template, 254–258, 261–265
malicious code, 229–230, 236
malware, 229–230
Matzko, Austin (developer), 360
media
  audio, 199, 202
  blogs, 18
  configuration, 142–144
  images, 188–196
  library, 148
  menus, 148
  organization, 199–201
  plugins, 202
  posts, 54–59
  uploader box, 59
  video, 197–198, 202
membership options, 130
memory limit checks, 333
Mendocino Beauty, 355
menus
  appearance, 87, 232
  comments, 76, 150, 181
  customization, 151
  links, 33–34, 149, 292
  media, 148
  menu bar, 32–34
  navigation, 35, 117, 128, 292–296
  plugins, 151
  posts, 51
  publishing status, 61
  settings, 72
  themes, 150

tools, 152
users, 70, 152
widgets, 87–88
metadata, 266
microcategories, 158
migration
  about, 369–371
  moving from other packages, 13, 373–378, 379–380
  preparing for, 371–372
  resources for, 380
  template conversion, 372–373
  from WordPress.com, 15, 378–379
Miller, Cory (designer), 238
Mini-Slides, 196
moderating
  comments, 37, 73–75, 120, 138–139, 150, 181–183
  posts, 69
  trackbacks, 183
modules, 35–40, 117, 173, 176
MommyCast, 354–355
monetization, 364
Mosaic Consulting, Inc, 352–353
Movable Type
  about, 2, 184
  backups, 371
  migration from, 13, 369, 370, 377–378
Moxie Design Studios, 355
Mozilla Firefox, 218
Mullenweg, Matt (developer), 78, 184, 195, 213, 224
multiple site hosting
  networks, 329–335
  plugins, 347–348
  resources for, 328–329
  super admin, 335–347
MySpace, 369
MySQL
  about, 16, 18–19
  backups, 360
  setting up, 105–107
  with templates, 247, 254
  with Web hosting, 101

• *N* •

names, 146, 154–156, 159, 311. *See also* user names
NamesDirect, 99
navigation
  with categories, 153
  Dashboard, 116–125

navigation *(continued)*
  menus, 128, 292–296
  shortcuts, 32, 34, 35, 49
  tools, 152
  WordPress.com, 32–34
N.Design Studio, 352
nested (threaded) comments, 73, 137
nested XHTML, 133
Network Solutions, 99, 101
networks
  configuration of, 16, 336–341
  multiple site hosting, 329–335
  Network Admin page, 341–342
  pings, 24, 72
  themes on, 345–346
  updating, 347
NextGEN Gallery, 196, 355
niche-specific blog networks, 16
Not Found, 258
Notepad, 262
notes, 68, 164
notifications, 72, 136–137, 183, 204

• O •

obsolescent links, 168
O'Caoimh, Donncha (developer), 360–361
1 Bit Audio Player, 202
one-click installation/upgrades, 105, 207–209
online services, 46
"out of memory" error, 372
open source environment, 204, 224–225
OpenID, 83–84
opening (expanding) modules, 35
options. *See also specific options*
  Dashboard, 128
  plugins, 221–222
  WordPress.com, 40–50
organization
  archives, 19–21
  blogs, 63–65
  links, 159–160
  media files, 143, 199–201
  posts, 177
Organizer, 196
Other WordPress News, 125

• P •

pages
  breaks, 73
  dynamic, 19
  layout, 87
  login, 113
  number of, 36, 118
  posts, 135, 149
  static, 78–80, 267, 299, 301–304, 306–309
  templates, 260, 306–309
parameters, 249–250, 319–322
parent categories, 154
passwords
  changing, 50, 147
  for installation, 110, 111
  post protection, 62, 179
  remembering, 32, 116
  strength of, 106, 147
  users, 152
  Web hosting, 103
PDF files, 54, 59
Pearl, Ori (designer), 368
permalinks
  about, 144–145, 165–171
  customization, 306
  with RSS feed coding, 172
  with search engines, 166–167, 322, 332
permissions, 108–109, 209, 219
personal journals, 17
personalization, 41–42, 49–50, 145–147
Pfaffenberger, Bryan (author)
  HTML, XML, and CSS Bible, 3rd Edition, 242
PhotoBucket, 198
photos, 45, 46–48, 54–59, 103, 193–196
PHP Hypertext Preprocessor
  about, 16, 18–19
  configuration, 333
  file transfer, 108
  functioning of, 105
  The Loop with, 256
  templates with, 247
  Web hosting with, 101
  widgets with, 90
ping service, 134
pitfalls
  domain names, 101
  installation, 114
  malicious code, 229–230, 236
  permalinks, 168
  plugins, 224
  publishing, 62, 179
  Web hosting limitations, 328–329
pixels (px), 297
planning blogs, 25
platform options, 10, 13–16
Plugin Buddy, 225

plugins
  about, 11, 204–206
  activating, 219–221
  Akismet (spam filter), 25, 37, 78, 183–184, 210–212
  audio, 202
  in the Dashboard, 121–122
  Easy Contact, 356
  examples
    All in One SEO Pack, 359
    Google XML Sitemaps, 362
    Hello Dolly, 213
    ShareThis, 358–359
    Subscribe to Comments, 358
    Twitter Tools, 361
    WordPress.com Stats, 362
    WP Print, 357–358
    WP Super Cache, 360–361
    WP-DB-Backup, 360
    WPtouch iPhone Theme, 360
  importers as, 371
  installation, 213–218
  menu, 151–152
  on networks, 347–348
  open source environment, 224–225
  options, 221–222
  for photo galleries, 196
  premium, 225
  in sidebars, 233
  third-party, 2
  uninstalling, 222–223
  updates, 207–209
  video, 202
  WordPress.com limitations, 15
  WP E-Commerce, 352
podcasting, 202
points (pt), 298
PollDaddy, 59, 198
polls, 54, 59
portals, 299
Posterous, 370
posts
  addresses. *See* permalinks
  archives, 272–274
  categories, 134, 154, 158, 310–311
  customization, 260–261, 315–321
  from Dashboard, 38
  drafts, 39
  editing, 180
  in front page displays, 80–82
  how to, 51–54
  linking, 38
  media files, 54–59

menus, 51
metadata, 266
notification of, 136–137
number of, 36, 118, 257
options, 176–178
pages compared with, 149
publishing, 61–62, 148, 178–180
refinements, 59–61
statistics for, 39
titles, 37
types of, 317–322
Visual Editor with, 49, 145
writing, 132–134, 173–180
Power Line Blog (Web site), 18
premium products, 225, 228, 236–238
previewing, 86–87, 178, 230–231
primary blogs, 50
printing, 357–358
privacy/publicity options, 62, 82–83, 134, 144, 164, 177, 179
private users, 93
ProBlogger blog (Web site), 18
professional bloggers, 18
profiles, 43–48, 50, 145–147
proofreading, 50
properties, CSS, 285–286
Proulx, Marcel (developer), 196
pt (points), 298
publicity/privacy options, 62, 82–83, 134, 144, 164, 177, 179
publishing
  archives, 19–21
  from Dashboard, 122
  posts, 60, 61–62, 178–180
  remote, 134
  scheduling, 179–180
  tools for, 148
px (pixels), 297

• *Q* •

Qik, 198
quality, permalinks, 166–167
Queensryche, 353–354
query post tags, 313
QuickPress module, 38, 122

• *R* •

Rabe, Alex (designer), 196, 355
Random Image Widget, 196

rating
  avatars, 76
  blogging, 164
  interactive, 353
  links, 68, 164
  photos, 48
RDBMS (relational database management
    system), 19
readability issues, 368
reader feedback, 21–22, 60
reading, 134–142
readme files, 218, 219
Really Simple Syndication. *See* RSS feeds
Reeder, Joelle (designer), 355
references to posts, 166
refinements, posts, 59–61
Register.com, 99
registration
  domain names, 97–98
  registrars, 99, 100
  users, 338–339
  widgets, 277–278
relational database management system
    (RDBMS), 19
remote publishing, 134
renewal dates, domain names, 99
replies, 77, 182
requirements, Web hosting, 15–16
retail blogs, 16
Revision3, 198
Right Now module, 35–37, 117–119, 125–126
Robinson, Dean J. (designer), 368
root directory, 108
rotation, clockwise/counter-clockwise, 57,
    190, 191
Rowse, Darren (blogger), 18
RSS feeds
  about, 22–24
  addresses, 67, 163
  backups, 372
  blogs, 171–172
  displays, 80–82
  migration with, 369, 378
  post information, 135
RSS import, 370
RSS widget, 91–92
Rust Roland (developer), 196

• S •

safe mode, 109
safe themes, 229–230
sans-serif fonts, 297

saving
  autosaving, 54, 175
  from Dashboard, 122
  drafts, 178, 179
  links, 68
  options, 61, 72
  posts, 54
  publishing options, 179
scaling images, 57, 191
Schuller, Jason (designer), 238
Scibd, 198
scripting, server-side, 19
scrolling background, 287
Search Engine Optimization For Dummies
    (Kent), 322
search engines
  blog visibility to, 62, 82, 112, 144
  optimization, 166–167, 322–326, 332, 359, 364
  permalinks designed for, 166–167, 168
  SEO (search engine optimization), 166–167,
    322–326, 332, 359, 364. *See also*
    search engines.
  tags with, 158, 250
searching
  by contact information, 342
  links, 165
  media files, 200, 201
  phrases, 39, 60–61
  plugins, 214
  results, 260
  themes, 230
security
  bug fixes, 224
  file permissions, 108–109, 209
  malicious code, 229–230, 236
  password strength, 50, 106, 111
  plugin updates for, 209
  public profile cautions, 44, 50, 147
  publicity/privacy options, 62, 82–83, 134,
    144, 164, 177, 179
  user names, 111
self-hosted versions, WordPress.org, 1, 13–14.
    See also specific topics
SEO (search engine optimization). *See* search
    engines
serif fonts, 297
ServerBeach (Web site), 18
server-side scripting, 19
settings
  configuration
    discussion, 136–142
    general settings, 128–132
    media, 142–144
    permalinks, 144–145

privacy options, 144
reading, 134–136
writing, 132–134
menus, 72
options, 41–50, 221–222
shared-server solution, 329
ShareThis, 358–359
shortcuts, 32, 34, 35, 49, 146
Show Avatars option, 76
sidebars
  categories in, 154
  coding, 258–259
  content, 91–92
  plugins in, 233
  tag parameters
    about, 265–266
    blogrolls (link lists), 270–272
    bookmarks, 270–272
    calendar, 267
    categories, 274–276
    list pages, 267–269
    post archives, 272–274
    widgets, 276–278
  templates, 245–246, 258–259, 262, 277–278,
    314–315
  toggling between, 87–88
  widgets, 78, 87, 210, 233, 276–278, 364
single post template, 260
Sites page, 342–344
sizing
  files, 59
  fonts, 296–298
  images, 142–143, 190
  limitations, 378
Skelton, Andy (developer), 362
Smart YouTube, 202
SmartFTP, 103
Smashing Magazine, 364–365
snippets, 37, 60
social networking sites, 46, 204, 359, 361, 364
software, Web hosting, 16, 18–19
space upgrades, 93
spam
  about, 24–25
  blocking, 183–184, 210
  blogging, 78
  comments as, , 24–25, 137, 150
  controlling, 73, 74–75, 137, 138–139
  deleting, 77, 182
  filtering, 75
  links as, 229–230
  network protection, 348
  statistics, 37
spellchecking, 53, 175
SQL (Structured Query Language), 19

standards for premium themes, 237
static background, 287
static HTML coding, 361
static pages, 78–80, 267, 299, 301–304, 306–309
statistics
  Network Admin page, 342
  plugins for, 204
  Sites page, 342
  types of, 35–37, 39
  from Web host, 100
  WordPress.com Stats, 362
sticky posts, 179, 315–317
Streamy Awards, 354
string parameters, 267
structure
  of blogs, 245–247
  of permalinks, 167–168
  of themes, 242–244
Structured Query Language (SQL), 19
StudioPress, 238
styles, 193, 296–298. *See also* Cascading Style
    Sheets (CSS)
subcategories, 63–65, 154
subdirectories, 331
subdomains, 331–332
subject organization, 63–65
submenus, expanding/collapsing, 35
Subscribe to Comments, 214, 215–217, 358
subscriptions
  to blogs, 76, 131, 337
  to comments, 75
  RSS feeds, 23, 171
super admin, 335–347
support forums, 12–13, 32

• *T* •

table prefix, 110
Tadlock, Justin (designer), 363–364
taglines, 41
tags
  about, 158
  customization, 315–317
  number of, 36, 118
  pages, 47
  with parameters
    about, 265–266
    blogrolls (link lists), 270–272
    bookmarks, 270–272
    calendar, 267
    categories, 274–276
    list pages, 267–269
    post archives, 272–274
    widgets, 276–278

tags *(continued)*
  posts, 177, 272–274
  as search feature, 60–61
teasers, 177
technical support
  support forums, 32, 100, 237–238
  themes, 237
  with Web hosting, 101
Technorati, 112, 204, 359
templates
  about, 11
  assembly simplification, 261–265
  backups, 371
  basics, 245–247
  coding of, 241–242
  conversion, 372–373
  in Dashboard, 300
  defaults, 303
  naming conventions, 311
  plugin modifications, 219
  post categories, 310–311
  sidebars, 245–246, 258–259, 262, 277–278,
      314–315
  static pages, 306–309
  tag parameters
    about, 265–267
    blogrolls (link lists), 270–272
    calendar, 267
    categories, 274–276
    list pages (bulleted lists), 267–269
    post archives, 272–274
    widgets, 276–278
  tags
    anatomy of, 247
    connecting, 244–245
    customization with, 260–261
    miscellaneous, 278–280
    query posts, 311
  themes, 16, 85–86, 242–243
  types of
    footers, 259
    headers, 248–254
    main index, 254–258
    others, 259–260
    sidebars, 258–259
text
  editors, 262
  files, 108
  widgets, 90
TextEdit, 262
Theme Garden, 238
themes
  about, 11
  activating, 36, 232–234

alignment in, 192–193
appearance, 150
assembly simplification, 261–265
backup, 19
basics, 242–244
changing, 37, 119
customization, 92–93
enhancements, 85–87
free price tag
  about, 227–232
  Carrington Blog, 366–367
  Corporate, 368
  designPile, 364–365
  Elegant Grunge, 365
  Gridline Lite, 368
  Hybrid, 363–364
  iTheme, 367
  P2, 365–366
  Redoable, 368
  Stargaze, 366
identifying, 119
installation, 234–236
menus, 150
on networks, 345–346
plugin modifications, 219
premium, 236–238
structure of, 245–247
tag parameters
  about, 265–267
  blogrolls (link lists), 270–272
  calendar, 267
  categories, 274–276
  list pages (bulleted lists), 267–269
  post archives, 272–274
  widgets, 276–280
templates for
  footers, 248, 259
  headers, 248–254
  main index, 248, 254–258
  others, 259–260
  sidebars, 248, 258–259
  tags, 247, 260–261, 278–280
as templates, 242
tweaking
  background color, 287–290
  Cascading Style Sheets (CSS), 281–286
  fonts, 296–298
  header images, 290–292
  navigation menus, 292–296
from Web host, 101
from WordPress user community, 16
WordPress.com limitations, 15
Themes Directory, 150

third-party applications
  plugins, 2
  premium products, 225, 228, 236–238
  WordPress as, 100
threaded (nested) comments, 73, 137
threads, 21–22, 60
thumbnails, 143, 190, 193–196, 353, 364
tiling images, 287
time settings, 42–43, 132
titles
  blog, 129
  meaningful, 51–52
  for search engine optimization, 322, 324
  tags, 250–253
Tittel, Ed (author)
  HTML 4 For Dummies, 5th Edition, 242
toggling between sidebars, 87–88
top-level domain extension, 98
Torbert, Michael (developer), 359
trackbacks
  about, 24, 60
  blogs, 181–184
  notification of, 72, 136–137
  in posts, 177
  spam, 24–25
transfer mode, 108
trash, 77, 150, 182
troubleshooting, 125. *See also* errors/error
    messages
Twenty Ten theme
  activation, 151
  as default, 227, 246
  DOCTYPE, 248
  files, location, 262
  header templates, 248–254
Twitter, 49
Twitter Tools, 361
TypePad, 369, 370, 371, 377–378
Tyson, Michael (designer), 365

• U •

uninstalling plugins, 222–223
Universal Resource Locators (URLs), 112,
    130, 171–172
unlimited private users, 93
unlinking, 53
unsafe themes, 229
unscrupulous theme designers, 230
updates/upgrades
  automatic, 208
  daylight saving time, 43
  network, 347
  notification of, 134, 207–209

plugins, 207–209, 224
  WordPress, 38, 119, 123–125
uploading
  definition, 105
  images, 57, 151, 188–192, 291–292
  media files, 143, 148
  plugins, 219–220
  size limitations, 378
  templates, 307–308
  WordPress files, 107–109
URLs (Universal Resource Locators), 112,
    130, 171–172
usability, 10
user names
  disallowed, 339
  for installation, 110, 111
  remembering, 32
  Web hosting, 103
users
  about, 152
  accounts, 130
  adding, 344–345
  comments from, 73
  inviting, 71–72
  menus, 70, 152
  network plugins, 348
  public/private, 82, 93
  types of, 69–70, 131
Users page, 344–345
UTC (Coordinated Universal Time), 43, 131
UTF-8 character encoding, 80–82, 135

• V •

values, CSS, 285–286
verified external services, 46
versions
  plugins, 216–217
  WordPress, 347
vertical flipping, 191
vertical tiling, 287
vetting for malicious code, 229–230, 236
Viddler, 198
video
  disk space for, 103
  embedding, 143
  inserting, 54, 59, 176, 197–198
  plugins for, 202
Video Embedder, 202
VideoPress, 92, 198
viewing
  comments, 37, 76, 120
  media files, 201
  posts, 39
  tags, 148

Vimeo, 198
Virtual Host, 332–333
Virtual Text Editor, 78
viruses, 229–230
visual editing, 52–53, 173
Visual Editor, 49, 145
Visual Text Editor, 175
VodPod, 59
Vox, 370

• W •

W3C standards, 248, 363
W3Schools (Web site), 289
Wallick, Scott Allan (developer), 356
Web hosting. *See also* multiple site hosting
    auto-installation, 215
    backups, 19
    bandwidth, 327
    blogging setup, 100–103
    disk space for, 327
    mail access, 100
    requirements, 15–16
    servers, 15–16, 100, 169–171, 219, 330–333
WebHost Manager (WHM), 332
WeblogsInc.com, 18
WebReference.com (Web site), 23
week start-day options, 43, 132
What You See Is What You Get (WYSIWYG), 52, 173
WHM (WebHost Manager), 332
widgets
    code, 359
    enhancements, 87–92
    in footers, 364
    links, 87
    managing, 150
    number of, 36, 119
    registering, 277–278
    removing, 89
    sidebars with, 78, 87, 233, 274–278, 364
    themes, 364, 366
wildcard records, 332
Windows server, 170
word processing, 174–175
WordPress. *See also* specific topics
    backups, 372
    benefits of, 9–13
    features of, 13–14
    files, uploading, 107–109
    migration from within, 378–379
    platform options, 13–16

upgrades, 119
    Web hosting support, 100
WordPress Codex, 12–13, 266, 267, 278
WordPress Development Blog, 123–125
WordPress MU (Multi User), 327
WordPress Planet (Web site), 125
WordPress Plugin Directory, 121, 151–152, 208, 213, 215–216
WordPress Theme Directory, 228–229, 230, 231, 246
WordPress user community, 2, 9–10, 12–13, 16, 204
WordPress.com. *See also* specific topics
    accounts, 29–32
    Dashboard, 34–40
    hosted versions at, 1, 13–15
    migration from, 369, 370
    navigation, 32–34
    options, 40–50
    updates, 38
WordPress.com Stats, 362
WordPress.org, 1, 13–14. *See also* specific topics
wordTube, 202
WP E-Commerce, 352
WP Print, 357–358
WP Super Cache, 360–361
WP-DB-Backup, 360
WPPlugins, 225
WPtouch iPhone Theme, 360
WP-Vidavee, 202
writing, 122, 132–134, 173–180
WS_FTP, 103
WYSIWYG (What You See Is What You Get), 52, 173

• X •

XHTML, 133, 197, 248
XHTML Friends Network (XFN), 67, 68, 162
XML-RPC publishing interfaces, 134

• Y •

Yahoo!, 171
YouTube, 59, 197, 198

• Z •

zip files, 105